Social Enterprise

CIVIL SOCIETY: HISTORICAL AND CONTEMPORARY PERSPECTIVES

Series Editors:

Virginia Hodgkinson *Public Policy Institute Georgetown University*

Kent E. Portney *Department of Political Science Tufts University*

John C. Schneider *Department of History Tufts University*

For a complete list of books that are available in the series, visit www.upne.com.

Janelle A. Kerlin, ed., *Social Enterprise: A Global Comparison*

Carl Milofsky, *Smallville: Institutionalizing Community in Twenty-First-Century America*

Dan Pallotta, *Uncharitable: How Restraints on Nonprofits Undermine Their Potential*

Susan A. Ostrander and Kent E. Portney, eds., *Acting Civically: From Urban Neighborhoods to Higher Education*

Peter Levine, *The Future of Democracy: Developing the Next Generation of American Citizens*

Jason A. Scorza, *Strong Liberalism: Habits of Mind for Democratic Citizenship*

Elayne Clift, ed., *Women, Philanthropy, and Social Change: Visions for a Just Society*

Brian O'Connell, *Fifty Years in Public Causes: Stories from a Road Less Traveled*

Pablo Eisenberg, *Challenges for Nonprofits and Philanthropy: The Courage to Change*

Thomas A. Lyson, *Civic Agriculture: Reconnecting Farm, Food, and Community*

Virginia A. Hodgkinson and Michael W. Foley, eds., *The Civil Society Reader*

Henry Milner, *Civic Literacy: How Informed Citizens Make Democracy Work*

Ken Thomson, *From Neighborhood to Nation: The Democratic Foundations of Civil Society*

Bob Edwards, Michael W. Foley, and Mario Diani, eds., *Beyond Tocqueville: Civil Society and the Social Capital Debate in Comparative Perspective*

Phillip H. Round, *By Nature and by Custom Cursed: Transatlantic Civil Discourse and New England Cultural Production, 1620–1660*

Brian O'Connell, *Civil Society: The Underpinnings of American Democracy*

EDITED BY JANELLE A. KERLIN

Social Enterprise
A Global Comparison

TUFTS UNIVERSITY PRESS
Medford, Massachusetts

Published by
University Press of New England
Hanover and London

TUFTS UNIVERSITY PRESS

Published by University Press of New England,

One Court Street, Lebanon, NH 03766

www.upne.com

© 2009 by Tufts University Press

Printed in U.S.A.

5   4   3   2   1

Library of Congress Cataloging-in-Publication Data
Social enterprise : a global comparison / edited by Janelle A. Kerlin.
    p. m. — (Civil society: historical and contemporary perspectives)
Includes bibliographical references and index.
ISBN 978-1-58465-789-7 (cloth : alk. paper)
ISBN 978-1-58465-822-1 (pbk. : alk. paper)
1. Social entrepreneurship—Case studies. 2. Social responsibility of
business—Case studies. 3. Non-governmental organizations—Case
studies. 4. Nonprofit organizations—Case studies. I. Kerlin,
Janelle A., 1969–
HD60.S585 2009
361.7'65—dc22   2009026948

For my husband, Clayton Bassett

Contents

List of Figures viii

List of Tables ix

Foreword *Jacques Defourny* xi

Contributors xix

Acknowledgments xxvii

1   Introduction *Janelle A. Kerlin* 1

2   Western Europe *Marthe Nyssens* 12

3   East-Central Europe *Ewa Leś and Marija Kolin* 35

4   Southeast Asia *Joel Santos, Leah Macatangay,*
        Mary Ann Capistrano, & Caroline Burns 64

5   United States *Janelle A. Kerlin & Kirsten Gagnaire* 87

6   Zimbabwe and Zambia *Absolom Masendeke &*
        Alex Mugova 114

7   Argentina *Mario M. Roitter & Alejandra Vivas* 139

8   Japan *Ichiro Tsukamoto & Mariko Nishimura* 163

9   A Comparison of Social Enterprise Models and Contexts
        Janelle A. Kerlin 184

Index 201

Figures

Figure 2.1 The EMES Ideal Type of Social Enterprise 14

Figure 3.1 Main Organizational Forms of Social Enterprises in East-Central European Countries 37

Figure 5.1 Selected Sources of Revenue for All Nonprofits (Excluding Hospitals and Higher Education Institutions), 1982–2002, in 2003 Dollars 96

Figure 6.1 DAPP Operations in Zambia 118–119

Figure 6.2 Crisis Situation for Social Enterprise in Zimbabwe 124

Figure 6.3 NGO Operational Requirements in Zimbabwe (2008) 128

Figure 6.4 The Rise and Fall of Informal Sector Social Enterprises in Zimbabwe 129

Figure 9.1 Relative Placement of Social Enterprise for Seven World Regions and Countries with Regard to Market, State, Civil Society, and International Aid 191

Figure 9.2 Countries Included in the Three World Regions 192

Tables

Table 1.1 Models of Third Sector Regime 4

Table 3.1 Accepted Examples of Social Enterprises Supplying Social and Community Services 38

Table 5.1 Common Types of Nonprofit Social Enterprises and the Extent of Nonprofit Involvement in Commercial Activity 91

Table 5.2 Common Types of Business Social Enterprise and the Extent of Business Involvement in Social Activity 94

Table 6.1 Evolution of Social Enterprises in Zimbabwe 120

Table 6.2 Performance by CSFS on Key Indicators, 2004–2005 136

Table 9.1 Comparative Overview of Social Enterprise in Seven World Regions and Countries 188

Table 9.2 The Emphasis of Social Enterprise in Four Areas: Market (M), Civil Society (CS), State (S), and International Aid (I) 190

Table 9.3 Ratings of the Socioeconomic Environments in Seven World Regions and Countries 193

Table 9.4 Comparative Overview of Social Enterprise Models and Four Socioeconomic Factors for Seven World Regions and Countries 196

Foreword

Field organizations, corresponding to what we now call "social enterprises," have existed since well before the mid-1990s when the term began to be increasingly used in both Western Europe and the United States. Indeed, the third sector, be it called the nonprofit sector or the social economy, has long witnessed entrepreneurial dynamics that resulted in innovative solutions for providing services or goods to persons or communities whose needs were met neither by private companies nor by public providers.[1] However, for reasons that vary from region to region as explained in this book, the concept of social enterprise is now the subject of a fast-growing interest, along with two closely related terms: "social entrepreneur" and "social entrepreneurship."

Until recently, those three "SE flags" were used more or less along the same lines: although this oversimplifies matters a little, one could say that social entrepreneurship was seen as the process through which social entrepreneurs created social enterprises. Since the early 2000s, however, a fast-growing literature has produced various definitions of and approaches to each of these three flags. A detailed analysis of these different approaches is clearly beyond the scope of this foreword, but a few features may be pointed out in order to stress some current trends and help avoid too much confusion.

The term "social entrepreneur" has been particularly emphasized by American foundations and organizations like Ashoka. Those entities identify and support in various ways individuals launching new activities dedicated to a social mission while behaving as true entrepreneurs in terms of dynamism, personal involvement, and innovative practices. Such a social entrepreneur brings about new ways of responding to social problems. Although this meaning of social entrepreneur is gaining some ground in Europe, the emphasis there has been much more often put on the collective nature of the social enterprise, as well as on its associative or cooperative form.

The notion of "social entrepreneurship" was conceptualized in rather precise ways in the late 1990s.[2] These conceptualizations stressed the social innovation processes undertaken by social entrepreneurs. However, the concept is increasingly being used in a very broad sense, as, for various authors, it now refers to a wide spectrum of initiatives, ranging from voluntary activism to corporate social responsibility (Nicholls, 2006). Between these two extremes, many categories can be identified: individual initiatives, nonprofit organizations launching new activities, public-private partnerships with a social aim, and so on. While scholars from business schools and consultants now tend to stress the "blurred boundaries" between institutional and legal forms as well as the "blended value creation" (profits alongside social value) that characterizes social entrepreneurship (Emerson, 2006), social science scholars underline the fact that social entrepreneurship most often takes place within the "third sector" (i.e., the private, not-for-profit sector). In any case, it seems clear today that of the three notions briefly described here, social entrepreneurship is the most encompassing.

As to the concept of "social enterprise," it took root in both the United States and Europe during the 1970s and 1980s. In the U.S., the nonprofit community began to set up and operate its own businesses as a way of creating job opportunities for the disadvantaged, the homeless, and other at-risk people. When an economic downturn in the late 1970s led to welfare retrenchment and cutbacks in federal funding, nonprofits began to expand commercial activities to fill the gap through market sales of goods or services not directly related to their missions (Crimmings & Kiel, 1983; Skloot, 1987). In Europe, new entrepreneurial dynamics clearly emerged within the third sector during the same period, though, as in the U.S., actual use of the term "social enterprise" was unusual. On the European scene, an emblematic step took place in Italy in the early 1990s, when the concept of social enterprise was promoted by a new journal entitled *Impresa Sociale*. The concept was introduced at the time in order to designate new types of initiatives for which the Italian parliament created the legal form "social cooperative," a type of enterprise that has achieved amazing success (Borzaga & Santuari, 2001). Various other European countries have since passed new laws to promote social enterprises (Defourny & Nyssens, 2008). Going well beyond legal issues in its pioneering comparative studies of all EU countries, the EMES[3] European Research Network stresses the positioning of European social enterprises "at the crossroads of market, public policies and civil society," especially to underline the "hybridization" of their resources: indeed, social enterprises in Europe combine income from sales or fees from users with public subsidies linked to their social mission and private donations and/or volunteering (Borzaga & Defourny, 2001; Nyssens, 2006; EMES, 2008). This clearly contrasts with a strong U.S. tendency to define social enterprises mainly as nonprofit organizations more oriented toward the market and developing "earned income strategies" as a response to increased competition for public subsidies and to the limits of private grants from foundations.

One of the first merits of the present book is that it clearly avoids mixing these three SE concepts and focuses clearly on organizational forms that may be designated as "social enterprises" around the world. Second, while fully acknowledging the "earned income" conception as the dominant view in the United States as well as its (varying) influence in other regions of the world, Janelle Kerlin has chosen the most honest research strategy to grasp what a social enterprise may mean around the world, including in regions where such a notion is not well known or even not used. It meant not imposing any specific conceptual framework that would have probably distorted the understanding of the grassroots conditions in which social enterprises emerge and develop. Likewise, the editor decided to rely on local researchers so as to use lenses representing the way local contexts view and may forge conceptions of social enterprise.

From an analytical point of view, such a research strategy is certainly neither the most comfortable nor the most elegant for theory building. It is, however, fully coherent with respect to the diversity of field actors and the quite different ways they build what they may call social enterprises. Incidentally, it is not surprising that the final comparative analysis made by the editor clearly refers to the "social origins" theory of the nonprofit sector, the most flexible theory framed to reflect the deep embedding of NPOS in their respective historical, cultural, economic, social, and political environments (Salamon, Sokolowski, & Anheier, 2000).

Although avoiding new conceptual debates on social enterprise, this book actually paves the way for further conceptual and theoretical work. Strikingly, it does so by reopening the fundamental question of the "social" qualification of such enterprises. While the dominant U.S. view usually refers to a general social purpose or a social mission, most regional overviews proposed by the book's chapters suggest that this social qualification may refer to quite different features.

Of course, the most common view of a social purpose or mission is to relieve social problems such as unemployment, poverty, underdevelopment, or handicaps of all kinds, among other factors, which may cause marginalization or exclusion of certain individuals, groups, or large communities. Such social challenges can be addressed through many strategies, ranging from social work or international aid to the setting up of various economic activities by enterprises deserving the label "social" when primarily focused on those problems. Many examples in this book may be viewed through such a lens, including the productive activities of various NGOs, the aid microfinance institutions give to small entrepreneurs in southern Africa, and the efforts of cooperatives for the handicapped in most Eastern European countries.

A second perspective on the "social" qualification of social enterprise focuses on the social sector as a whole, or the spectrum of services from education to health or social care services, which are not generally considered parts of the "true" economic sphere because they are not provided by companies or markets. Creating social enterprises could thus mean marketizing such services and/or adapting management techniques from the business world to at least part of the social sector. The U.S. scene probably provides the best illustration of such social enterprises, although market income may also be generated through products other than the social services themselves. Of course, some overlap can exist between these two first social qualifications, but their respective emphasis on specific disadvantaged groups and on fields of activity is different.

A third approach refers to the decision-making power local groups or communities want to keep in order to better take their destiny into their own hands. Such "empowerment" is often sought through the development of cooperatives, workers' collectives, or other types of producers' groupings, which may then be described as social enterprises, as they are in chapters focusing on Southeast Asia and Latin America. Although production remains central in such enterprises, it cannot be disconnected from a political or ideological dimension or, broadly speaking, a quest for economic democracy.

On the basis of such a collective control or in order to meet legal requirements, a fourth approach may stress the socialization of the enterprise's surplus when the surplus is allocated to the benefit of the community or when the distribution of profits to individual members is subject to limitation, as it is in the case of cooperatives. Still referring to financial means, a fifth related conception underlines the social or societal choice of elected governing bodies to finance the provision of some services in order to make the services available to all citizens. In Western Europe, the importance of such societal support through public subsidies or public contracts, as well as through private giving or volunteering, may lead nonprofit providers to be named social enterprises.

In addition to this diversity of social qualifications, let us also note the general public's strangely narrow association of the term "enterprise" with a market orientation. Of course most enterprises sell their products on the market. This does not mean, however, that a full reliance on market income is a necessary condition of being qualified as an enterprise. We do not debate this point in depth; we just note here that an enterprise is at least about producing and/or providing goods or services as well as doing so by bearing some risks. Such risks are often linked to the uncertainty of the level of costs and incomes from the market, but they may also be related to a more complex mix of resources from the market, the state, international aid, and private philanthropy. From such a fundamental perspective, one cannot be sure that an organization should be considered to be more of an enterprise if it gives more importance to market income. We realize how provocative such an assertion may be, but the latter is supported by common sense when one considers a business as a commercial enterprise, not just an enterprise.

These remarks on the meaning of social enterprise should not be confusing. As already stressed by the editor in an earlier work, conceptions of social enterprise vary considerably between the United States and Western Europe[4] as well as within those regions. This book simply illustrates how diverse local contexts may be around the world and, therefore, how large the spectrum of social enterprise conceptions may also be. It therefore invites the reader to keep in mind the relative value of U.S. or European conceptualizations. Notwithstanding, most organizational forms listed hereafter in the regional overviews (nonprofits, NGOS, cooperatives, foundations, religious-based associations, social purpose companies, etc.) actually support the idea that the bulk of social enterprises around the world do belong to the third sector, provided that the third sector is considered to be larger than a nonprofit sector strictly defined by the traditional nondistribution constraint. Although the very notion of a third sector does not make sense everywhere, this finding means that further international comparative research on social enterprise may certainly be fruitfully devel-

oped against the background of strong theoretical and empirical litera-
tures that have already been built on those various types of organizations.

JACQUES DEFOURNY
Centre for Social Economy, HEC-ULg, University of Liège, Belgium
President of the EMES European Research Network

NOTES

1. A major part of the literature on the nonprofit sector since the mid-1970s deals
   with the conditions under which NPOs have emerged and developed in modern economies. In such a context, the issue of entrepreneurship was particularly raised by authors such as Young (1983, 1986), among others.
2. Especially by Dees (1998).
3. EMES is the acronym of the network's first major research program on the
   "emergence of social enterprise," carried out from 1996 through 2000. For
   more information, see www.emes.net.
4. Kerlin (2006), further developed by Defourny & Nyssens (2009).

REFERENCES

Borzaga, C., & Defourny, J. (Eds.). (2001). *The emergence of social enterprise.* New
   York: Routledge.
Borzaga, C., & Santuari, A. (2001). Italy: From traditional cooperatives to
   innovating social enterprises. In C. Borzaga & J. Defourny (Eds.), *The
   emergence of social enterprise* (pp. 1–28). New York: Routledge.
Crimmings, J. C., & Kiel, M. (1983). *Enterprise in the nonprofit sector.* Washington,
   DC: Partners for Livable Places.
Dees, J. G. (1998). The meaning of social entrepreneurship. Working paper,
   Kauffman Center for Entrepreneurial Leadership.
Defourny, J., & Nyssens, M. (Eds.). (2008). Social enterprise in Europe: Recent
   trends and developments. EMES Working Papers Series, No. 08/01.
——. (2009). Conceptions of social enterprise in Europe and the United States:
   Convergences and divergences. EMES Working Papers Series, No. 09/01.
Emerson, J. (2006). Moving ahead together: Implications of a blended value
   framework for the future of social entrepreneurship. In A. Nicholls (Ed.),
   Social entrepreneurship: New models of sustainable social change (pp. 391–406).
   New York: Oxford University Press.
EMES European Research Network. (2008). *Social enterprise: A new model for
   poverty reduction and employment generation.* Bratislava: UNDP Regional
   Bureau.

Kerlin, J. (2006). Social enterprise in the United States and Europe: Understanding and learning from the differences. *Voluntas*, 17(3), pp. 247–263.

Nicholls, A. (Ed.). (2006). *Social entrepreneurship: New models of sustainable social change.* New York: Oxford University Press.

Nyssens, M. (Ed.). (2006). *Social enterprise: At the crossroads of market, public policies and civil society.* New York: Routledge.

Salamon, L. S., Sokolowski, W., & Anheier, H. K. (2000). Social origins of civil society: An overview. Working paper of the Johns Hopkins Comparative Nonprofit Sector Project, no. 38. Baltimore: Johns Hopkins Center for Civil Society Studies.

Skloot, E. (1987). Enterprise and commerce in non-profit organizations. In W. W. Powell (Ed.), *The Non-profit Sector: A Research Handbook.* New Haven, CT: Yale University Press.

Young, D. (1983). *If not for profit, for what?: A behavioral theory of the nonprofit sector based on entrepreneurship.* Lanham, MD: Lexington Books.

——. (1986). Entrepreneurship and the behaviour of non-profit organizations: Elements of a theory. In S. Rose-Ackerman (Ed.), *The economics of non-profit institutions* (pp. 161–184). New York: Oxford University Press.

Contributors

Caroline Burns is the executive director of the Entrepreneurs School of
Asia Foundation, the Institute for Social Entrepreneurship Education,
in Quezon City, Philippines. Before this she was the executive director
of the Assumption Lay Volunteer Programme, an international organization that sends volunteer workers to developing countries. Ms. Burns
is a British national who has been working in the Philippines for the
last three years. She has traveled and/or lived in many countries in
Africa, Latin America, and Asia. She has a BSC (Hons) in international
studies from the Open University/University of London and has at-
tended the Asia Institute of Management in Manila.

Mary Ann Capistrano is Dean of Instruction at the Entrepreneurs School
of Asia in Quezon City, Philippines. She has a BS in management
engineering from Ateneo de Manila University and an MS in Computer Methods Applied to Management from the University of Paris in
France under a French government scholarship grant. For over fifteen
years Capistrano taught at Ateneo de Manila University, where she was
assistant professor, chair, and program director. In her over twenty
years of tertiary-level teaching, she required applied projects with a
social focus of helping less privileged members of the business sector,
in particular, blue-collar workers. Her operations focus exposes her
to laborers, while her computer training allows her to look into job
designs that help lift the skills and improve productivity of human
resources. Capistrano has also been a seminar leader for the Asian
Development Bank and a systems consultant for D&L/OFI, Canon Marketing, and the Philippines Women's University.

Jacques Defourny is a Professor of Economics at HEC-ULg, University
of Liège (Belgium), where he is also director of the Centre for Social Economy (www.ces-ulg.be). Since 1996, he has been acting as
the founding coordinator and then the president of the EMES European Research Network, which gathers ten university research centers
and individual scholars working on social enterprise across Europe

(www.emes.net). His work focuses on the emergence of social enterprise in various parts of the world and on conceptual and quantitative analyses of the third sector in developed and developing countries. Besides numerous articles in academic journals, he has authored or edited ten books, including *The third sector: Co-operative, mutual and non-profit organizations* (1992), *Tackling social exclusion in Europe: The role of the social economy* (2001), and *The emergence of social enterprise* (2001 and 2004).

Kirsten Gagnaire is principal and founder of Social Enterprise Group, LLC, a company in Seattle, Washington (United States), that specializes in assisting organizations and individuals with developing and sustaining ventures that meet social, environmental, and financial bottom lines. She has a broad background in developing and conducting strategy and business planning for clients in all sectors who are integrating both social mission and profitability. In partnership with Bainbridge Graduate Institute, she created the comprehensive social enterprise business planning methodology, Sustayne. In addition, Gagnaire is vice chair of the board of the Social Enterprise Alliance (a professional association for social enterprise practitioners) and is a member of the faculty at Bainbridge Graduate Institute.She was named one of the Puget Sound area's Top 40 Under 40 businesspeople in 2003, and her company was also named as a finalist for the Stevie Awards Best Overall Service Business in 2004.She has worked at the Russian-owned world trade center in Moscow and as a Peace Corps volunteer in Mali, West Africa, in small enterprise development.

Janelle A. Kerlin is an Assistant Professor in the Andrew Young School of Policy Studies at Georgia State University in Atlanta, Georgia (United States). Kerlin's areas of research include the study of domestic and comparative social enterprise and international nongovernmental organizations. Current research focuses on the influence of culture on innovation in social enterprise, trends in nonprofit commercial activity in the United States, and U.S.-based diaspora philanthropy. She is author of a number of book chapters and journal articles and the book *Social service reform in the postcommunist state: Decentralization in Poland* (2005). Kerlin holds an MS from Columbia University and a PhD in political science from the Maxwell School at Syracuse University. She has also worked as a research associate in the Center on Nonprofits and

Philanthropy at the Urban Institute and as a visiting research scholar at the Woodrow Wilson International Center for Scholars, both in Washington, D.C.

Marija Kolin is a social scientist at the Institute for Social Sciences in Belgrade, Republic of Serbia. Her work includes national and international research projects focused on social policy, social economy, and civil society. At present she is conducting the research project "Supporting European Integration through Promotion of Alternative Economy and Social Cohesion in Serbia" in cooperation with the European Movement in Serbia and the Olof Palme Foundation. In addition to her scientific research, Kolin is known as a national expert, lecturer, trainer, and evaluator on European Union and UNDP projects. Kolin earned her MA and PhD at the University of Belgrade. During 2002–2003 she was awarded a Fulbright Visiting Scholar Fellowship at Georgetown University in Washington, D.C. Kolin has published several papers on the social economy and related issues. She is author of the books *Non-profit organizations—New social partners*, *Social enterprises in Serbia* and *The role of alternative economy in European integration process*.

Ewa Leś is a Professor of Political Science and Social Welfare at Warsaw University in Poland. She is also the founder and chair of the Research Center on Non-Profit Organizations at the Polish Academy of Sciences as well as chair of the Postgraduate Programme on Nonprofit Management at Collegium Civitas of the Polish Academy of Sciences. Leś has master's and PhD degrees in political science and social policy from Warsaw University. She has worked as project leader on several national and international research projects, including principal local associate for Poland under the Johns Hopkins Comparative Nonprofit Sector Project. Most recently she completed a large Europe Union project carrying out the country's first comprehensive survey of the social economy sector. Her most recent books include *The voluntary sector in post-communist East-Central Europe*, *Voluntary organizations: A comparative study* and *From philanthropy to subsidiarity*. She also edited the book *Pictures of social economy* and coedited three working papers on aspects of the theory and practice of social enterprise.

Leah Macatangay is the Faculty Research and Development Head of the Entrepreneurs School of Asia (ESA) in Quezon City, Philippines, where she lectures as an Associate Professor of business ethics and operations management. She is also the head of the school's mentoring program, which serves as the source of integration for the students. Macatangay has worked as a project and business consultant and manager for a number of businesses and has written cases for the Asian Institute of Management. She has worked for more than twenty years on projects in youth and women development with nonprofit organizations that include the Philippine Foundation for Cultural and Educational Development, People Engaged in People Projects Foundation, Inc., and the Dalayrayan Social Enterprise. She has BS and MS degrees in industrial engineering from the University of the Philippines and a master's degree in values education from the University of Asia and the Pacific.

Absolom Masendeke is currently working as a regional program team leader for the Reducing Vulnerability Programme at Practical Action Southern Africa (formerly ITDG) based in Zimbabwe. His sixteen years of development work have largely focused on community-based enterprise planning and management, linking communities with local government and local economic development. Masendeke has practical field development experience in Zimbabwe, Mozambique, Malawi, Uganda, Kenya, Bangladesh, Sudan, and Peru. He has published work in the areas of community-based planning, citizen participation in smallholder agriculture, sustainable partnerships, social enterprises, community-based natural resources management, and land and agricultural governance. Masendeke holds an MSC in population and development studies (UZ) and an MA in leadership and management from the Africa Leadership Management Academy. Masendeke is currently contributing to a regional publication, *Making Change Real: Transforming the Development System to Promote Sustainable Livelihoods*, which is being coordinated by Khanya-Africa Institute for Community Driven Development and the University of KwaZulu-Natal in South Africa.

Alex Mugova holds an MA in economic development and planning from the United Nations Institute for Economic Development and Planning (IDEP), based in Dakar, Senegal. He also holds a postgraduate diploma in development studies from the University of Cambridge, England, and a BA in economic history from the University of Zimbabwe. Mugova has worked for the Ministry of Foreign Affairs and for the Ministry of Labour in Manpower Planning and Social Welfare as a senior research and planning officer, and for the Forestry Commission, where he worked as a corporate planner in charge of strategic and business planning. In 1994, Mugova took an appointment as program team leader with Practical Action, an international nongovernmental organization based in the U.K. Since then, he has been stationed with Practical Action's Regional Office for southern Africa, based in Harare, Zimbabwe, where he is responsible for project design, implementation, review, and evaluation. His keen interest is in small enterprise development and promotion, and social enterprise in particular. He has conducted numerous consultancy assignments in project design and evaluation in many countries across Africa, Asia, and Latin America.

Mariko Nishimura is a Professor of Public Policy in the Faculty of Law at Meiji-Gakuin University in Tokyo, Japan. She specializes in public policy, especially health care policy and social welfare policy for the elderly. Her particular research interests include nonprofit organizations in the field of social care services, commercialization, reconciliation between public benefit and business activities, and the social impact of nonprofit agencies and public-private partnerships. Nishimura has been involved in a large government-funded research project that studies and compares nonprofit partnerships and overlapping boundaries of the nonprofit sector with public and business sectors in Japan, the United Kingdom, and the United States. She has published numerous articles on public policy, health care policy, and partnerships between nonprofits and government. She is author of the book *Social policy* (2008) and contributor to the book *Social enterprise: Philanthropy to business* (2008).

Marthe Nyssens is a Professor in the Department of Economics at the Catholic University of Louvain, Belgium, where she is the coordinator of a research team on third sector and social policies within the Centre de Recherches Interdisciplinaires sur la Solidarité et l'Innovation Sociale. She is a founding member of the European Social Enterprise Research Network (www.emes.net). Her work focuses on conceptual approaches to the third sector in both developed and developing countries as well as the links between third sector organizations and public policies. She has published numerous scientific articles and has edited several books in French, English, and Spanish, including *Social enterprise: At the crossroads of market, public policies and civil society* (2006).

Mario M. Roitter has been a senior researcher at the Center for the Study of State and Society (CEDES) in Buenos Aires, Argentina, since 1995. He is director of the project "Arts and Recreation as Tools for Social and Local Development," which is aimed at generating knowledge and providing technical assistance for youth initiatives in Latin America. He also coordinates the project "Strengthening the Latin American nonprofit sector through incorporating the measurement of its size and scope into the system of national accounts" within the framework of the UN Nonprofit Handbook Project—Center for Civil Society Studies, Johns Hopkins University. Roitter conducts research on "recuperated companies" in the field of social economy and also works in the Corporate Social Responsibility Program at the University of San Andrés. He has also acted as a consultant for UNDP, UNICEF, ECLAC, the Ford Foundation, and various corporate foundations in Argentina and Latin America. He is an instructor in a postgraduate nonprofit management program sponsored by the University of San Andrés and CEDES. Roitter has published works on different topics related to nonprofit organizations and corporate social responsibility.

Joel Santos is cofounder and president of the Entrepreneurs School of Asia in Metro Manila, Philippines. Santos initially worked as a marketing executive with Proctor and Gamble and then became a venture capitalist investing in several businesses in distribution, logistics, advertising, and publishing. In 1998, Santos sold his businesses and cofounded the Entrepreneurs School of Asia (ESA), Southeast Asia's first college focused on entrepreneurship education. Santos is a founding director of the Institute for Social Entrepreneurship and Empowerment (14SEE) and also part of the executive committee of the Philippine Center for Entrepreneurship, the country's leading advocate for entrepreneurship development. He was the Philippine representative for the Global Entrepreneurship Monitor, a consortium of universities in forty countries that conduct research on entrepreneurship worldwide. Santos was also cochairman of the region's first Forum on Social Entrepreneurship, held in Hangzhou, China. He has an undergraduate degree from Ateneo de Manila University in the Philippines and an MSC in Responsibility and Business Practice from the University of Bath (U.K.).

Ichiro Tsukamoto is a Professor of Public Management at Meiji University in Tokyo, Japan. He is also head of the Institute of Nonprofit and

Public Management Studies, which he founded. His research interests are in the areas of nonprofit management and strategic collaboration between nonprofits and other sectors. He is particularly interested in the organizational change of nonprofit agencies that is influenced by collaborations with the business and public sectors and the pressures of commercialization. Tsukamoto has been involved in a large, government-funded research project that studies and compares partnerships and overlapping boundaries of the nonprofit sector with public and business sectors in Japan, the United Kingdom, and the United States. He has published numerous articles and edited books about the third sector. His edited books include *Social enterprise: Philanthropy to business* (2008).

Alejandra Vivas is a research assistant in the Civil Society and Social Development Department at Centro de Estudios de Estado y Sociedad (CEDES) in Buenos Aires, Argentina. She is currently studying for a master's degree in economic sociology at the University of San Martín. She has a bachelor's degree from the School of Economics, University of Buenos Aires, 2003. She has given several research presentations at international and regional research conferences on the topics of intersectoral relations and volunteering. She was a coauthor with González Bombal and Mario Roitter on the article "Empleo y voluntariado en las organizaciones del sector no lucrativo de la Ciudad Autónoma de Buenos Aires."

Acknowledgments

This book is the culmination of many dedicated people's efforts over many years. First and foremost I am indebted to the book's initial editor, Ellen Wicklum, who encouraged the idea of the book in the first place and supported it through the review process at Tufts University Press. I am also grateful to the many others at the press who subsequently gave of their time and patiently guided me through the process of putting together an edited volume. I especially appreciate the efforts of Julie Fisher and Alex Murdock, who reviewed the book for the press and provided excellent comments and suggestions for revisions.

There would of course be no book if it were not for the contributions, and also the patience, of the many authors involved in its development. Ewa Leś is a good friend and respected colleague whom I met while doing dissertation research in Poland and have known for many years. I am grateful to her for introducing me to Marija Kolin, who has provided much insight into social enterprise elsewhere in East-Central Europe. Jacques Defourny and Marthe Nyssens have provided ongoing inspiration since I first met them in Paris at the beginning of my comparative work on social enterprise. Isabel Vidal, whom I met relatively recently, has helped round out the picture of social enterprise in Western Europe in many ways. Many thanks also go to Joel Santos, whom I met at a conference in China and who suggested a chapter on Southeast Asia. He then put together a dedicated team of colleagues to help write it: Mary Ann Capistrano, Leah Macatangay, and Caroline Burns. I have also greatly appreciated the scholarly exchange I have had with Ichiro Tsukamoto and Mariko Nishimura, who provided many valuable insights into social enterprise in Japan during my visit there. Then there are those who agreed to devote their time to the project without ever meeting in person. Mario Roitter, Alejandra Vivas, Absolom Masendeke, and Alex Mugova graciously agreed to contribute chapters after others pointed me in their direction. I am heavily indebted to all of the authors for their endurance through multiple drafts and revisions over the span of several years.

Many others also provided background support for the project. The

Center on Nonprofits and Philanthropy at the Urban Institute supported the project's initial stages and provided much-needed overhead support. One of my colleagues there, Kendall Golladay, was instrumental in shaping the title for the book. My gratitude also goes out to the Department of Public Management and Policy at Georgia State University, which continued to cover the many ancillary costs of the project, including research and index assistance. Indeed, most of the research and editorial support for the book was provided by my graduate research assistants funded by the department: Geoff Edwards, Susan Manikowski, and Jasmine McGinnis. Very special thanks go to Susan Manikowski in particular, who provided excellent, detailed English and reference editing on every chapter in the volume. I am also grateful to the Nonprofit Studies Program at Georgia State University, especially Dennis Young, who provided insightful discussions on topics related to the book and supported its overall development. I appreciate most my husband, who has supported me in every way through this project.

JANELLE A. KERLIN

1 Introduction

Social enterprise has been a growing global phenomenon for over two decades.[1] Though the concept of using market-based approaches to address social issues is not new in many societies, use of the term "social enterprise" to describe specific, often innovative, types of this kind of activity is new. Around the world, common activities associated with social enterprise include, among others, civil society organizations that receive earned income in exchange for products or services, microcredit lending institutions and activities, and cooperative ventures that engage the unemployed. Increasing interest in social enterprise has been spurred on by the belief that market-based approaches for social benefit can contribute significantly to the self-determination and long-term sustainability of programs serving the disadvantaged, particularly in regions where funding from government and private sources is limited or unavailable. Indeed, policy makers and international development strategists alike have begun looking to social enterprise to regenerate communities, deliver public services, and promote a new, socially responsible economic engine.

However, one of the major barriers to the discussion, investigation, and promotion of social enterprise has been a lack of understanding of the concept itself. Though large amounts of time, energy, and ink have been spent on efforts to define social enterprise and its counterpart, "social entrepreneurship,"[2] consensus has not been reached on what social enterprise is, and confusion is still the norm at gatherings for social enterprise actors and scholars, especially in international settings. Part, though not all, of the problem is due to the fact that different areas of the world have begun associating the term "social enterprise" with their own distinct models and activities. Thus, cross-regional discussion on the topic is often difficult because everyone speaks from their own regionally defined version of the concept. Moreover, isolated, regional development has meant that innovative ideas for social enterprise originating in one area of the world are rarely known of in other regions.

In an attempt to address these problems, this volume brings together descriptions of social enterprise in seven regions and countries around the world: Western Europe, East-Central Europe, Southeast Asia, the United States, Zimbabwe and Zambia, Argentina, and Japan. Chapters covering each of these regions and countries were written by local social enterprise researchers, most with social science backgrounds, as well as development consultants, in the case of Zimbabwe and Zambia. They examine the conceptualization, history, legal frameworks, supporting institutions, and latest developments and challenges for social enterprise in their region or country and provide several examples of typical social enterprises. The intent is to provide a basis for cross-regional understanding and exchange using existing definitions and discourses in a region or country.

Indeed, the book does not call for consensus around one narrow definition of social enterprise. As Mair, Robinson, and Hockerts state in their discussion of social entrepreneurship, "Narrowing [social entrepreneurship] down to a uniformly agreed upon definition would probably make it applicable only to a limited set of problems and issues" (2006, p. 7). As this volume demonstrates, social enterprise has begun to be associated with a wide variety of not only problems and issues but also forms, resources, and institutions that are connected to an immediate country or region context. Thus, a narrow definition of social enterprise would limit not only the kinds of problems and issues it could address but also the kinds of environments where it would be appropriate or even feasible.

Given its focus, the volume fills a gap in the literature on social enterprise from an international comparative perspective. Of the limited set of books available on social enterprise internationally, most focus on a single country or region and/or rely heavily on case studies. In addition, aside from the Europe-focused texts, almost all tend to overlook the broader environment in which the social enterprise activity is emerging (Alter, 2002; Borzaga & Defourny, 2001; Dacanay, 2004; NESsT, 1997; Nyssens, 2006; SEKN, 2006). While a related discourse on social entrepreneurship has been more international in scope (Bornstein, 2004; Nicholls, 2006b), it tends to focus on the highly innovative social accomplishments or ideas of a few individuals, and it too often uses case studies.

Alternatively, this book focuses on a global comparison of the different grassroots conceptualizations and contexts of the social enterprise organization. With much of the international literature focused on individual social entrepreneurs and case studies, broad organizational trends in social enterprise associated with particular regions or countries have been overlooked. Such organizational trends are important because they signal what is currently the easiest route for social enterprise activities in a given context. The book also focuses on the context in which organizational trends operate in order to examine the broader environment's role in shaping and maintaining those trends. Thus, the volume identifies distinct regional and country organizational trends in social enterprise; examines their historical, institutional, and socioeconomic contexts; and considers how that context has shaped the kind of need, purpose, activity, form, legal structure, and process involved in their creation.[3]

The cross-regional information collected in this volume lends itself to social science research that deals with how societal context shapes social institutions in different places. An important part of this discussion is how existing social institutions and patterns constrain the options available for the development of new institutions (Salamon, Sokolowski, & Anheier, 2000). Most relevant to the research in this volume is the social origins approach to understanding international variation in the development of nonprofit sectors. This approach, developed by Salamon, Sokolowski, and Anheier (2000) and Anheier (2005), is based on research the Johns Hopkins Comparative Nonprofit Sector Project conducted in twenty-two countries during the 1990s. Its main premise is that variations in nonprofit sectors across different countries in scale, composition, and financial base can largely be explained by their differing social, economic, and political contexts.

Salamon, Sokolowski, and Anheier's analysis focuses on four possible traits of nonprofit sectors: the large or small size of the nonprofit sector and high or low government social welfare spending. Using different combinations of these characteristics they created four models of third sector regimes: liberal, statist, corporatist, and social democratic. They also tested the models using data on nonprofit employment (as a proxy for nonprofit sector size) and government social welfare spending for twenty-two countries and found that the countries fall into the four different regimes in predictable fashion (see table 1.1).

Salamon, Sokolowski, and Anheier then analyzed the formation of

TABLE 1.1. *Models of Third Sector Regime*

		Nonprofit Scale	
		Small	Large
Government Social Welfare Spending	Low	Statist (e.g., Argentina, Japan)	Liberal (e.g., United States, Australia)
	High	Social democratic (e.g., Hungary, Slovakia)	Corporatist (e.g., Netherlands, Belgium)

Source: Salamon, Sokolowski, & Anheier (2000)

these regimes in terms of the historical forces shaping both the size of the nonprofit sector and social welfare spending. To understand factors behind the size of nonprofit sectors, they drew on Barrington Moore's (1966) work on the social origins of different government regimes to help explain how different forces, namely the interrelationships between different classes, create the conditions that result in large or small civil societies. They then turned to Esping-Anderson (1990) and his study of the origins of the modern welfare state to examine the forces creating different levels of government welfare spending. They conclude that "certain circumstances are . . . more congenial to the blossoming of nonprofit institutions than others, and the shape and character of the resulting nonprofit sector is affected by the particular constellation of social forces that gives rise to it" (Salamon, Sokolowski, & Anheier, 2000, p. 21).

Salamon, Sokolowski, and Anheier's social origins approach provides a starting point for examining the factors associated with the development of social enterprise around the world. In addition to civil society and government traits that characterize nonprofit sectors, social enterprise researchers have put forward two additional factors as essential in characterizing social enterprise: the market and international aid. In particular, Nyssens (2006) and Nicholls (2006a) include the concept of market in their discussions on how social enterprise/entrepreneurship appears to be positioned differently in different societies relative to civil society, government, and the market. Research collected in this volume identified international aid as a possible fourth influential factor. The underlying assumption in this model is that social enterprise in a given society is more or less strongly associated with the four factors of civil society, state capacity, market functioning, and international aid depending on their strength or weakness in the surrounding environment.

The concluding chapter in this volume takes a first step toward establishing a link between regional/country social enterprise models and these four characteristics in their environments. Drawing on information from the preceding chapters, it identifies different models of social enterprise for each region/country based on how much social enterprise is associated with market, international aid, state, and civil society in a number of areas. The models are then matched with their regional and country socioeconomic data on market functioning, international aid, state capacity, and civil society drawn from a number of international social and economic databases. Results show that, in almost a one-to-one correspondence, social enterprise models match the strengths of their given country or region across the four socioeconomic areas.

The findings provide evidence that current differences in social enterprise found in various areas of the world are, in part, reflections of the socioeconomic contexts of the regions making use of the term. This suggests that social enterprise practitioners are developing their activities by building off the particular strengths of their environments, which helps shape different models and activities. Specifically, region-specific factors may have shaped the broad conceptualization of social enterprise, including its uses, organizational forms, supportive environment, and strategic development base.

The book's final construction was determined by a number of factors. Areas of the world were initially selected based on their perceived activity in the sphere of social enterprise. Thus, areas such as the Middle East, Russia, China, and northern Africa were not included because during the initial stages of the book's development these regions either had no known social enterprise movements or such movements had not achieved a broadly recognizable form. Also, at times only single countries were chosen from some regions due to difficulty in finding researchers willing to take on a regional analysis because of lack of easily accessible information.

Local social enterprise researchers and consultants were recruited to write the region/country chapters because they were deemed to be the most familiar with both social enterprise activities and contexts in their areas. The book is distinctive in this approach because, aside from the European country studies (see Borzaga & Defourny, 2001; Nyssens, 2006), most published research comparing social enterprise across different countries has been conducted by outside observers. The authors contributing to the volume were found by different means through an extended process. Authors for the Western Europe, Southeast Asia, and Japan chapters were identified at nonprofit research conferences during discussions on social enterprise. For southern Africa and South America, connections through research networks led to the two development consultants who wrote on Zimbabwe and Zambia and also to a team of civil society researchers who contributed a chapter on Argentina. A colleague and leading East European scholar on social enterprise from Poland wrote the chapter on East-Central Europe with another colleague from Serbia.

The authors were asked to discuss a common set of topics in their chapters, including the concept(s) of social enterprise in the region/country; organizational forms; history of the recent trend toward social enterprise (including underlying political, economic, and other forces); legal frameworks used for social enterprise; institutional support for the development of social enterprise; and an assessment of social enterprise. They were also asked to provide several case examples of common forms of social enterprise found in their region or country. Though the authors all address the same set of topics in their writing, they were given considerable freedom to write the chapters in a way that best reflects social enterprise and the information available in their region or country. Thus, the author for Western Europe provides a systematic overview drawing on a considerable amount of research on social enterprise already completed in her region. The Argentina team, on the other hand, devotes much attention to the historical development of social enterprise, which helps explain why new, distinct forms of the activity have emerged in their country. Overviews of the country/region chapters follow.

Chapter 2, on Western Europe, was authored by Marthe Nyssens, a professor at Université Catholique de Louvain, Belgium, and reviewed by Isabel Vidal, a professor at Universidad de Barcelona, Spain. This chapter is the most analytical of all the country/region chapters due to the advanced nature of both social enterprise and the research being conducted on the topic in Western Europe. It follows the common outline for the chapters, but in contrast to the others, it presents a highly developed framework for understanding and conceptualizing social enterprise. It also provides an in-depth analysis of the sphere social enterprise occupies in Western Europe in relation to government and the market. In particular, it discusses the relatively high involvement of both national governments and the European Union in not only supporting the development of social enterprise but also using it to further their own policy agendas, particularly with regard to work integration for the hard-to-employ. This chapter also provides one of the most in-depth assessments of the state of social enterprise in the region.

Chapter 3, covering East-Central Europe, was coauthored by Ewa Leś, a professor at the University of Warsaw and director of the Research Center on Nonprofit Organizations, Polish Academy of Sciences, Poland, and Marija Kolin, a senior researcher at the Institute of Social Sciences in Belgrade, Serbia. This chapter shows how the influence of Western Europe as well as the lingering influence of communism and its collapse are shaping the concept of social enterprise in East-Central Europe. It discusses how much of the movement is being pushed forward by a situation of high rates of unemployment, poverty, and unequal access to social safety nets brought on by the fall of communism. The chapter discusses how small, self-help groups in this region, in contrast to other regions, are being created for the purpose of earned income generation. However, it acknowledges that access to government resources (with the exception of European Union funds for new EU members) and private funds is limited in this region and the development of social enterprise is largely supported by international donors. The chapter notes how the East-Central Europe region has been about as strong as Western Europe in the passage of legislation that creates new legal forms for social enterprise organizations.

Chapter 4, on Southeast Asia, was written by a team of educators from the Entrepreneurs School of Asia in Quezon City, Philippines, headed up by Joel Santos, the school's president. The study of social enterprise in this region too is still relatively new, thus much of the discussion in this chapter is built on many examples of social enterprises, particularly large operations, such as the Grameen Bank in Bangladesh, founded by Nobel laureate Dr. Mohammad Yunus, and their efforts at poverty reduction. The authors discuss how historical events such as colonial rule and the failure of government-led poverty initiatives have shaped and spurred on the development of a combination of civil society and market-based solutions to address poverty issues in the region. The chapter covers the broad range of organizational forms that social enterprises operate: cooperative enterprises, civic foundations of corporations, religious-based organizations, and associations. It also introduces new roles for social enterprise: peace-building and war reconstruction.

Chapter 5, on the United States, was coauthored by the editor, an assistant professor at Georgia State University, and Kirsten Gagnaire, founder and principal of the Social Enterprise Group, LLC, a social enterprise consulting firm in Washington State. It discusses the closing of a divide between academics and nonprofit practitioners in the understanding of social enterprise in the United States. These groups have coalesced around the idea that social enterprise includes both nonprofit and business forms. The chapter then discusses the many different organizational arrangements available for nonprofit and business social enterprise in the U.S. The authors also provide data on the amount of earned income attributed to nonprofit social enterprise, showing in graph form a significant rise in the commercial activity of U.S. nonprofits over a twenty-year span. The chapter highlights how private philanthropy, rather than government, is providing support for the development of social enterprise. The authors conclude with a review of some of the major concerns regarding social enterprise as it is presently developing in the United States.

In contrast to the others, chapter 6 on Zimbabwe and Zambia was written by two community development consultants, Absolom Masendeke and Alex Mugova, both program team leaders for Practical Action in Southern Africa, headquartered in Zimbabwe. Consultants were chosen to author this chapter because social enterprise is rapidly changing on the local level in this region and is still largely understudied at universities. The authors discuss how social enterprise in this part of the world is currently expanding in conjunction with international aid projects. As such, its conceptualization is currently tied to ideas expressed by the international development community, including microcredit lending institutions and the small businesses they support. The chapter discusses how high unemployment and the negative social impact of structural adjustment reforms promoted by international financial institutions are the leading reasons behind the recent movement toward social enterprise solutions. The chapter also highlights the need for market intermediation for products of social enterprise, the limiting effect the lack of appropriate national-level legislation can have on social enterprise operation, and the negative impact of too much financial support by international donors.

Chapter 7 was written by Mario Roitter, director and senior researcher, and Alejandra Vivas, researcher, both of the Civil Society and Social Development Department, Center for the Study of State and Society (CEDES), Buenos Aires, Argentina. This chapter provides a strong historical analysis of the development of social enterprise in Argentina. The authors note how early social enterprise included mostly cooperatives and mutual benefit societies following models inherited from European immigrants. More recently, economic decline and high unemployment tied to structural adjustment programs prompted variations of these forms, including the rise of so-called "regained companies": failed companies that have been reorganized into self-managed cooperatives, at times in opposition to local authorities. The authors identify 170 regained companies that have been formed since the end of the 1990s and discuss the factors behind their creation as well as the process involved in their restructuring. They conclude with a discussion of the prospects for social enterprise as a more dynamic process for development than what is currently in place in the country. Overall, the chapter points to a more politicized discourse for social enterprise in Argentina than other areas.

Chapter 8, on Japan, was written by Professor Ichiro Tsukamoto of the School of Business Administration, Meiji University, and Professor Mariko Nishimura, Faculty of Law, Meiji-Gakuin University. They note that in Japan, the term "social enterprise" is still relatively new. Nonetheless, since 2000, it has increasingly attracted the public interest as an alternative business model for nonprofit organizations and corporate social responsibility. In recent years, the national government and local authorities have become interested in the potential of social enterprise, particularly for local-level regeneration and social integration. In this context, new intermediary organizations have engaged in building networks among social enterprises, in part to disseminate new ideas for social innovation. The authors write, however, that broad awareness of social enterprise in Japanese society is limited, supporting institutions and networks have been poorly created, and in most cases, entrepreneurship related to successful marketing and sustainable income generation tends to be lacking.

While the book provides a first step in understanding social enterprise and its context from an international perspective, it does not attempt to assess its effectiveness or overall impact. Authors of the individual region/country chapters were asked to provide a general discussion of the known benefits and challenges to social enterprise in their geographic areas. However, these are only preliminary reflections, often based on limited information. Indeed, a common finding in this research has been that there is great need for the systematic investigation of social enterprise in almost every country and region in the study. The book is also not meant to be the definitive source of information on social enterprise in the represented regions and countries. Although the authors made every effort to capture the broad understanding and context for social enterprise in their given locations, some perspectives and activities may have been overlooked. Also, their work represents only a snapshot in time in what is, in many areas, a dynamic and changing movement.

NOTES

1. See Salamon (2004); Smallbone et al. (2001); Nicholls (2006a) for evidence and discussion of the rise in social enterprise/social entrepreneurship.
2. See Nicholls (2006a) and Mair, Robinson, and Hockerts (2006) for discussions of the many participants and publications that have introduced different definitions of these terms.
3. In the process, the book begins to address research questions raised by Austin (2006), specifically those involving a comparison of social entrepreneurship across dimensions of place and form.

REFERENCES

Alter, S. K. (2002). *Case studies in social enterprise: Counterpart International's experience.* Washington, DC: Counterpart International.

Anheier, H. (2005). *Nonprofit organizations: Theory, management, policy.* New York: Routledge.

Austin, J. E. (2006). Three avenues for social entrepreneurship research. In J. Mair, J. Robinson, & K. Hockerts (Eds.), *Social entrepreneurship* (pp. 22–33). New York: Palgrave Macmillan.

Bornstein, D. (2004). *How to change the world: Social entrepreneurs and the power of new ideas.* Oxford: Oxford University Press.

Borzaga, C., & Defourny, J. (Eds.). (2001). *The emergence of social enterprise.* New York: Routledge.

Dacanay, M. (2004). *Creating a space in the market: Social enterprise stories in Asia.* Makati City, Philippines: Asian Institute of Management (AIM) and Conference of Asian Foundations and Organizations (CAFO).

Esping-Anderson, G. (1990). *The three worlds of welfare capitalism.* Princeton: Princeton University Press.

Mair, J., Robinson, J., & Hockerts, K. (2006). Introduction. In J. Mair, J. Robinson,

& K. Hockerts (Eds.), *Social entrepreneurship* (pp. 1–13). New York: Palgrave Macmillan.

Moore, B., Jr. (1966). *Social origins of dictatorship and democracy: Lord and peasant in the making of the modern world.* Boston: Beacon Press.

NESsT. (1997). *The NGO-business hybrid: Is the private sector the answer?* Washington, DC: The Johns Hopkins University, Nitze School of Advanced International Studies.

Nicholls, A. (2006a). Introduction. In A. Nicholls (Ed.), *Social entrepreneurship: New models of sustainable change* (pp. 1–36).Oxford: Oxford University Press.

Nicholls, A. (Ed.). (2006b). *Social entrepreneurship: New models of sustainable change.* Oxford: Oxford University Press.

Nyssens, M. (Ed.). (2006). *Social enterprise: At the crossroads of market, public policies and civil society.* New York: Routledge.

Salamon, L. S., Sokolowski, W., & Anheier, H. K. (2000). Social origins of civil society: An overview. Working paper of the Johns Hopkins Comparative Nonprofit Sector Project, no. 38. Baltimore: Johns Hopkins Center for Civil Society Studies.

Salamon, L. et al. (2004). *Global civil society: Dimensions of the nonprofit sector, volume two.* Bloomfield, CT: Kumarian Press.

Smallbone, D., Evans, M., Ekanem, I., & Butters, S. (2001). *Researching social enterprise.* London: Middlesex University.

Social Enterprise Knowledge Network (SEKN). (2006). *Effective management of social enterprises: Lessons from businesses and civil society organizations in Iberoamerica.* David Rockefeller/Inter-American Development Bank.

2 Western Europe

DEFINITION

In Western Europe, according to Defourny and Nyssens (2006, p. 4), the concept of social enterprise "made its first appearance in the early 1990s, at the very heart of the third sector, following an impetus that was first Italian, linked closely with the cooperative movement." Indeed, according to European tradition (Evers & Laville, 2004), the third sector brings together cooperatives, associations, mutual societies, and, increasingly, foundations, or, in other words, all not-for-profit organizations (organizations not owned by shareholders) that are labeled the "social economy" in some European countries.[1]

Specifically, in 1991, the Italian parliament adopted a law creating a specific legal form for "social cooperatives," stimulating their extraordinary growth. These cooperatives arose primarily in response to needs that had been inadequately met or not met at all by public services or private enterprises (Borzaga & Santuari, 2001). More than ten years later, the government in the United Kingdom defined social enterprises as "businesses with primarily social objectives whose surpluses are principally reinvested for that purpose in the business or in the community, rather than being driven by the need to maximize profit for shareholders and owners" (DTI, 2004), and a new legal form, the "community interest company," was approved by the British parliament in 2004.

European researchers noticed the existence of similar initiatives in several other European countries. These initiatives were given a variety of labels and legal forms. In 1996, researchers from a number of these countries decided to form a network to study the emergence of social enterprises in Europe. This group became known as the EMES Research Network. Covering all fifteen countries that at the time comprised the European Union, this network of researchers carried out its initial work over a four-year period and gradually developed a common approach to the study of social enterprise in Europe (Borzaga & Defourny, 2001b).

In the European public debate, the concept of social enterprise has different meanings and is still unclear. One school of thought stresses the social entrepreneurship dynamic developed by firms seeking to enhance the social impact of their productive activities. In this school the literature often highlights innovative approaches to tackling social needs developed by individuals who are fostering businesses (Grenier, 2003), mostly in the nonprofit sector but also in the for-profit sector (Nicholls, 2005). In the latter case, social entrepreneurship has to do, at least partially, with the "corporate social responsibility" debate. Another stream of thought uses the concept of social enterprise only for organizations belonging to the third sector and therefore builds on the specificities of the sector. In such social enterprises, generally of the cooperative or associative type, the social impact on the community is not merely a consequence or a side effect of economic activity; it is the motivation itself (Defourny & Nyssens, 2006).

The EMES approach (Borzaga & Defourny, 2001a; Nyssens, 2006) falls within this latter framework. EMES defines social enterprise as not-for-profit organizations providing goods and services, directly related to their explicit goal of benefiting the community. They generally rely on collective dynamics involving various stakeholders in their governing bodies, and they place a high value on independence and economic risk-taking related to ongoing socioeconomic activity (Defourny & Nyssens, 2008). This research effort is, among other things, establishing an "ideal type" of social enterprise with the understanding that even social enterprises that do not precisely adhere to the "ideal type" are nonetheless included in the sphere of social enterprise.

This perspective on social enterprise differs on at least three points from the U.S. rationale for social enterprise (Defourny & Nyssens, 2006). First, the EMES framework places the emphasis on the multidimensional character of the governance of social enterprises. This point of view is far richer than the sole nondistribution constraint or the limitation on profit distribution, which constitutes the central feature around which most of the nonprofit literature has been built. In comparing it with social enterprise in the United States, Young and Salamon state, "In Europe, the notion of social enterprise focuses more heavily on the way an organisation is

FIGURE 2.1. *The EMES Ideal Type of Social Enterprise*

The EMES definition distinguishes between criteria that are more economic and criteria that are predominantly social.

The economic dimension
a) A continuous activity, producing and selling goods and/or services
b) A high degree of autonomy
c) A significant level of economic risk
d) A minimum amount of paid work

The social dimension
e) An explicit aim to benefit the community
f) An initiative launched by a group of citizens
g) A decision-making power not based on capital
h) A participatory nature, which involves the various parties affected by the activity
i) A limited profit distribution

Source: Defourny, 2001, pp. 16–18

governed and what its purpose is rather than on whether it strictly adheres to the nondistribution constraint of a formal nonprofit organisation" (2002, p. 433). The EMES definition of social enterprise also integrates this feature by its "limited profit distribution" criterion. However, other aspects are central to characterizing social enterprise's governance structure. One of these is the existence of a collective dynamic of entrepreneurship involving people who belong to a community or to a group that shares a well-defined need or goal. This does not exclude the possibility that some leader or charismatic entrepreneur plays a key role in the enterprise, but generally these persons are supported by a group whose members are responsible for the public benefit mission of the social enterprise. This view contrasts with the emphasis on social entrepreneurship (see Dees, 2001), "which reflects a shift toward focusing on individuals and away from traditional emphasis on the community and collective found in community development and the co-op movement" (Grenier, 2003, p. 4).

The EMES definition also stresses the involvement of different stakeholders in the governance of the organization through formal channels, such as participation on the board, or more informal ones. Defourny states, "In many cases, one of the aims of social enterprises is to further democracy at a local level through economic activity" (2001, p. 18). What sets them apart is the involvement of stakeholders through the representation and participation of workers, customers, or beneficiaries, that is, the use of a democratic management style, which is not a requirement of social enterprise in the United States. For example, some cooperatives are commonly understood as a basic type of social enterprise. Indeed, in some European countries, such as Italy, the term "social cooperative" came into common usage before the term "social enterprise" (Bengtsson & Hulgard, 2001).

Moreover, regarding the involvement of stakeholders, the concept of "multiple stakeholder ownership" has been developed (Bacchiega & Borzaga, 2001) in reference to the fact that different types of stakeholders can be represented on the board of an organization. Governing bodies are made up of a diverse group of stakeholders that may include beneficiaries, employees, volunteers, public authorities, and donors, among others. Moreover, multi-stakeholder cooperatives, as a distinct legal form of cooperative, are becoming increasingly popular in Europe and are even recognized in some national-level legislation (see legal forms below) (Münkner, 2003; Levi, 2003; Lindsay et al., 2003). A recent analysis (Nyssens, 2006) based on more than 160 European social enterprises shows that 58 percent of them involve more than one type of stakeholder on their board. Moreover, the data collected seem to indicate that "the participation of stakeholders in these social enterprises leads to the exercise of a real influence within boards" because of the "balanced governance structure" (Campi, Defourny, & Grégoire, 2006, p. 46). This dynamic, which links people with different backgrounds, is also reflected in the fact that a lot of social enterprises are founded through local partnerships across different types of stakeholders, which can consequently enhance the development of bridging social capital.

Second, though widely assumed in the U.S. and U.K. debates on social enterprise, the economic dimension of the concept does not necessarily refer to the growing importance of a trading activity. The central idea in Europe is, rather, that the financial viability of the social enterprise depends on the efforts of its members to secure adequate resources to support the enterprise's social mission. These resources can have a hybrid character and come from trading activities, from public subsidies, or from voluntary resources obtained thanks to the mobilization of social capital.

Though the EMES list of criteria does not make this explicit, the third way the European conception differs is related to the nature of the continuous activity of the social enterprise. The production of goods and/or services should in itself (and not only indirectly through the income it generates) constitute support of the social mission of the organization. In other words, the nature of the economic activity must be connected to the social mission: if the mission of the social enterprise is to create jobs for low-qualified people, the economic activity itself supports the work-integration goal; if the mission of the social enterprise is to develop social services, the economic activity is the delivery of these social services. By contrast, in the U.S. or U.K. conception of social enterprise, the trading activity is often considered simply a source of income, and the nature of the trade does not necessarily matter (Dees, 1998).

HISTORY OF THE RECENT SOCIAL ENTERPRISE MOVEMENT

In Europe, the trend toward social enterprise was focused on the simultaneous development of public interest services and diversification of revenue generation, mainly in the third sector. With the decreased economic growth and increased unemployment that began at the end of the 1970s and continued into the 1990s, many European welfare states experienced a crisis. Budgetary constraints were the main cause, but the crisis was also in terms of the effectiveness and legitimacy of state welfare programs (Borzaga & Defourny, 2001b; Spear et al., 2001; Borzaga & Santuari, 2003). Legitimacy was particularly undermined in the area of unemployment as policies, especially for the long-term unemployed (including the disadvantaged and low-skilled), proved not very effective (Borzaga & Defourny, 2001b).

In this context, an increasing number of socioeconomic initiatives, mainly inside the third sector, appeared in response to emerging needs, including: solutions to the housing problems of increasingly marginalized groups; child-care services to meet new needs created by socioeconomic changes; new services for the elderly, given the rapid aging of the population and changes in family structures; urban regeneration initiatives; employment programs for the long-term unemployed, and so on. Social actors did not find adequate public policy schemes to tackle these problems and pointed to the limits of traditional public intervention practices. The first pioneering social enterprises in Europe were founded in the 1980s by civil society actors including social workers, associative militants, representatives of more traditional third sector organizations, sometimes with the excluded workers themselves. In some countries with a tradition of cooperative entrepreneurship, some pioneering initiatives were launched by the workers themselves relying on a self-help dynamic. Sometimes the groups launching social enterprises had links to public bodies, which probably reflected, in countries such as Germany or Denmark, the interwoven nature of the third sector and the public sector (Laville, Lemaitre, & Nyssens, 2006).

Although these innovative initiatives were not labeled "social enterprises," they were characterized by a new entrepreneurial spirit focused on social goals. Comparing social enterprises to traditional third sector organizations reveals some differences. In contrast to traditional cooperatives, social enterprises are more open to the local community and place more emphasis on the dimension of general interest because they serve the broader community and not just their own members (such as organizations combating poverty and exclusion or protecting the environment). Moreover, social enterprises are initiated by a group of citizens and often combine different types of stakeholders in their membership, whereas traditional cooperatives are usually single-stakeholder organizations. Compared to traditional associations, social enterprises place a higher value on economic risk-taking related to an ongoing productive activity. Social enterprises are, therefore, new organizations that may be regarded as a subdivision of the third sector but that also reflect a process at work within older experiences inside the third sector (Defourny & Nyssens, 2006).

As previously stated, social enterprises operate in a wide range of activities. However, one type of social enterprise is widespread across Europe: "work integration social enterprises" (WISE) (Nyssens, 2006). The persistence of structural unemployment among some groups, the difficulties of integrating some workers by means of traditional active labor policies, and the need for more active integration policies have naturally raised questions concerning the role that social enterprises can occupy in combating unemployment and fostering employment growth. The major objective of these work-integration social enterprises is to help poorly qualified, unemployed people who are at risk of permanent exclusion from the labor market. These enterprises integrate them into work and society through productive activity. In almost all European countries, this type of social enterprise has driven the development of specific public schemes, causing the concept of social enterprise to be associated with this type of employment-creating initiative.

In some cases, social enterprises adopt existing legal forms, including the association, cooperative, companies limited by guarantee, or, for example, the Industrial and Provident Societies in the U.K. However, most social enterprises fall under the legal forms of associations or cooperatives. Social enterprises are established as associations in those countries where the legal form of association allows a degree of freedom in selling goods and services on the open market. In countries where associations are more limited in this regard, such as the Nordic countries, social enterprises are more often created under the legal form for cooperatives (Borzaga & Defourny, 2001a).

Besides these traditional legal forms, a number of national governments have created new legal forms specifically for social enterprises with the goal of promoting their development. In 1991, Italy became the first to create a legal form of "social cooperative" status that has been successful in increasing the number of this type of organization. The law distinguishes between two types of social cooperatives: those delivering social, health, and educational services, called "type A" social cooperatives, and those providing work integration for disadvantaged people, called "type B" social cooperatives. In 2006, an Italian law on social enterprise was enacted that opened this label to various legal forms (not just social cooperatives) and fields of activities, provided that the organization complied with the nondistribution constraint and involved certain categories of stakeholders, including workers and beneficiaries. In Portugal, Greece, Spain, and France, these new legal forms are of the cooperative type. Portugal created the "social solidarity cooperative" in 1998, and Greece created the "social cooperative with limited liability" in 1999. As for Spain, a national law created the label of "social initiative cooperative" in 1999. Any type of cooperative providing social services or developing an economic activity working toward the work integration of socially excluded persons can use this label. Twelve autonomous regions in Spain have since developed their own legislation linked to this national law. France introduced the "société co-opérative d'interêt collectif" in 2002. In Belgium, the "social purpose company" legal framework, introduced in 1996, does not focus on the sole cooperative tradition, although it is often combined with it. Most recently, the U.K. approved the "community interest company" in 2004. Less than two years after its implementation, the number of community interest companies reached one thousand.

Some of this legislation, including the new French laws, was supported by the European Commission's Digestus Project, which began in October 1998. The project proposes legal changes to member states with the goal of promoting social enterprise along the Italian model of cooperative enterprise (Lindsay et al., 2003). All of these countries' legal forms define social enterprise by the social purpose of the company and its limited way of distributing profit. All of them except the U.K. also define a specific governance model regarding the involvement of various stakeholders and the democratic decision-making process of the board. For example, in Italy, the 1991 Law 381 established the social cooperative with three main categories of share/stakeholders: lending or funding members (65 percent), volunteer members (20 percent), and beneficiary/user members (5 percent) (Thomas, 2004). The French legal form of the "société coopérative d'intérêt collectif" also defines a multi-stakeholder strategy (see Lindsay & Hems, 2004).

SUPPORTIVE INSTITUTIONS

In Europe, the institutional environment for strategic support of social enterprise is more tied to regional or national government and European Union support for the subject than in other world regions.[2] While the various legal forms are open to a wide spectrum of social purposes, almost all the specific public programs and public financing linked to social enterprises are focused on the work-integration social enterprise (WISE).

Indeed, the institutionalization of WISEs has to be studied in the context of the boom of active labor policies. During the 1980s, public bodies, faced with high rates of unemployment and a crisis of public finances, developed active labor policies that tried to integrate the unemployed into the labor market (through professional training programs, job subsidy programs, etc.) instead of relying only on passive labor policies based on a system of allocation of cash benefits to the unemployed. In this context, it seems that WISEs have increasingly represented a tool for implementing these active labor market policies, a kind of "transmission belt" of active labor market policies. Indeed, they were pioneers in promoting the integration of excluded persons through productive activities. The first WISES actually implemented active labor policies before such policies institutionally came into existence.

However, we can observe that, at least in the beginning of the public institutionalization of WISES, some countries that are characterized by a long tradition of social policies and active labor policies, such as Sweden and Denmark, used types of programs other than employment programs to sustain such pioneering initiatives; one example is the "social development program" in Denmark. In other cases, the WISES, whose main target groups are disabled people, have also been recognized through traditional social policies. In some countries, such as the United Kingdom or Spain, where welfare spending is generally lower and labor policies in particular are less developed, pioneering initiatives received little or no public support.

The 1990s saw the development of specific public programs targeting social enterprise in many countries. This recognition by public authorities of the integration through work performed by social enterprises usually allows more stable access to public subsidies, but in a limited way. Usually only temporary subsidies are granted to start the initiative and to compensate for the "temporary unemployability" (i.e., the difficulty in obtaining employment due to the deterioration of a person's skills following his or her extended absence from the labor market) of the workers. Examples of public programs on the national level include "empresas de inserção" in Portugal, "entreprise d'insertion, association intermédiaire" in France, the "social economy program" in Ireland, and social enterprise in Finland. On the regional level there have been public programs such as "enterprise d'insertion," "enterprise de formation par le travail," and "sociale werkplaats" in Belgium, and "empresas de insercion" in Spain. In 2006, Poland also passed an Act on Social Cooperatives specifically intended for the work integration of groups in particular need, such as ex-convicts, the long-term unemployed, disabled persons, and former alcohol or drug addicts. In 2007, Spain's national parliament passed a law on work-integration enterprises. It should be noted that these different pieces of legislation do not define any new legal form; rather, they create a tool, like an official register, for social enterprises.

In some countries, the persistence of a social economy sector or cooperative sector that still maintains some of its original features influences the environmental perception of these new social enterprises and the building of organizational identities and institutions along this tradition (Bode, Evers, & Schultz, 2006). The influence has been reciprocal: the emergence of these social enterprises, whose official recognition was in some respects made easier by the existence of a social economy or cooperative sector, has often brought new life into this sector. For example, the development of new public programs targeted at social enterprise in the field of work integration fostered the creation of social economy units inside public authorities at the national or regional level in Belgium, France, and Ireland. In Sweden, the minister of the social economy, whose existence is probably linked to the tradition of a cooperative movement in this country (Stryjan, 2004; Hulgård, 2004), supports the development of new social enterprises, even though there is no official accreditation of them.

In the United Kingdom, the Blair government launched the Coalition for Social Enterprise and created a Social Enterprise Unit in the Department of Trade and Industry (DTI) to improve knowledge about social enterprises and, above all, to promote the development of social enterprises throughout the country. The Social Enterprise Unit is specifically responsible for implementing a three-year program called "Social Enterprise: A Strategy for Success." The objective is to create a supportive environment for social enterprise through a coordinated effort by DTI, regional development agencies, government offices, and local government. This unit also makes tax and administrative regulatory recommendations for social enterprises and supports public and private training and research in the area (DTI, 2004). In 2006, this social enterprise unit was transferred to the cabinet office, where it was linked with government responsibilities for the voluntary sector.

Another way for public authorities to support the mission of social enterprises is by contracting out the provision of goods or services (Laville, Lemaitre, & Nyssens, 2006). Indeed, sales to public bodies can be organized in different ways. One way is that of traditional market sales, organized, for instance, through traditional calls for bids where the offer with the lowest price for the level of quality required is chosen. A second way is that of sales motivated by "social criteria" (Gardin, 2006). On the one hand, in small markets, usually with local public bodies, sales motivated by "social criteria" can occur in a discretionary way: the public bodies simply "privilege" some social enterprises they know when they have to buy a product or a service in order to support them and their social mission. These types of sales motivated by a social mission can occur when the amount of the market is, in financial terms, lower than the threshold established by the European Community law; public bodies are then allowed to contract directly with social enterprises without issuing a call for tender. On the other hand, in the case of more important markets, some social dimensions can be introduced in these public markets. For example, they can be introduced in the form of social clauses that allow calls for bids of other types of criteria than market criteria, such as the importance of the integration of disadvantaged workers (Navez, 2005). Thus, there are regulated and unregulated ways to support social enterprises.

The European Union (EU) has also been a strong actor in promoting research through programs developed by the Directorate-General for Research and providing program support for social enterprise. The EU views social enterprise as a business model that can simultaneously address issues of economic growth, employment, and quality of life (Thomas, 2004). The European Commission's Directorate-General for Enterprise has supported social economy enterprises such as cooperatives and mutuals since 1989 and is currently focusing on their "enterprise aspects." The Directorate-General for Enterprise supports research, helps draft European Union statutes, consults with organizations, and forges links with public officials in member countries who are working on regulation in this area (European Union, 2004). The European Union also provides financial support for social enterprise in individual member countries. Ireland is an example of a country in which the EU has been especially active. Beginning in 1992, Ireland received a Global Grant from EU Structural Funds "to support local development and enterprise initiatives and to promote integrated economic, social, and community development of local areas" (O'Hara, 2001, p. 156). The EU LEADER program for rural development provided similar support. Other EU initiatives in Ireland provide direct and indirect support for local social enterprise, including INTEREG, NOW, INTEGRA, and URBAN. As O'Hara summarizes, "This support for local development has either helped to create the conditions for the emergence of new social enterprises or has afforded existing enterprises the opportunity to broaden or consolidate their activities through participation in such programs" (2001, p. 156).

Membership organizations for social enterprises are emerging along with the rise of social enterprise. For example, in the U.K. between 1997 and 2003, several umbrella organizations of social enterprises or social entrepreneurs were established (Grenier, 2003), including the Community Action Network, Social Enterprise London, and the Social Enterprise Coalition. The Community Action Network is a membership association for social entrepreneurs that is roughly equivalent to the United States–based Social Enterprise Alliance. It is oriented broadly on the promotion of social entrepreneurship, especially the exchange of ideas. The Community Action Network states, "We focus on the practical delivery of the social entrepreneurial approach, whilst continuing to stimulate government, public and private sector thinking, both on the method and the importance of this approach for social regeneration" (Community Action Network, 2004). The Social Enterprise Coalition is a national network of social enterprises located in the social economy.

The development of such umbrella organizations can be seen in all European countries. They can have key roles in negotiating contracts either with private enterprises or with public bodies, in exchanging best practices not only at the national level but also between different European countries, and in interacting with public bodies for the construction of specific public programs. Indeed, public policies in this field are the result of interactions between social actors, particularly between the promoters of social enterprises and representatives of the public bodies. In other words, public programs are not the result of top-down processes only; they are the result of a co-construction between representatives of social enterprise and those of public bodies (Laville, Lemaitre, & Nyssens, 2006).

In Europe, initial research on social enterprise was conducted almost exclusively in social science departments. Much attention was placed on the contribution of these organizations to the work integration of the unskilled and to care services. Now, however, some business schools, such as the Skoll Centre in the Oxford business school, have begun to explore the field through a focus on social entrepreneurship (Nicholls, 2006). There is also a concerted effort in Europe, through the work of the EMES Research Network described previously, to unify definitions and research on social enterprise in European Union countries (Defourny, 2001; Nyssens, 2006, Defourny & Nyssens, 2009). Current research also includes the development of theoretical approaches to the study of social enterprise: this is work that often draws on economic theory (Bacchiega & Borzaga, 2001; Laville & Nyssens, 2001b; Sacconi & Grimalda, 2001; Badelt, 1997) and sociology and political science theory (Evers, 2001; Evers & Laville, 2004).

How should the role of social enterprises be analyzed in the different welfare state contexts of European countries? Are they a sign of a retrenchment of the welfare state? The answer is complex and naturally varies depending on the welfare state model and its existing relationship with the third sector.

European welfare states have a long tradition of partnership with third sector organizations, even if the relationships vary according to the type of welfare mix (Evers & Laville, 2004). In corporatist states like Germany, France, and Belgium, there is a lasting tradition of partnership in the provision of social services between the state and associations (Salamon & Anheier, 1998; Laville & Nyssens, 2001a). Associations have often taken a pioneering role in clearing the way for meeting emerging social needs. Later, public authorities arrive to regulate their activities, providing financial support, among other things. Therefore, associations still retain an important role in the provision of social services in these corporatist models, beyond the phase of social innovation. The state has to respect the autonomy and the role of associations and support them in achieving their objectives that are linked to the public good. In the Nordic model of the welfare state, the state is responsible for regulating and providing social services. The key role for associations in this social democratic model is advocacy rather than service provision. Finally, scientists usually classify the U.K. as a liberal model (Salamon & Anheier, 1998). In this model, a lower level of government social spending is associated with a relatively large voluntary sector, and the public sector provides less financial support to voluntary organizations than in the corporatist model. However, in the U.K. the situation is mixed. Indeed, the experience of the two World Wars led national public authorities to develop various social programs with universal coverage, and charities were supported through public subsidies (Lewis, 1999). This approach was challenged in the 1970s and 1980s by a new public management approach that stressed quasi-market design to increase efficiency in service provision. With the development of the compact framework in the late 1990s, the types of relationships between the state and the voluntary sector were once more at issue. Indeed, this agreement between the public authorities and the voluntary sector recognizes the specific role of the voluntary sector as complementary to the state in the development and the provision of public policies and services (Craig, Taylor, & Carlton, 2005).

Does the recent trend in the development of social enterprises affect the nature of relationships between third sector organizations and public bodies? It seems that it is not the level of social expenditures that is challenged but the instruments through which government supports social enterprises in particular and third sector organizations more generally. More and more, public money across the different models of the welfare state takes the form of contracts and third-party payments instead of grants. Public policy is looking to increase efficiency by introducing competition among different types of providers using quasi-market logic. As a result, social enterprises, for-profit enterprises, and public organizations are increasingly on equal footing regarding contracts. The key question is whether social enterprise can preserve its social innovation role in this type of financing framework. Regarding this question, the discussion around the compact in the U.K. could be seen as a way of recognizing the specific voluntary sector role in social innovation, which was somewhat denied in the quasi-market logic implemented through the new public management model in the 1980s.

In the Nordic countries, the emergence of social enterprise is a sign of an increasing collaboration between the third sector and public bodies. This is quite a new phenomenon for these countries, where the third sector is traditionally viewed as having an advocacy role rather than a service-provider role. In countries where welfare provision of services was low, such as Italy, social co-ops pioneered the implementation of active labor policies and the delivery of some social services before their existence in governmental programming. If social enterprises addressed particular areas for which the welfare state had not been able to meet demand, we cannot attribute their development to a reduction in social services. Instead, we can attribute their development to new forms of partnership and funding strategies with the third sector whose advantages and drawbacks have to be carefully evaluated.

Social enterprise in Europe faces a set of challenges that stem from Europe's historical approach to social enterprise. Many observers' largest concern is the narrow range of services currently supported by social enterprises. Having become associated with work integration and, to a lesser extent, personal social service provision, social enterprise is being underutilized as a viable strategy for supporting other nonprofit activities (Borzaga & Defourny, 2001a).

This problem stems from the difficulty of reconciling social enterprise views with those of public bodies due to the contested nature of the mission of social enterprises (Bode, Evers, & Schultz, 2006). Active labor policies increasingly constitute the framework within which social enterprises are developed, and as such, they somewhat frame the objectives and actions of social enterprises. Public programs tend to recognize the social mission in the field of work integration in a rather narrow way, but social enterprises usually have a much more complex blend of goals (Evers, 2001). This blend of goals includes three different categories (Campi, Defourny, & Grégoire, 2006): social goals, connected to social enterprises' particular mission to benefit the community, which is not restricted to work integration of excluded workers; economic goals, connected to the entrepreneurial nature of social enterprises; and sociopolitical goals, connected to the fact that social enterprises come from a sector traditionally involved in sociopolitical action. This last goal can be included in the wider perspective of producing social capital. Concretely, the achievement of the "social capital goal" by social enterprises may appear not only in the will to cooperate with many economic, social, and political actors through the development of various networks, but also in the implementation of democratic decision-making processes in specific working conditions (e.g., little hierarchy, participation of the workers, trust atmosphere, etc.), and in the promotion of volunteering, and so on (Davister, 2004). As a matter of fact, within these organizations, the production and mobilization of social capital can be goals in themselves and not merely instruments for achieving other objectives (Evers, 2001).

The difficulty of valorizing their multiple-goal missions explains, on the one hand, why some pioneering initiatives chose not to adopt these social enterprise–specific public programs; this is the case with "local development" initiatives in Ireland that did not adopt the "social economy" program. On the other hand, it should be noted that if public programs encourage some initiatives, they also exclude others. In France, for instance, the institutionalization process recognized and favored initiatives launched by professional and associative militant actors aiming to integrate disadvantaged populations through work opportunities, whereas the initiatives originating from these populations themselves were in most cases neglected. In other countries, such as Portugal, work-integration social enterprise emerged with the creation of a specific public program, partly under the pressure of the "national plans for employment" developed within the framework of the European Commission. These organizations are only weakly embedded in the social fabric and rely on a public program that appears somewhat artificial (Perista & Nogueira, 2004).

In a context where the sector of services (more specifically, that of personal services) is on the rise—for example, through the development of voucher systems—the analysis of the specific characteristics of social enterprises must go beyond the field of work integration. Indeed, personal services are provided by a variety of operators, including for-profit private enterprises, traditional nonprofit bodies, social enterprises, and public sector organizations, which have specific organizational forms and modes of governance. The development of these services generates many expectations based on the collective benefits they can produce. These expected benefits include equity and the creation of high-quality jobs. Therefore, it is important that the question of the value added to models of social enterprises, which are driven by their explicit goal of benefiting the community, be studied more thoroughly in the European context.

EXAMPLE I: THE GROUPE TERRE

Overview

The Groupe Terre, located in Belgium, is an association of social enterprise organizations that serves two key purposes. The first purpose is the creation of jobs for unemployed and underprivileged workers in Belgium. The second is the support of sustainable development projects for disadvantaged groups in both the Northern and Southern Hemispheres. The Groupe Terre has decentralized many management functions, giving some of them to the underprivileged workers for whom it provides jobs. A weekly program provides consultation services, training, and professional education to these workers involved in the group's decision-making process.

Structure

The Terre ASBL NPO legal form in Belgium manages most of the commercial activities of the Groupe Terre and thus also contains the General Assembly, which has final decision-making authority for the entire organization. This General Assembly is composed of Groupe Terre employees who have been on staff for at least one year. Inclusion in the assembly is voluntary. At present, the seventy-five employees who meet these requirements and ten outside volunteers assemble three times annually to make strategic decisions for the group as a whole.

Activities

All social enterprise activities of the Groupe Terre are organized under the Wallonia Project, aimed at providing approximately 280 underprivileged workers with stable jobs, training, and educational opportunities; most of these workers collect and recycle secondhand clothing, paper, and cardboard.

Two enterprises in Groupe Terre, Récol' Terre safs (a social purpose company) and Tri-Terre safs, organize the collection and sorting of paper and cardboard. The latter organization, Tri-Terre safs, has partnered with a private operator. This partnership has allowed the social enterprise to sustain production and increase employment.

Two other social enterprise companies within the Groupe Terre are Pan-terre and Co-terre safs, manufacturers of insulation material made from recycled paper and straw by means of a process that does not use any resins or chemicals. The patents and licenses behind the product and its production process were developed by the group.

The Autre Terre ASBL is the NGO of the group. It manages development projects in the Southern Hemisphere, population education initiatives in the Northern Hemisphere, and a new project that researches potential development activities for the group. The Groupe Terre currently supports a dozen projects throughout the Southern Hemisphere in which the group partners with local cultures to adapt the sustainable social enterprise model, which provides employment and sustainability. Development workers from the group often serve as indispensable links between the workers of Groupe Terre and those of the Southern Hemisphere projects, helping to nurture cross-cultural worker solidarity. The Autre Terre ASBL draws support from donations and the work of volunteers in addition to income generated from the Groupe Terre's other enterprises. The Belgian General Direction to Cooperation and Development (DGCI) and other regional bodies also provide substantial financial support, comprising 75 percent of the total budget.

The Future

The environmental sector is subject to greater competition from service multinationals. As such, new projects of the Groupe Terre have been limited by the challenges of maintaining current employment levels. Though preserving existing jobs is as important and difficult as creating jobs, such efforts are rarely recognized by European, federal, or regional directives.

EXAMPLE 2: SOCIAL COOPERATIVES OF THE
CONSORZIO PER l'IMPRESA SOCIALE[3]

More than twenty years ago, the Italian government began to implement a plan for the deinstitutionalization of state psychiatric hospitals. An innovative young psychiatrist, Dr. Franco Basaglia, was given the task of closing the large state hospital in Trieste and establishing necessary placements in the community for former patients (called consumers). Basaglia and the consumers quickly came to believe that finding jobs would be the best way to integrate the consumers into Triesten society. Unfortunately, the citizens of Trieste discriminated against the consumers by denying them employment. Basaglia, not easily daunted, decided to look for more innovative means of employment.

During this same time period, the direct care employees at the hospital were earning very poor wages, and many of them were forced to take on second jobs to subsidize their incomes. These second jobs ranged from carpentry and small agricultural enterprises to more skilled work, such as bookbinding. Basaglia began to encourage these direct care workers, who were also more open to interacting with people with psychiatric disabilities, to employ consumers to assist them in their second jobs. In a short time, a few of the small enterprises began growing into larger businesses. More and more consumers were employed as these businesses became successful. As the need for space for these growing businesses began to grow, Basaglia arranged for empty hospital wards to be renovated into office and manufacturing space. The old state hospital's central location, accessible by public transportation, proved ideal for these purposes.

The environment, today called the "business park," no longer bears any resemblance to a hospital. The park's small businesses are run as six "social cooperatives," and consumers are full partners in the enterprises. Employees are organized into small unions, better known as guilds, and a majority of the partners must be consumers. Out of the four hundred partners in these cooperatives, half have psychiatric disabilities. Furthermore, there are more than sixty trainees, whose wages are equal to those of their fully employed colleagues. The cooperatives all belong to the Consorzio per l'Impresa Sociale, a special association established in 1991 to support their administrative and corporate functions, and all of the cooperatives operate under free-market principles. Over the years, these social cooperatives have expanded from carpentry and agricultural ventures to include high-tech businesses and enterprises requiring highly skilled labor. Here are descriptions of the six social cooperatives:

1. The Lavoratori Uniti Cooperative, founded in 1972, is the oldest cooperative and now employs more than 120 workers and has annual revenue of about 3 billion lire. This cooperative provides various services, including transportation, cleaning, and bookbinding.
2. The La Collina Cooperative Sociale is considered the artistic cooperative because it works in the fields of photography, graphics, theater, video, and carpentry. In the carpentry division, furniture is manufactured for schools and hospitals. There are only eight persons in this cooperative, all of whom are consumers, and their revenues exceed 2 billion lire a year.
3. The Il Posto Delle Fragole Cooperative provides tourist services throughout Trieste, operates several restaurants, runs a hotel on the seaside, manages several pubs, and runs a hairstyling center. There are twenty-one members, of whom eleven are consumers.
4. The Crea Cooperative Sociale, the most recently established cooperative, operates a building renovation business.
5. The Agricola M.S. Pantaleone Cooperative works in the gardening sector. In addition to contracting with various businesses and private homeowners, this cooperative also contracts to care for the campus of the business park.
6. The Agenzia Socialle assists persons experiencing psychiatric and/or drug addiction problems. In addition to selected case management tasks, this cooperative also provides in-home health services.

By law, none of the cooperatives may share its profits with the various partners or stakeholders. Rather, all profits are reinvested into the cooperative and therefore are not subject to taxes. At the same time, the partners are the legal owners. When new partners join a cooperative, they pay an associative fee, which is returned if they depart from the cooperative. The sum of all of the partners' shares makes up the company's capital. In other words, all of the partners are entrepreneurs and run the risk of losing their investment. Also, all of the partners have one vote each, regardless of how many shares they own. At an annual Board of Directors meeting, the officers are elected, and it is mandatory that the majority of the officers be active working partners with psychiatric disabilities.

Italian Law 381 governs the cooperatives, defining them as "corporate entities" aimed at "pursuing the general interests of the community in human promotion and social integration, by managing different activities, with the aim of providing jobs for disadvantaged people." Today, the six social cooperatives thrive economically and serve as a symbol of the consumer's ability to pursue entrepreneurial efforts and participate in a competitive marketplace.

ACKNOWLEDGMENTS

Isabel Vidal of the University of Barcelona, Spain, assisted with the development of this chapter by providing an in-depth review of an earlier draft.

NOTES

1. For a discussion of this concept see Defourny (2001).
2. This section is developed more fully by Laville, Lemaitre, and Nyssens (2006).
3. The Italian example is adapted from Goegren (n.d.).

REFERENCES

Bacchiega, A., & Borzaga, C. (2001). Social enterprises as incentive structures: An economic analysis. In C. Borzaga & J. Defourny (Eds.), *The emergence of social enterprise*. New York: Routledge.

Badelt, C. (1997). Entrepreneurship theories of the non-profit sector. *Voluntas*, 8(2), pp. 162–178.

Bengtsson, S., & Hulgard, L. (2001). Denmark: Cooperative activity and community development. In C. Borzaga and J. Defourny (Eds.), *The emergence of social enterprise*. New York: Routledge.

Bode, I., Evers, A., & Schultz, A. (2006). Social enterprises: Can hybridisation be sustainable? In M. Nyssens (Ed.), *Social enterprises at the crossroads of market, public policies and civil society*. New York: Routledge.

Borzaga, C., and Defourny, J. (2001a). Conclusions: Social enterprises in Europe: A diversity of initiatives and prospects. In C. Borzaga & J. Defourny (Eds.), *The emergence of social enterprise*. New York: Routledge.

———. (2001b). *The emergence of social enterprise*. New York: Routledge.

Borzaga, C., & Santuari, A. (2001). Italy: From traditional cooperatives to innovative social enterprises. In C. Borzaga & J. Defourny (Eds.), *The emergence of social enterprise* (pp. 166–181). London: Routledge.

———. (2003). New trends in the non-profit sector in Europe: The emergence of social entrepreneurship. In OECD (Ed.), *The non-profit sector in a changing economy*. Paris: OECD.

Campi, S., Defourny, J., & Grégoire, O. (2006). Multiple goals and multiple stakeholder structure: The governance of social enterprises. In M. Nyssens (Ed.), *Social enterprises at the crossroads of market, public policies and civil society.* New York: Routledge.

Community Action Network. (2004). About us. Retrieved April 16, 2004, from www.can-online.org.uk/about.

Craig, G., Taylor, M., & Carlton, N. (2005). The paradox of compact: Monitoring the implementation of compacts. Home Office Research Development and Statistics, online report, February. Retrieved from www.homeoffice.gov.uk/rds/pdfs05/rdsolr0205.pdf.

Davister, C. (2004). Capital social dans les entreprises d'insertion: Un modèle à développer. *Reflets et perspectives de la vie économique, 42*(3).

Dees, J. G. (1998). Enterprising nonprofits. *Harvard Business Review*, January–February, pp. 55–67.

———. (2001). The meaning of social entrepreneurship. Retrieved from www.fuqua.duke.edu/centers/case/leaders/resources.htm.

Defourny, J. (2001). Introduction: From third sector to social enterprise. In C. Borzaga & J. Defourny (Eds.), *The emergence of social enterprise.* New York: Routledge.

Defourny, J., & Nyssens, M. (2006). Defining social enterprise. In *Social enterprises at the crossroads of market, public policies and civil society.* New York: Routledge.

———. (2008). Social enterprise in Europe: Recent trends and developments. *Social Enterprise Journal 4*(3), pp. 202–228.

———. (2009). Conceptions of social enterprise in Europe and the United States: Convergences and divergences. EMES Working Papers, *9*(1).

Department of Trade and Industry (DTI). (2004). Social enterprise. Retrieved February 6, 2004, from www.dti.gov.uk/socialenterprise.

European Union. (2004). Who we are and what we do. Retrieved March 26, 2004, from http://europa.eu.int/comm/enterprise/entrepreneurship/coop/social-history/social-history.htm.

Evers, A. (2001). The significance of social capital in the multiple goal and resource structure of social enterprises. In C. Borzaga & J. Defourny (Eds.), *The emergence of social enterprise.* New York: Routledge.

Evers, A., & Laville, J. L. (2004). *The third sector in Europe: Globalization and welfare series.* Northampton, MA: Edward Elgar.

Gardin, L. (2006). A variety of resource mix inside social enterprises. In

M. Nyssens (Ed.), *Social enterprises at the crossroads of market, public policies and civil society*. New York: Routledge.

Goegren, R. (n.d.). The social cooperative. Retrieved March 2005 from www.mentalhealth.org/publications/allpubs/KEN-01–0108/social.asp.

Grenier, P. (2003). Reclaiming enterprise for the social good: The political climate for social entrepreneurship in U.K. Presentation at the 32nd Annual ARNOVA Conference, Denver, CO.

Hulgård, L. (2004). Work integration social enterprises in Denmark. EMES Working Papers, 4(8).

Laville, J. L., Lemaitre, A., & Nyssens, M. (2006). Public policies and social enterprises in Europe: The challenge of institutionalisation. In M. Nyssens (Ed.), *Social enterprises at the crossroads of market, public policies and civil society*. New York: Routledge.

Laville, J. L., & Nyssens, M. (2001a). *Les services sociaux entre associations, Etat et marché, L'aide aux personnes âgées*. Paris: La Découverte, MAUSS, CRIDA.

———. (2001b). The social enterprise: Towards a theoretical socioeconomic approach. In C. Borzaga & J. Defourny (Eds.), *The emergence of social enterprise*. New York: Routledge.

Levi, Y. (2003). Single vs. multi-stakeholding, the "restitution" of the economic to cooperatives and the social enterprise. In *Communication to the International Conference of the EMES Network*, University of Trento, Italy.

Lewis, J. (1999). Reviewing the relationships between the voluntary sector and the state in Britain in the 1990s. *Voluntas, 10*(3), pp. 255–270.

Lindsay, G., & Hems, L. (2004). Sociétés coopératives d'intérêt collectif: The arrival of social enterprise within the French social economy. *Voluntas, 15*(3), pp. 265–286.

Lindsay, G., Hems, L., Noges, H., Liret, P., & Margado, A. (2003). Societal cooperative d'interet collectif: A research methodology. In *Communication to the 32nd Annual ARNOVA Conference*, Denver, CO, November.

Münkner, H. (2003). Multi-stakeholder cooperatives and their legal framework. In *Communication to the International Conference of the EMES Network*, University of Trento, Italy.

Navez, F. (2005). Marchés publics et évolution du droit européen: Quelles possibilités de soutien pour les entreprises d'économie sociale. In Première conférence européenne d'ISTR et EMES (Concepts of the third sector: The European debate). Paris, April 27–29.

Nicholls, A. (2005). Measuring impact in social entrepreneurship: New accountabilities to stakeholders and investors? Seminar on Social Enterprises, Milton Keynes University. Milton Keynes, U.K., July 2–3.

Nicholls, A. (Ed.) (2006) *Social entrepreneurship: New models of sustainable social change*. Oxford: Oxford University Press.

Nyssens, M. (2006). *Social enterprises at the crossroads of market, public policies and civil society*. New York: Routledge.

O'Hara, P. (2001). Ireland: Social enterprises and local development. In C. Borzaga & J. Defourny (Eds.), *The emergence of social enterprise*. New York: Routledge.

Perista, H., & Nogueira, S. (2004). *Work integration social enterprises in Portugal*. EMES Working Papers, 4(6).

Sacconi, L., & Grimalda, G. (2001). The constitution of the nonprofit enterprise: A game theoretical account based on conformist utilities and reciprocity. In *Communication to the International Conference of the EMES Network*, University of Trento, Italy.

Salamon, L., & Anheier, H. (1998). Social origins of civil society: Explaining the nonprofit sector cross-nationally. *Voluntas 9*(3), pp. 213–247.

Spear, R., Defourny, J., Favreau, L., & Laville, J. (2001). *Tackling social exclusion in Europe*. Aldershot: Ashgate.

Stryjan, Y. (2004). Work integration social enterprises in Sweden. EMES Working Papers, 4(2).

Thomas, A. (2004). The rise of social cooperatives in Italy. *Voluntas, (15)*3, pp. 243–264.

Young, D., & Salamon, L. M. (2002). Commercialization, social ventures, and for-profit competition. In L. M. Salamon (Ed.), *The state of nonprofit America* (pp. 423–446). Washington, DC: Brookings Institution.

EWA LEŚ & MARIJA KOLIN

3

East-Central Europe

THE CONCEPT OF SOCIAL ENTERPRISE

Social enterprise in East-Central Europe has emerged from the concepts of the third sector, nonprofit organizations, and the social economy, including both institutionalized entities such as associations, foundations, and cooperatives and noninstitutionalized entities such as self-help groups and other initiatives without legal identity (see figure 3.1). Social enterprises consist of new, emerging organizations that have developed between the market and the state to pursue social goals by economic activities. A range of social and economic criteria of social enterprises, known collectively as the EMES criteria (Borzaga & Defourny, 2001), have been identified by researchers of the EU-15. In recent years these criteria have been adopted and modified to fit within an East-Central European context. This approach defines a social enterprise as an organization that fulfills certain minimum economic and social criteria. These basic economic criteria include both the production of goods or the provision of services on a continuous basis and a trend toward paid work, involvement of economic risk, and autonomy. This means that associations, foundations, and other organizational forms of social enterprise have neither an advocacy function nor the redistribution of financial flows as a major goal. Instead, social enterprises are predominantly involved in producing goods or providing services on a longer-term basis. Moreover, although the provision of paying jobs is not a requirement, social enterprises in East-Central Europe usually aim to hire a paid staff.

A number of criteria are essential to defining social enterprise within East-Central Europe. Social enterprises generally serve a specific group of people by meeting special needs or providing a service or set of services to the community. Social enterprises in the region also rely on new models of decision-making power that are not based on capital ownership or maximizing profits. These new decision-making models distinguish East-

Central Europe's social enterprises from regular third sector organizations and usually include democratic management styles, customer representation and participation, and an orientation toward stakeholders. The last of these promotes decision-making input and a high degree of participation by stakeholders. Another feature distinguishing social enterprises from ordinary voluntary organizations is that social enterprises include not only organizations characterized by total nondistribution constraints, but also organizations that share some percentage of their profits.

Most studies argue that there is not yet a common definition of social enterprise in East-Central Europe. For example, in Poland the concept of social enterprise has received initial recognition among government officials, professionals, academics, and the third sector due to EU programs on social inclusion and economic reintegration, such as EQUAL and Human Capital. The model for social enterprise consists of both mutual-interest and general-interest organizations. The main legal forms of the third sector in Poland that closely correspond to the concept of social enterprise include foundations, associations, and other voluntary organizations, cooperatives, shelter enterprises, and social cooperatives. Additionally, several entities have no legal form but are close to the EMES ideal type and act as substructures for associations, foundations, and other voluntary organizations—for example, vocational enterprises for the handicapped (ZAZ),[1] social integration centers (CIS),[2] social integration clubs (KIS),[3] and vocational therapy workshops (WTZ).[4] A closer look at Serbian social enterprise development shows that the following forms of organizations correspond to the concept of social enterprise: associations of citizens, cooperatives, social cooperatives, vocational enterprises for persons with disabilities, spin-off enterprises in the form of limited and joint-stock companies, incubators, and agencies for small and medium-sized enterprises (Babovic et al., 2008). In reality, the forms of organizations listed in figure 3.1 do not entirely correspond to the ideal type of social enterprise model and vary significantly in their degree of similarity with the EMES model. For example, social cooperatives in Poland and Serbia are very close to the model, whereas others do not meet some of the criteria due to such reasons as the dearth of paid work in associations and foundations and the low degree of empowerment and democratic procedures and management in cooperatives and religious-based organizations.

The majority of social enterprises in East-Central Europe consist of service-oriented initiatives, work-integration organizations, and other

FIGURE 3.1. *Main Organizational Forms of Social Enterprises in East-Central European Countries*

- Associations
- Foundations
- Cooperatives
- Social cooperatives
- Mutual benefit funds
- Public benefit companies
- Social integration centers and clubs

entities that strengthen local development in economically depressed locations through initiatives such as facilitating access to information technologies (IT) or providing access to capital in rural areas. In most East-Central European countries, social enterprises have developed within the social and community service fields, partly as a result of welfare gaps that emerged from shrinking public welfare programs and new emerging needs for services and partly as a product of the contract culture and welfare partnership paradigms (see table 3.1). While social enterprises provide direct social services, treatment, and other types of nontraditional activities, they have more often developed from bottom-up initiatives and the influence of international actors and pilot projects than from social policy reform strategies. Most of these efforts have been facilitated by EU policies and international donors' programs in close cooperation with government bodies, the relevant ministries, local authorities, academics, experts, and civil society groups.

Additionally, social enterprise, as a model of work integration and at least partially self-financed job creation through productive activities, began developing throughout the region since the beginning of the transition period in 1989. Whereas the term "WISE" (work integration social enterprise) is a West European import, social innovations promoting the socioeconomic integration of hard-to-employ or low-income groups by third sector organizations is indigenous to the region. For example, the Polish Foundation of Mutual Help, "Barka," initially a humanitarian organization with relief for the homeless as its mission, has developed a set of work integration social cooperatives with wide implementation of work integration modes.

TABLE 3.1. *Accepted Examples of Social Enterprises*
Supplying Social and Community Services

Serbia	Self-help groups specializing in welfare and social protection of the most vulnerable are representative of social enterprises in their initial stages of development.
Poland	Alternative preschool centers operated by local governments and nonprofit organizations. The involvement of parents helps cover the costs of the centers.
Slovenia	Nonprofit organizations that provide services in the fields of science, education, culture, sport, health, and social affairs. Their main sources of income are commercial activities and public support in the form of annual subsidies and project financing through grants.
Bulgaria	Social service nongovernmental organizations that conduct income-generating activities including day-care agencies for the disabled, organizations that provide nursing care, and other facilities for the aged.
Romania	Telecenters—i.e., community-based nongovernmental organizations that facilitate rural communities' access to information and communication technologies and support training, consultancy, and assistance services in social, cultural, educational, and economic fields.

Despite their increasing yet gradual development in East-Central Europe, social enterprises are rarely a subject of research and public discourse; moreover, they have only been partially integrated into policies and laws. This may be because the primary goal of the economic transition has been the institutionalization of a market economy. The public debate has paid little attention to innovative solutions for reconstructing welfare systems or for moving the new dynamic of the third sector toward monetary production of services in a managerial way. However, due to dramatic increases in poverty and unemployment during the transition, the third sector began to see how it could target programs for groups most at risk for unemployment, poverty, and unequal access to basic social services. Some of these responses have come in the form of social enterprises understood as a subtype of the third sector and as a new wave within the sector, covering existing organizations as well as new types. This turn toward more economic activities within third sector organizations contributed to their more entrepreneurial position, particularly the production of social services for women, the disabled, and other vulnerable groups, as well as the promotion of alternative modes of employment generation primarily for those workers who became unemployed during the transition. Most analyses of the region point out that policy papers have only recently focused attention on these emerging issues (Leś & Jeliazkova, 2007).

Research evidence suggests that most of the countries in the region are currently trying to find ways to help improve the overall social situation, provide social and community services, create jobs, integrate services, and initiate other innovative and supplementary programs (Borzaga et al., 2008). Preliminary studies confirm, however, that networks of new enterprises with social objectives do not have an adequate institutional framework to encourage the creation of new opportunities for them or the provision of new social services. However, there is the general conviction that social programs and activities corresponding to social enterprises have resulted in pilot projects in which key actors are learning how to enhance solidarity and cohesion in areas where traditional, investor-driven enterprise structures and the public sector are not sufficient to resolve unemployment and other side effects of the market transition. In short, the third sector in East-Central European countries has significant but still untapped potential for developing social enterprise activities.

HISTORY OF THE RECENT SOCIAL ENTERPRISE MOVEMENT

Despite popular opinion, social enterprise in East-Central Europe is not a product of the political and economic breakthroughs of 1989; foundations, associations, and cooperatives have long traditions in the region (Leś, 1994). Most reports argue that prior to World War II, foundations, associations, credit cooperatives, and other cooperatives played a significant role in the First Czech Republic, Hungary, Poland, Lithuania, Romania, the Kingdom of Serbs, Croatia, and Slovenia, though the third sector's size and scope of activity varied significantly from country to country. The main role of these organizations was to promote the interests of disadvantaged populations through institutions such as credit cooperatives, which were popular among poor farmers all over the region.

After World War II, third sector organizations and the cooperative movement were strongly influenced by communism's push to collectivize the private sector. Cooperative ownership was transformed into "public" enterprise, thus breaking a long history of social entrepreneurship. Their activities were under strict political and administrative control. The communist authorities dissolved most foundations and associations and also deprived cooperatives and the remaining voluntary organizations of their greatest strengths, which included defining democratic principles, meeting needs, and representing interests independently from government. As a result, social enterprise institutions became important instruments for the nationalization of social welfare systems and collectivization of agriculture, crafts, and trade in the region (Bubnys & Kaupelyte, 2004; Kolin, 2004; Huncova, 2004; Leś, 2004). They also played the role of quasi-public agencies in nationalized economies, where the central governments, instead of markets, became the main providers and organizers of goods and services. With no or very reduced civic involvement, they were an integral component of the totalitarian regime and planned economic system.

There were considerable differences by country, however, regarding the extent to which the communist state interfered with the function of social enterprise organizations. In comparison to other East-Central European countries prior to 1989, the former Yugoslav communist regime was fairly liberal, and its system allowed self-organizing on a local level, especially if associations organized recreational activities and other supplements to state programs.

The growth of social enterprise organizations in East-Central Europe after 1989 can be attributed mostly to democratization, decentralization, and the structural changes that resulted in rapidly growing unemployment rates and widening welfare gaps due to the scaling down of public welfare states. Their growth can also be attributed to European Union policy recommendations that accessioning countries address problems of social exclusion and unemployment. Indeed, since the late 1990s the majority of East-Central European countries have focused primarily on their accession into the European Union, highly anticipating the positive economic consequences, social benefits, and open society of such rapid reforms. Other forces contributing to the recent emergence of the social enterprise phenomenon in East-Central Europe include (1) the churches' and religious communities' involvement in production or service delivery both for disadvantaged groups (e.g., economic integration) and for the general public (e.g., child care and elderly care); and (2) foreign aid, which has provided technical assistance, know-how, and financial backing for the third sector.

For most of the countries, the last twenty years of transition have seen unprecedented growth in some subsectors of social enterprise organizations, such as foundations, associations, and religious organizations. During this same period, however, most of the East-Central European cooperative sector did not experience a similar upsurge or political and legal institutionalization. For example, a comprehensive research project conducted in 2005 in Poland (one of the few countries in the region with a new record of third sector organizations) found that between 1997 and 2005 the number of cooperatives decreased from 19,700 to 9,500. During the same period, most branches of the cooperative sector saw employment drop by half, from 642,000 employed in 1995 to 320,000 in 2005. The East-Central European political elites (i.e., Poland, Lithuania, Serbia, and the Czech Republic) have not yet taken a clear position on whether the cooperative sector is a part of the market economy. Nevertheless, the cooperative form has recently regained its position in some of its classical functions (e.g., credit cooperatives in Poland, housing cooperatives in Estonia, and the agriculture sectors in Lithuania and Hungary).

During the last decade, the number of associations has expanded 123 times in Slovakia, 81 times in the Czech Republic, 14 times in Poland, and 3 times in Hungary. This renaissance of citizen organizations was particularly strong during the first years of transition (Nałęcz & Bartkowski, 2006). For the first time in many years, "hibernating" reserves of participatory and self-help motivations in East-Central European societies could finally succeed. Even in countries like Serbia, which lacked the main prerequisites for civil society development (i.e., a democratic environment, supportive laws, and other preconditions for civil movements), a great number of voluntary, nonprofit, self-organized, and other civil groups were organized there in the 1990s. The third sector created a foundation for social change and played a direct political role as an important tool for fostering the values of democracy. Less crucial though still important is the alternative and innovative role played by the third sector, which subsequently developed into a network that was complementary or parallel to public organizations. This network will form the basis for the future role of the third sector, especially in the domain of social welfare.

LEGAL FRAMEWORK FOR SOCIAL ENTERPRISES

The environments supporting the expansion of social enterprise and the degree to which social enterprise is legally recognized in the region vary widely. Considering existing legislation for third sector organizations, cooperatives, and other forms of organizations relating to social enterprises, it is obvious that this legal base is insufficient for the successful functioning, fund-raising, and sustainability of social enterprise programs. By some estimates, all countries in East-Central Europe suffer from incomplete and unstable legal and fiscal frameworks, making them less suitable for social enterprise. The general impression is that there is a need for fiscal systems and support services for social enterprises comparable to those established for small and medium enterprises (SMES) and other innovative solutions that are promoted in the region (Borzaga et al., 2008; Leś, 2008).

After the turbulent political changes of 1989, new legislation was created that was conducive to the development of third sector organizations (Leś, 1994). This legislation enabled the restoration and establishment of legal and fiscal structures for this set of institutions. Thus, the political and legal institutionalization of the East-Central European nonprofit subsector might be viewed as complete for the vast majority of countries in question (exceptions include Belarus, Russia, and the CIS countries). The growth in the formation of foundations, associations, and other third sector groups after 1989 was mainly due to the lifting of political and legal restrictions on these organizations.

Most social enterprises in East-Central Europe operate within the legal framework of associations, foundations, or cooperatives. Along with regular third sector organizations, special voluntary institutions have been formed, such as public benefit companies in Hungary, Slovakia, and the Czech Republic and microfinance organizations in Bosnia. Moreover, some countries have introduced new legal forms specifically for social enterprises. For example, Lithuania recently issued a regulation that allows Soviet-period workshops for the disabled to be transformed into social enterprises. As of April 2006, Poland's Act on Social Cooperatives allows selected hard-to-employ groups, including ex-convicts, the long-term unemployed, disabled persons, and former alcohol or drug addicts to establish social cooperatives. It is an important policy innovation in the area of employment for these disadvantaged groups. Among the provisions introduced by the Act on Social Cooperatives are entitlements to perform public tasks similar to associations and foundations and to produce goods and services on a not-for-profit basis. Hungary has also introduced new legal forms in this area.

Most East-Central European countries do not allow third sector organizations to conduct economic activity as their primary activity. The permissibility of economic activities is limited to activities consistent with the public interest. This is the case in the Czech Republic, Estonia, Poland, and Slovenia (Borzaga et al., 2008). It is noteworthy that most countries under study here (Albania, the Czech Republic, Hungary, Latvia, Poland, Slovenia, and Bosnia and Herzegovina) have issued a nondistribution constraint principle (Golubovic & Bullain, 2006). Tax incentives are another key element of the legal and fiscal environment for social enterprises. Taxation policy varies significantly among East-Central European countries. The Czech Republic, Hungary, Romania, Slovakia, Serbia, Montenegro, and Macedonia use tax thresholds/hybrid tests as the basis for third sector taxation. Poland and Kosovo apply the destination of income test. Estonia and Latvia use a relatedness test. In Albania, Bulgaria, and Slovenia, third sector economic activities are fully taxed; in Macedonia, direct economic activities are prohibited (ECNL, n.d.; ICNL, n.d.).

In most countries of the region, regulations conducive to social enterprise exist, but further active policies are needed in the areas of framework regulation, taxation, financing infrastructure, governmental incentives and subsidies, the contracting out of services, and improved awareness of social enterprises. New laws that attempt to legitimize social enterprise have been enacted in Poland and Hungary (social cooperatives); the Czech Republic, Slovakia, and Hungary (public benefit companies); Slovenia (not-for-profit institutes); and Lithuania (social enterprises). In other countries (e.g., Bulgaria, Croatia, and Serbia), the legislative framework does not yet recognize a legal form of social enterprise, and the understanding of their role is rather poor and based on existing cooperative law.

To illustrate this, a closer look at the cooperative legal base in Serbia reveals that it is inherited from socialism and is composed of major cooperative principles. In addition, the main direction of the evolutionary trend is focused on the further improvement of cooperative legislation, tax policy deductions, and favorable loans for cooperative support programs. The new initiatives are based on a new legal framework that would properly define cooperative property, protect the interests of cooperative members, and facilitate sustainable development of cooperatives and other activities in terms of policy improvement measures (Kolin, 2004). However, the income-generating activities of NGOs in Serbia are not regulated (Babovic et al., 2008).

Political debates in East-Central Europe have only recently recognized the new potential of the third sector as a social service provider and employment generation tool. Most of the East-Central European governments have started to design a legal and financial environment that allows associations, foundations, cooperatives, and other third sector entities to act as a social service producer for target groups and the broader public, a provider of goods, and an employer (a role attributed mainly to cooperatives). In Serbia, for example, the government facilitates the collaborative role of self-help groups and other third sector organizations involved in general social reconstruction. In an emerging system in which local government and third sector entities operate in place of a state monopoly at the local level, self-help organizations have begun to obtain formal recognition as partners with public authorities and professional groups in policy implementation. Problems with these collaborations, however, include financial shortages of governmental bodies, misunderstandings, confusion, and a lack of confidence in the professional competence of new actors.

Based on existing but very limited data on social enterprises in East-Central European countries, legislation in most countries allows third sector organizations to receive state government contracts for service delivery. In the Czech Republic, the subsidy can reach 70 percent of the actual costs of the organization. Moreover, in Hungary, Lithuania, Poland, Romania, and Slovakia there are percentage laws providing citizens with the right to devote 1 or 2 percent of their income to socially useful causes (public benefit) that they particularly want to strengthen. This income goes to third sector organizations as well as public sector institutions (in the case of Hungary). In Bulgaria, Macedonia, and Croatia, the lottery, and other games of chance also finance third sector activities.

Nevertheless, further development of social enterprises must overcome organizational and legal barriers. Cooperatives often complain about unequal treatment in comparison to private companies. A new approach toward social enterprises should recognize their potential in performing direct social services, treatment, and other types of nontraditional activities, such as household and community services. Recent best practices for enabling a social enterprise environment in Poland include the Regional Public Fund for Support of the Social Economy (which renders small grants of approximately 4,000 Euros each), the state Fund of Citizen Initiatives, and the newly created state program for Social Cooperatives Support Centers, which combines training and advisory services with an investment fund. Access to funds from local and European programs is still limited. In

Poland only 3 percent of foundations and associations have financed their activities with EU structural funds (Gumkowska & Herbst, 2006).

EUROPEAN CAPACITY FOR BUILDING STRUCTURES
FOR SOCIAL ENTERPRISES IN EAST-CENTRAL EUROPEAN
COUNTRIES

The OECD LEED Trento Centre for Local Development in Trento, Italy, is the key network for East-Central Europe's social enterprise sector and scientific community. Indeed, the center was designed to have a special focus on local capacity-building activities in the countries of East-Central Europe. Social entrepreneurship and innovation are at the core of its line of analysis, and in 2004, it created a scientific advisory group on social economy and social innovation (Centre for Entrepreneurship, SMEs and Local Development, n.d.).

The European Research Institute on Cooperative and Social Enterprises (EURICSE) at the University of Trento is another capacity-building initiative used by the East-Central European social enterprise community. EURICSE is an associational foundation with the goal of promoting and developing research on cooperatives, social enterprises, and nonprofit organizations more generally, and their contribution to economic and social development from an international and multidisciplinary perspective. EURICSE also promotes the cultural and professional growth of social and cooperative entrepreneurs, as well as the managers and administrators of those organizations, by supporting their innovative strategies and practices. The training activity is directed toward young people—European and Italian managers of cooperatives, social enterprises, and nonprofit organizations. Promotion and consultancy is directed in particular at these types of organizations and their representative bodies, as well as to subjects intending to undertake cooperative, social, and nonprofit initiatives (EURICSE, n.d.). EURICSE promotes these organizational forms, particularly those initiatives undertaken with a view to promote international solidarity and cooperation for development. Its goal is to contribute to the economic and social growth of countries encountering difficulties and delays in development.

Training and Research Structures

With the growth of the third sector, training programs for leaders and staff of third sector organizations have developed in higher education institutions of several academic centers in East-Central Europe. Among academics and policy makers there is also a growing interest in carrying out systematic studies on the potential of the third sector and its effectiveness in service delivery.

Poland has been a leader in implementing training programs specifically for social enterprise leaders and staff. In March 2006, the EQUAL project, We Have Jobs, instituted a pilot training and educational program for social enterprise managers at the Institute of Social Policy at Warsaw University in Poland. Other innovative programs and educational institutions in Poland include the Post-graduate Study Program in Social Economy Management at Warsaw University's Institute of Social Policy; Summer and Winter International Schools of Social Economy; and workshops on social entrepreneurship for local community development leaders, administrators, and managers of social enterprises. These educational and training programs were developed, implemented, and adapted to meet the needs of various types of participants. New perspectives and practical tools were also introduced at Warsaw University, including the concept of socially responsible territory, participatory needs assessments of communities, and an interdisciplinary teaching curriculum. In addition, some Polish universities (both state and private) have included social entrepreneurship and the cooperative movement in their general studies curricula (mainly in departments/institutes of economics, agriculture management, law, and social policy). Some of them also organize postgraduate studies on these topics.

Several cooperative and other third sector organizations often conduct training courses for the managers, employees, and administrators of social enterprises. Many of these courses address subjects such as accounting, taxes, marketing, quality control, and personnel management. Most of these courses are financed by the participants themselves (sometimes with the support of the organizations where they are members or employees). Sometimes the courses are organized under the framework of EU or national projects.

OVERVIEW AND ASSESSMENT OF SOCIAL ENTERPRISE IN POLAND

The last twenty years of the Polish transition have witnessed a renaissance of third sector organizations, particularly foundations and associations. These organizations are the basis for many new social enterprises in Poland. From 1990 to 1999, the number of foundations grew twenty times, and the number of associations expanded nearly fifteen times, an increase comparable only to that of the period immediately after World War II. More recently, from 1997 to 2005, the number of operating foundations and associations registered in the public statistics system grew from 3,600 to 5,000, while the number of associations grew from 35,900 to 56,400. The cooperative sector, however, saw the opposite trend: the number of cooperatives decreased from 19,700 to 9,500 during the same period (Leś, 2008).

The Third Sector as a Social Enterprise Employer
Overall, the third sector in Poland has created significant job opportunities, which now constitute 3.4 percent of all persons working in the national economy (including employers and self-employed workers) and 4.5 percent of hired employment of the Polish national economy. However, the role of particularly Polish nonprofits as an employer continues to be weak. From 1997 to 2005, the number of permanent jobs in the association and foundation subsector grew slightly (by 14 percent or over 12,000 jobs), increasing its share of hired employment in the labor market from 1.0 to 1.1 percent, while temporary hires grew by 28 percent. Indeed, the percentage of temporary jobs in the nonprofit sector was much higher than it was for cooperatives and the national economy as a whole (23, 11, and 11 percent, respectively). The overall result has been that most foundations and associations noted a decrease in permanent employees from 1997 to 2005. In 1997, 25 percent of those organizations employed at least one staff person on a permanent basis, but this number dropped to barely 16 percent in 2005. During the same period, the number of organizations not paying their staffs any type of wage grew from 55 to 63 percent.

This data indicates that Polish social enterprises originating from the nonprofit sector rely to a large extent on temporary hires. This situation inhibits them from being a viable producer of goods and services and therefore hampers their growth. Thus, one of the major obstacles preventing Polish nonprofits from developing social enterprises is their low capacity to sustain permanent, paid staff.

Cooperatives, on the other hand, remain a significant third sector employer in Poland despite their weakening role (Leś, 2004). A drop in employment by half (from 642,000 jobs in 1995 to 320,000 in 2005) was observed in most branches of the cooperative sector. Nonetheless, cooperatives still account for about 3.5 percent of all hired employment in Poland and 2.6 percent of all paid employment in the national economy and thus provide the largest base for employment in Poland's third sector.

As social enterprises, many Polish cooperatives play an important role in generating employment for groups with lower employability potential, such as disabled persons, women, older people, and low-skilled workers. Cooperatives employ 12 percent of workers with disabilities (compared with 4 percent in the economy as a whole), 59 percent of women (compared with 45 percent in the entire working population), 53 percent of workers in immobile (45+) age groups (compared with 37 percent in the entire working population), and 46 percent of workers with primary education and vocational training (compared with 41 percent in the economy as a whole) (Nałęcz, 2008). This indicates that classic cooperatives act like work integration social enterprises that sustain jobs for the hard-to-employ.

In addition, the Polish cooperative sector is also active in social cohesion projects. Every fifth cooperative is active in organizing vocational training and internships and assisting with employment. In 2005, approximately 137,000 people participated in such vocational activation programs conducted by co-ops. Another important feature of cooperatives as social enterprises is their contribution to local economic and social development. The local market represents 78 percent of the average share in cooperatives' sales, and 63 percent of cooperatives indicate that they sell over half of their production on the local market. Furthermore, over one-third of cooperatives point out that they are significant suppliers for the local market, as well as buyers of local production, local employers, and patrons or leaders of local social initiatives in culture, sports, education, and religion (Nałęcz, 2008).

The Funding Base for Social Enterprise

A significant feature of the third sector in Poland is its extremely high economic polarization. According to the research findings of the EQUAL Development Partnership, We Have Jobs,[5] one-sixth of nonprofit organizations with hired paid staff accessed 87 percent of the financial resources available to nonprofits, while the remaining five-sixths accessed only 13 percent of the funds at the disposal of the sector (Leś, 2008).

In 2005, the main sources of revenue for the Polish cooperative subsector were almost entirely revenues from selling goods and services (over

96 percent). The largest part of the nonprofit sector's revenues (48 percent) is generated from market sources (selling goods and services), but this is a major source of income for only one-fourth of the nonprofit sector. The second important funding base (42 percent) for the nonprofit subsector is revenue from public subsidies and private giving. Over half of nonprofit organizations rely on these revenues. Public funds alone comprise 29 percent of Polish nonprofits' revenue. The low level of contracting out of services to the third sector is partly a result of the lack of effective pressure by the federations representing them in the areas of coproducing and contracting public services. Consequently, slow progress in government-contracted services and third sector implementation of government-mandated public services (especially in comparison to Western EU countries) is a major obstacle to a sound social enterprise subsector in Poland.

Obstacles to Growth

Certainly the development of the third sector and social enterprises in Poland would be incomparably greater if not for legal and institutional barriers and problems securing support services and financing (including access to capital). Associations and foundations that evolve toward social enterprises are especially affected because they conduct activities "from grant to grant" and thus cannot afford to contribute significantly to the job market. Moreover, Polish reforms of the public welfare state favor a strategy of commercialization of core welfare services (health, education, social services) over a strategy of a mixed economy of supply based on a pluralistic model of social welfare production and delivery that includes state, for-profit institutions as well as third sector and social enterprises.

The political and legal reinstitutionalization of the advocacy and social service role of the third sector has been much more advanced than the employer role of the third sector. As mentioned, the contracting out of services to third sector organizations is low, and the sector is still perceived as a "shunting yard" for acute social problems rather than as a full-fledged partner in regular public service delivery. In general, the structure of the Polish third sector and social enterprise paid workforce reflects both the legacy of the socialist welfare state (where these organizations did not play the role of a structurally independent service provider) and a weak institutional recognition of their ability to deliver public services over the last twenty years of Polish reforms. To some extent, however, third sector organizations have often been seen as cheaper and more flexible modes of service delivery than the public or private sector (Golinowska, 2002), but this has not yet been translated into the delegation of public tasks on a permanent basis, except in a few subfields.

As discussed earlier, in April 2006 Poland introduced a new legal entity specifically for social enterprises through its Act on Social Cooperatives. However, new social cooperatives established under this law have faced profound legal and fiscal barriers that have led to their stagnation and even decrease. This situation has led to efforts to amend the Act on Social Cooperatives in the Polish parliament.

Despite these obstacles, recent development dynamics indicate that social enterprises are slowly growing in the fields of social and work integration, selected personal services, and some community services. Social enterprises developed in response to the mass increase in unemployment and poverty during the transition and the welfare gap created by the shrinking public welfare system. All categories of work integration social enterprises, such as transitional occupations, creation of permanent self-financed jobs, and socialization through productive activities, have started to grow. Some of these efforts have been facilitated by European Union policy recommendations and structural funds to address problems of social exclusion and unemployment (e.g., Local Employment Development and the EQUAL Programme), by donor programs, and in cooperation with some local authorities, relevant ministries' authorities, academics, experts, and third sector initiatives. Generally speaking, however, Poland is similar to other countries in the region: social enterprise is rarely a subject of public discourse and has only been partially integrated into policy and law. Social enterprises operate in some service fields, but their potential, particularly as employers, still remains untapped.

OVERVIEW AND ASSESSMENT OF
SOCIAL ENTERPRISE IN SERBIA

In the absence of reliable statistics on third sector actors related to social enterprise in Serbia, we have preliminarily mapped the social institutions that are strengthening work integration or providing new types of service provision. Our initial focus was on different types of citizen associations (self-help groups in particular), religious groups, and cooperative networks (Kolin, 2004, 2005). More recent research on social enterprises in Serbia (Babovic et al., 2008) recognizes a broader scope of actors, along with citizen associations and cooperatives. This research also assessed vocational enterprises for persons with disabilities, spin-off enterprises in the form of limited and joint-stock companies, business incubators, and agencies for development of small and medium-sized enterprises. The report showed that cooperatives represent the largest part of these networks (79 percent), followed by citizen associations (14 percent) and enterprises for persons with disabilities (3 percent).

Citizen Associations: Self-Help Groups

Self-help groups are a subset of the much larger category of citizen associations that include sports clubs, cultural and artistic organizations, humanitarian and charity associations, professional organizations, and others. According to evidence provided by the Center for Non-Profit Sector Development (CRNPS),[6] more than 3,000 autonomous nongovernmental organizations (NGOS) are registered under the 1989 Law on Associations (2002). However, data provided by Civil Initiatives, another NGO think tank, suggests that only 900 NGOS were active in 2005. In addition, the same source argued that around 300 to 400 NGOS are self-help groups specializing in welfare and social protection for the most vulnerable groups. These organizations provide great potential for social cohesion through programs for job creation and service provision, so they correspond to the East-Central European definition of social enterprise.

The main subcategories in the social enterprise segment of the third sector are refugee groups and self-help groups for women and people with disabilities. The latter represent a well-organized, traditional segment of voluntary organizations focused on programs for the handicapped population (blind, deaf, developmentally delayed, paraplegics, and disabled veterans). Self-help groups for women stimulate business activities and job creation and promote the social inclusion of vulnerable women. Some minority groups that strengthen the social inclusion of their members by means of production also fit the definition of social enterprise. Their activities often include sewing, weaving, or pottery making and at times involve marginal minority groups such as the Roma people.

Religious Groups

The renaissance of religious groups in Serbia started during the 1990s, when many renewed their programs after several decades by providing direct relief and support to war victims. A key task of these organizations has been the distribution of humanitarian aid provided by numerous international organizations. After democratic changes in the fall of 2000, religious groups started to provide social services, particularly to vulnerable and marginalized groups. The elderly population comprises the main beneficiary group of these religious organizations; they receive assistance ranging from nursing and medical treatment to nutrition, food provision, and home assistance. Chronically sick individuals with weak family support are also supported by religious groups because many were extremely marginalized during the transition. Programs are tailored to support these vulnerable groups with different services and protection measures organized at the local level.

Generally, religious networks consist of a small number of thirty to fifty medium NGOs operating in Belgrade or other regional centers (such as Nis, Uzice, and Novi Sad). Caritas, the biggest religious network in Serbia, is supported by international welfare organizations of the Catholic Church. Philanthropy, the humanitarian organization of the Serbian Orthodox Church, is one of the most influential religious groups involved in the provision of services for the elderly and sick. It is argued in third sector research studies (Kolin, 2005; Kolin & Petrusic, 2008) that because these organizations provide direct social services and treatment and thus fill the welfare gap that emerged from shrinking public welfare programs, they could be considered social enterprises. The majority of religious-group activities are heavily dependent on resources provided by international organizations and foreign money, but government funds, fees, commercial activities, and local donor contributions will be an important issue for the future of religious groups in Serbia.

Cooperatives

After the democratic turnover, economic restructuring sparked a renaissance of the cooperative movement as an important opportunity for the open labor market and the integration of disadvantaged workers. The most important aspects of the cooperative movement are that it promotes economic activities at lower costs, enables active participation of its members in management, favors different small-scale entrepreneurship programs, and strengthens the enthusiasm, motivation, and activism of its members to improve business. A closer look shows that their self-help character dominates and social responsibility is naturally built into their missions.

According to official data provided by the Cooperative Union of Serbia (2002), Serbia has approximately 1,200 cooperatives on record, with approximately 120,000 members. The majority of these cooperatives, however, have frozen their businesses because of political reasons and other difficulties. There are credit, consumer, youth, and trade cooperatives, but farmers' cooperatives are most widespread. The main challenges of farmers' cooperatives include inadequate agrarian policy, unresolved cooperative ownership, or the neglect of cooperatives' principles and usurpation of power inside the cooperatives. Due to these and other reasons, traditional cooperatives have undergone a period of stagnation, and according to the source above, only half of those registered (around six hundred) are still functioning. It is estimated that only a small number are able to perform nontraditional functions.

On the other hand, around fifty to sixty newly created cooperatives have begun to develop an entrepreneurial dynamic focused on social goals such as services for the elderly or integrative programs designed for the disabled (Kolin, 2004, 2005). In addition to social service provision organizations, there is a small network of ecological cooperatives that promote healthy food, and organic, environmentally safe agriculture. There are also so-called "women cooperatives." Women cooperatives search for ways to provide jobs and reduce the poverty and unemployment of vulnerable groups of women, including those who were laid off during the transition, the long-term unemployed, less-qualified persons, and the elderly.

Enterprises for Vocational Training and
Employment of Persons with Disabilities
Sheltered workshops are enterprises that offer vocational training and alternative employment for persons with disabilities. There are various legal forms of organization for these enterprises according to a 1996 law. This type of enterprise can be established by associations of persons with disabilities and may obtain relative autonomy from their founders. In addition, these organizations can be established by profit-driven enterprises when such companies employ people with disabilities, primarily those with disabilities due to work-related incidents. According to 2006 data from the Ministry of Labour and Social Policy, fifty-two enterprises for the professional rehabilitation and employment for persons with disabilities have been established, and these companies employ a total of 2,926 persons with disabilities, of which 60 percent are persons with disabilities

due to work-related incidents, 21 percent are persons with mental disorders, and 12 percent are persons with hearing disorders (UNDP-BRC, 2006).

Agencies for the Development of Small and Medium-Sized Enterprises

Entities in Serbia that are fostering employment through the development of small and medium-sized enterprises have been supported by a European Union program since 2001, when the Law on the Agency for the Development of Small and Medium-Sized Enterprises (SMES) was passed. According to this law, the establishment of these entities must promote partnership among the public, private, and nongovernmental sectors (UNDP-BRC 2006). The Strategy for Development of SMES (2003) and its Action Plan (2005) underlined the fact that regional centers have been recognized as important partners for fostering employment through SMES. The missions and functioning of these entities correspond to the definition of social enterprises, as they are described in the same report. Similar to these entities are business incubators, designed to accelerate the growth and success of entrepreneurial companies through an array of business support programs and services.

Obstacles and Opportunities

Overall, third sector actors that fit the definition of social enterprise have the potential to generate new jobs, either through direct employment or by offering job services that improve the quality of life and increase the social integration of disadvantaged groups. In the context of their social and economic dimensions, some of the social actors already described (some types of citizen associations, self-help and religious groups, enterprises for training and employment of the people with disabilities, and some types of cooperative) have more potential to satisfy the demands that characterize social enterprise. Others (agriculture cooperatives, business incubators, agencies for SMES development), however, are questionable because their essential characteristics fulfill social enterprise principles in a situation where these organizations have a low degree of autonomy or when their economic performance dominates over social activism and community-building activities.

As one Serbian analysis has reported, "[In Serbia] most of the social enterprise-like activities of NGOS so far have been in training and social care services. [A] main characteristic of the third sector is a low potential for employment" (UNDP-BRC, 2006, p. 38). The general observation is that Serbian social enterprise initiatives are struggling with an inappropriate legal framework and tax deduction measures, with ineffective promotion and support by local government, and with prejudices and negative attitudes toward cooperatives inherited from the past. Recent efforts to promote social enterprises are focusing on a legal framework that would properly define the enterprises and facilitate sustainable development of their programs, but these initiatives are still in the preparation phase. Most programs undertaken by the UNDP European Movement in Serbia and the Ministry of Labour and Social Policy are focusing not only on improving legislation but also on necessary education and training to be coordinated by support centers and umbrella organizations. As social enterprises begin to attract the attention of governmental and nongovernmental organizations, it is assumed that new support measures will be implemented parallel to further research and analysis, publishing, and university education in this area.

CONCLUSION

A number of factors have inhibited the further growth of social enterprise as a poverty-reduction mechanism, as a model of employment generation, and as an instrument of local socioeconomic development. The following issues have been the key obstacles:

- Insufficient employee ownership structures such as cooperative property (producer-owned, consumer-owned, nonprofit-owned), the prevalence of the neoliberal concept of market economy based on investor-owned enterprises, a bipolar economic system consisting of employees and employers, and a bipolar social welfare system based on the public and for-profit sectors
- The lack or insufficiency of an enabling environment for social enterprises at the national and local levels
- Low or inadequate number of social enterprise advisers, instructors, leaders, administrators, managers, social entrepreneurs, and paid staff of third sector organizations delivering social and community services
- Problems of a fragile political system that hinder the building of enterprises and medium- and long-term strategies
- Low level of contracting out of services

- Underpaid or poorly paid public contracts
- Need for the general education system and training courses to develop social enterprise staffs' entrepreneurial, administrative, and managerial skills
- Emerging shortage of leaders for social enterprises / work integration social enterprises
- Chronic financial instabilities on the part of social enterprises, including a lack of funds for running services and hiring paid staff on a permanent basis
- Overregulated application procedures for structural funds
- Restricted access to small grants from EU structural funds for grassroots initiatives
- Narrow scope of EU structural funds programs, with a focus exclusively on employment-generation issues and the underestimation of gaps in social and community services
- Lack or insufficiency of capital within third sector / social enterprise structures
- Incomplete and unstable legal and fiscal frameworks

Among recommendations toward a more enabling legal and institutional framework, the following issues merit attention:

- Delegation of public tasks and contracting out of services in favor of social enterprises
- Need for a fiscal system and support services for social enterprises comparable to those established for SMES
- Fair compensation for the production and delivery of goods and services by social enterprises
- Need for SES' managers and moderators of their support structures to be educated and trained in order to sustain the organizations' growth

Other support policies social enterprises should work toward are:

- Innovative grassroots and territorial initiatives and different local citizen structures as primary mechanisms of social inclusion and community development
- Strengthening the local potential in the field of socioeconomic self-help and development

- Promotion of new, alternative, and community financing through community foundations, partnerships and trusts, lotteries, and community third sector funds and the development of innovative local financial institutions supporting third sector / social enterprise goals, among others

EXAMPLE I: LASTAVICA NGO AND COOPERATIVE IN SERBIA

The story of Lastavica, which was initially founded as a nongovernmental organization (NGO), is very similar to many other self-help refugee groups organized in Serbia since 1992. Lastavica was founded in 1996 according to the Law on Associations as a response to the extremely difficult situation in which many single women refugees in Serbia found themselves. The association started as a joint project of the Autonomic Women Centre in Belgrade and the British humanitarian organization OXFAM. Its primary aims are to provide residence, psychosocial support, education, and economic empowerment for this vulnerable segment of Serbian society. The association helps women refugees who are alone, without family support, and vulnerable in other ways by creating collective houses, shelters, and other social support measures. The name Lastavica ("swallow") was selected to describe the collective houses in which the women refugees reside and to symbolize their temporary accommodation.

NGO Social Services

When it was founded, Lastavica's volunteers and professionals provided social and health care services, advocacy, legal advice, and other kinds of help to support the refugees' integration in a new environment, to encourage them to return home, or to support their migration process to a third country (if this solution was the most appropriate for them). The activities of the organization have now changed, and today the association has multiple objectives. In dealing with programs for refugees, Lastavica discovered that many local people were themselves marginalized and needed different kinds of help and services. The organization now conducts different programs for both vulnerable groups: refugees and the local population. Activities for refugees now include computer courses, English-language learning, sewing, weaving, and communication skills building. Special programs directed at the elderly consist of psychosocial support, work therapy, recreation and health programs, and humanitarian support. During its twelve years of existence, Lastavica has had several thousand beneficiaries of various types of services.

Cooperative Catering Service

Lastavica's catering service has developed into one of the most successful economic reinforcement programs. According to current law in Serbia, nonprofit organizations cannot organize for-profit production, so the women's association decided to establish Lastavica-Catering as a cooperative association that can generate earnings through business activities. Lastavica-Catering prepares, distributes, and arranges food for cocktails, receptions, banquets, birthdays, and other celebrations. The initial group of thirteen women participated in a three-month training program and perfected their culinary skills with the help of a professional caterer. The firm is designed to provide benefits for its members, and its institutional characteristics are typical for an enterprise with social goals.

The cooperative association has a democratic character due to its decision-making process and the prevalence of solidarity and mutuality in the distribution of income over capital. The women earn their living through their own efforts and work. Although this business does not have a strong impact on unemployment, catering services could be a solution for the massive unemployment among women in Serbia. These organizations also have social potential, and with some stimulating measures they could, in time, be capable of performing different functions in line with social responsibility inclusion.

Capacity building has been one of the most important parts of Lastavica-Catering's internal strategy. Through this effort, Lastavica-Catering professionals and volunteers learned about project preparation and implementation, the research process, monitoring and evaluation, partnership building, networking, and other skills and techniques important to the sustainability of their programs. The organization's greatest concern is the sustainability of its programs in situations where the government is not able to replace foreign aid, especially in some programs directed toward women's equality issues.

EXAMPLE 2: WWW PROMOTION SOCIAL COOPERATIVE IN POLAND

The start-up of www Promotion was promoted by the target group itself: the Association for Vocational and Social Reintegration of the Handicapped (ACTUS). The association, located in Wrocław, Poland, included the physically handicapped who were looking for jobs, who had not been formally unemployed, and who had lived on disability pensions. Initially they set up an informal group, www Promotion, that focused on information technologies. In May 2005, they became formally established as a social cooperative. The two sources used to establish the cooperative were the Regional Fund for Social Economy (set up in 2005 by the Ministry of Social Policy), which gave seed money of approximately 4,000 Euros, and revenues from the sale of their products.

At time of writing (2008), the cooperative had thirteen members, twelve of whom are handicapped with various kinds and degrees of disabilities. www Promotion is a single-stakeholder organization created predominantly by one category of stakeholders (handicapped persons). The group is composed of both men and women from twenty-one to sixty-four years old. The mission of the cooperative is explicitly aimed at promoting the interests of the handicapped group itself (mutual-interest orientation). It focuses on the economic and social integration and empowerment of its members by offering temporary jobs and self-help support. In 2008 the cooperative employed five members on a temporary basis and encouraged several more to find jobs in the open market. Its products include Web positioning, Web designing, Web mastering, and Web hosting. These services are sold to the market. Among its clients is the Regional Office of Social Policy in Wrocław. Most recently the cooperative obtained a grant for the years 2009–2010 financed by the EU Operational Programme Human Capital. The task is to create Web promotion for the social cooperatives in the region of Lower Silesia. The grant has also enlarged the opportunity for employment in the cooperative, allowing it to employ four more members as staff persons and increase its longer-term sustainability.

CASE STUDY 3: ŁUKSJA SHELTERED ENTERPRISE
FOR THE DISABLED IN POLAND

The disabled workers' cooperative in Łuków, Łuksja, is fifty-five years old. It was established on January 3, 1950, by thirteen founding members consisting mainly of disabled World War II veterans and was incorporated on March 30, 1950, under the name "Disabled Workers Cooperative."

The profile of the cooperative's production has evolved over time. In its early stages, it rendered various kinds of services to the local community: mainly ladies' and gentlemen's tailoring, shoemaking, bookbinding/ papermaking, and small-scale trade activity.

At the time of writing the Łuksja cooperative acts in the form of a sheltered enterprise. It employs about five hundred workers, of which over 60 percent are disabled persons. About 95 percent of the production is exported, mainly to France and Germany. Among the cooperative's business partners are the companies Tristano Onofri, Kokai, and Max Mara. Łuksja manufactures fashionable ladies' clothing, bed-linen items, and textile products for hotels. It has preserved its papermaking plant, which currently employs thirty workers and manufactures cardboard boxes for the cooperative's own use as well as for sale in the local market.

The decisions in the cooperative are made democratically according to cooperative principles and values. All member-employees of Łuksja are entitled to attend the General Assembly and to be elected to the cooperative's supervisory council. The day-to-day activities are managed by the board of directors.

The key to the success of Łuksja has been the effective integration of social functions with the business performance of the cooperative. It has proven that not only private companies but also cooperatives employing handicapped workers from a small, provincial town are able to operate successfully in a competitive market. The main barrier to development for Łuksja and other sheltered enterprises has been the frequent changes to regulations regarding employment of the disabled.

NOTES

1. ZAZ is a type of internally oriented structure that provides transitional and permanent sheltered employment for the disabled.

2. CIS is a type of externally oriented organization that provides its services, including access to social, psychological, and vocational services, to various target populations as a means of creating economic integration through the generation of new jobs and social inclusion.

3. KIS is another type of externally oriented organization that focuses on economic and social integration and empowerment of low-skilled groups by offering self-help support, legal advice, and temporary jobs.

4. WTZ (vocational therapy workshop) is another form of transitional and permanent sheltered employment for the disabled.

5. The "Tu Jest Praca" ("We Have Jobs") project funded by the European Social

Fund and the Polish government has laid the foundations for a resurgence of social enterprises in Poland. Working at a national level from its base at the Institute of Social Policy at Warsaw University coordinated by Ewa Leś, it has carried out the country's first comprehensive survey of the third sector. This survey was directed by Sławomir Nałęcz at the National Social Economy Observatory at the Institute of Political Studies, Polish Academy of Sciences.

6. The Center for Non-Profit Sector Development (CRNPS) is a think tank established in 1996 by the Soros Foundation to support the building of autonomous civil organizations within Serbia.

REFERENCES

Babovic, M., Cvejic, S., Nusik, O., & Pavlovic, O. (2008). Promoting the role of social enterprise in Serbia. In *Social enterprise: A new model for poverty reduction and employment generation: An examination of the concept and practice in Europe and the Commonwealth of Independent States.* UNDP and EMES.

Borzaga, C., & Defourny, J. (Eds.). (2001). *The emergence of social enterprise.* New York: Routledge.

Borzaga, C., Defourny, J., Galer, G., Leś, E., Nogales, R., Nyssens, M., et al. (2008). Part III. Recommendations on how to support social enterprises. In *Social enterprise: A new model for poverty reduction and employment generation: An examination of the concept and practice in Europe and the Commonwealth of Independent States.* UNDP and EMES.

Bubnys, S., & Kaupelyte, D. (2004). Development of co-operative enterprises in Lithuania. In C. Borzaga & R. Spear (Eds.), *Trends and challenges for cooperatives and social enterprises in developed and transition countries* (pp. 253–264). Trento, Italy: Edizioni 31.

Center for Non-Profit Sector Development (CRNPS). (2002). *Directory of nongovernmental, non-profit organizations in former Yugoslavia.* Belgrade: Center for Non-profit Sector Development.

Centre for Entrepreneurship, SMEs and Local Development. (n.d). OECD LEED Trento Centre for Local Development, Italy. Retrieved from www.oecd.org/document/21/0,3343,en_2649_34417_18647829_1_1_1_1,00.html.

Cooperative Union of Serbia. (2002). Rezolucija o razvoju zemljoradnickog zadrugarstva (Resolution on agriculture cooperative development). Retrieved from www.zssrbije.co.yu/frameset.htm.

European Center for Not-for-Profit Law (ECNL). (n.d.). Resource materials. Retrieved from www.ecnl.org.hu.

European Research Institute on Cooperative and Social Enterprises (EURICSE). (n.d.). Why a study centre on cooperative and social enterprise? Retrieved from www.euricse.eu.

Golinowska, S. (2002). The system of social assistance: The main challenges of changes and reforms. In E. Leś (Ed.), *Social assistance: From paternalism to participation.* Warsaw: Aspra-JR Publishing House.

Golubovic, D., & Bullain, N. (2006). Perspective on regulatory issues for social enterprise development in CE. Paper presented at the International Seminar Emerging Models of Social Entrepreneurship "Possible Paths for Social Enterprise Development in Central East and South East Europe," OECD-Leed Programme, USAID, ISSAN, Zagreb, September 28–29.

Gumkowska, M., & Herbst, J. (2006). *Basic facts on the NGO sector in Poland 2006.* Warsaw: Klon/Jawor.

Huncova, M. (2004). The Czech co-operative reality and its social aspects. In C. Borzaga & R. Spear (Eds.), *Trends and challenges for cooperatives and social enterprises in developed and transition countries* (pp. 211–228). Trento, Italy: Edizioni 31.

International Center for Not-For-Profit Law (ICNL). (n.d). Online library. Retrieved from www.icnl.org/index.htm.

Kolin, M. (2004). The evolution of cooperative principles and the emerging third sector activities in Serbia. In C. Borzaga & R. Spear (Eds.), *Trends and challenges for cooperatives and social enterprises in developed and transition countries* (pp. 197–210). Trento, Italy: Edizioni 31.

———. (2005). Socijalna ekonomija i integracija ugrozenih grupa (Social economy and integration of vulnerable groups). In Institute for Social Sciences (Ed.), *Pojedinac i drzava.* Belgrade: Institute for Social Sciences.

Kolin, M., & Petrusic, N. (2008). Socijalna preduzeca i uloga alternativne ekonomije u procesima evropskih integracija (Social enterprises in Serbia and the role of alternative economy in European integration process). Belgrade: European Movement in Serbia.

Leś, E. (1994). *The voluntary sector in post-communist East Central Europe, World Alliance for Citizen Participation.* Washington, DC: CIVICUS.

———. (2004). Co-operatives in Poland: From state-controlled institutions to new trends in co-operative development. In C. Borzaga & R. Spear (Eds.), *Trends and challenges for cooperatives and social enterprises in developed and transition countries* (pp. 185–196). Trento, Italy: Edizioni 31.

———. (2008, forthcoming). The third sector in post-transition Poland. *Revista Espanola del Tercer Sector.*

Leś, E., & Jeliazkova, M. (2007). The social economy in Central and South East Europe. In *The social economy: Building inclusive economies*. Trento, Italy: OECD.

Nałęcz, S. (2008). Role of cooperatives in Poland. Paper presented at the Conference of International Cooperative Alliance (ICA) "The Role of Cooperatives in Sustaining Development and Fostering Social Responsibility," Riva del Garda, Italy, October 15–18.

Nałęcz, S., & Bartkowski, J. (2006). Is there an organisational base for civil society in Central Eastern Europe? Social and economic potentials of civil society organizations in CEE after 1989. In S. Eliaeson (Ed.), *Building democracy and civil society east of the Elbe* (pp. 163–195). New York: Routledge.

UNDP-BRC. (2006). Study on promoting the role of social enterprises in CEE and the CIS, Serbian case study. SeConS—Development Initiative Group Report.

JOEL SANTOS, LEAH MACATANGAY
MARY ANN CAPISTRANO, & CAROLINE BURNS

4 Southeast Asia

THE CONCEPTUAL FRAMEWORK

In Southeast Asia, the conceptual framework for social enterprise varies from country to country. Dr. Eduardo Morato of the Philippines created a theoretical framework in 1994 when social enterprise was a relatively unused concept. He postulated that "the social enterprise exists for a community of worker-owners who seek to jointly improve their lot through collaborative, cooperative and prosperity-sharing mechanisms" (Morato, 1994, p. 2). Further, he writes that a social entrepreneur is an innovative person or institution who promotes the successful creation and operations of enterprises or livelihood endeavors for those who are in need. Social entrepreneurs assist the poor by enabling them to undertake better livelihood activities or run their enterprises viably (Morato, 1994).

Joel Santos, founder of the Entrepreneurs School of Asia, provides a definition of social enterprise embodied in the school's motto: "Social entrepreneurs are individuals who use their skills, talents, and resources to create enterprises that have service to society as one of their primary objectives" (Santos, 2002, p. 1). This service to society can be providing jobs, food, and shelter to the poor; health programs; training for livelihoods and economic independence; and environmental interventions. These enterprises are business enterprises (usually for-profit or in some cases nonprofit) that are directed toward more than financial goals; they use other measures to gauge success. These include social benefits for the community and environmental sustainability.

Professor Marie Lisa Dacanay (2004) of the Asian Institute of Management (AIM) identifies three main strategies social enterprises can adopt: resource mobilization, empowerment, and intermediation. The resource mobilization strategy is primarily concerned with generating income from the sale of products or services to finance an organization's operations or the core program of its parent organization. The empowerment strategy addresses the need for the poor or marginalized to own and control the social enterprise themselves. Its most usual form is the cooperative, where members own the enterprise. Finally, the intermediation strategy provides stakeholders access to critical services (financial, product development, trading and marketing, technological services, etc.). This strategy has had a larger reach than the empowerment strategy. A social enterprise chooses its strategy mainly on the basis of its objectives. In reality, a social enterprise may have a dominant strategy that it may combine with one or two other strategies.

Through the study of two social enterprises supported by the Sasakawa Peace Foundation (Japan)—namely, the Juboken Enterprises, headed by Dr. Justino Arboleda (Philippines), and the Wongpanit Company, headed by Dr. Somthai Wongcharoen (Thailand)—Kaori Kobayashi (2006) provides another framework for social enterprise, that of a wealth-creating organization that combines financial sustainability and service to achieve development objectives. Arboleda established Juboken Enterprises as a pilot coconut fiber company. His strategy was to provide rural communities with the technology for geotextile production made from coconut-coir fiber. This strategy allowed people to turn what is basically a waste product into something useful as well as address an environmental concern by providing an organic solution to the erosion of slopes and riverbanks. He did a tie-up with a nongovernmental organization (NGO) to develop a community-based joint venture called Cocotech. Through partnerships with both government agencies and NGOs, Cocotech is realizing its corporate mission of rehabilitating the environment while empowering marginalized coconut-farming communities. Aside from bioengineering advances in coconut coir fiber production, Cocotech provides training, technical support, and marketing assistance to beneficiary communities, which is clearly the result of resource mobilization and intermediation strategies.

Similar to Arboleda, Somthai Wongcharoen also took an interest in the same issues (use of waste materials, the environment, and employment for the poor) but developed a different type of social enterprise. In 1974, when he was eighteen years old, Somthai founded the Wongpanit Garbage Recycling Separation business, going from village to village collecting and buying garbage. The business grew through the years, and in 1994 Somthai established a facility to recycle solid wastes such as paper, plastics, metals, and e-waste. The recycling business has expanded to 153 branches employing 10,000 persons across Thailand (WorldAware, 2004; Wongpanit, 2006).

Somthai has always believed that waste management is the responsibility of both the people and the government. He has undertaken campaigns to educate people about separating their waste, realizing the value of waste recycling, and selling waste to Wongpanit. Additionally, waste banks have been established in schools to educate children and staff. Environmentally, the plant has significantly reduced the amount of solid waste sent to landfills and has properly disposed of toxic wastes and e-wastes. The business need for a large stable supply of recyclable waste has made networking and alliances essential. Somthai has close working relationships with manufacturing industries, local authorities, NGOs, hospitals, schools, and religious institutions. He helps his franchisees grow their businesses and provides employment for the poor, who can work as tricycle drivers, scrap shop owners, junk shop owners, and so on. Somthai exemplifies implementing interlinking strategies of empowerment, intermediation, and resource mobilization (WorldAware, 2004; Wongpanit, 2006).

In Singapore, the government's Social Enterprise Committee identifies social enterprises as small to medium-sized businesses with a social mission: either to help disadvantaged people through employment or to generate profits used for services to the needy. This national committee recognizes the resource mobilization and intermediation strategies.

The practical framework of social enterprise in Southeast Asia can also be seen in the pioneering efforts of Nobel laureate Mohammad Yunus, founder of the Grameen Bank in Bangladesh. His vision of social enterprise focuses on three major strengths: a pressing social need, such as credit; a disadvantaged or underrepresented sector, like women; and a working mechanism—in this case, group credit. Yunus saw the need to reconceptualize the business world to contribute to the creation of a more humane society in Bangladesh. Yunus stressed that social business enterprises are a new kind of nonloss organization aimed at solving social, health, and environmental problems while utilizing the market. Yunus started the Grameen Bank based on the voluntary formation of morally bound groups of five people to serve as guarantees in lieu of the collateral required by conventional banks. The assumption was that if individual borrowers are given access to credit, they will be able to identify and engage in viable income-generating activities (including simple processing such as paddy husking and lime making; manufacturing such as pottery, weaving, and garment sewing; and storage, marketing, and transport services). Grameen Bank is almost completely owned by its constituents, demonstrating the use of a dominant empowerment strategy, in combination with resource mobilization and intermediation (Grameen Bank, 2006).

Nhev Sitsophary, founder of Digital Divide Data (DDD) Laos, provides another practical framework, with training and employment as the backbone of the organization. Together with a group of international advisers, DDD provides opportunities for underrepresented sectors in Cambodia and Laos. One of the most important components of DDD's mission is its long-term impact on its employees' lives. While these individuals work for DDD, they gain computer, information technology, and English skills, earn money to support their families, attend school part-time with scholarships for 50 percent of tuition, and build friendships and relationships with people who share their disadvantages. DDD hires talented workers from some of Cambodia's most disadvantaged groups, such as land mine victims and women, to provide them with opportunities they cannot normally access. DDD operates as a self-sustaining cooperative, with all profits going back into the business to provide fair salaries, ongoing training, and health services for its employees. This social enterprise benefits from the interplay of three strategies: resource mobilization, empowerment, and intermediation.

THE RECENT SOCIAL ENTERPRISE MOVEMENT IN SOUTHEAST ASIA

Social enterprises in Southeast Asia are often influenced by or are a result of historical, political, sociological, and cultural realities across the region. Certain characteristics of the people and their past account for the growth, development, and trends of social enterprises. What most Southeast Asian countries have in common is their colonial pasts; what differentiates them from each other are their unique cultures, heritage, and composition of races.

Philippine Business for Social Progress

The Philippines was a colony of Spain and the United States. The U.S. taught democracy, while the Spanish colonizers taught the Filipinos to rely strongly on the government and to adopt mercantilism. There was a great dependence on government to provide jobs, social security, subsidies, and industry protection. Beginning in the late 1960s, the experience of dealing with crony-laden leadership and an inefficient and graft-ridden bureaucracy fostered the initiative of the private sector and civil society, partly resulting in the generation of nongovernmental organizations and social enterprises. Civil society and the private sector took up the challenge of providing social services to supplement inadequate government performance and address the problems of poverty and underdevelopment (Mercado, 1974).

The formation of the Philippine Business for Social Progress (PBSP) in 1970 started the social development movement in the Philippines. PBSP, a nonprofit organization, aims to improve the quality of life of the Filipino poor in traditional communities, marginal upland farmers/forest dwellers, lowland small farmers, the urban poor, sustenance fishermen, and landless rural workers. It was founded by a group of businessmen from fifty Philippine corporations and served as a collective business response to the social and economic needs of the people. It began with projects such as the resettlement of urban poor, a social housing project for low-income earners, applied nutrition and feeding services, and the training of unemployed persons and organizing of farming households and their adoption of appropriate technologies (PBSP, 2000). As it evolved, social enterprise at PBSP was an approach used to encourage the poor to help themselves.

PBSP's first foray into social enterprise activities occurred between 1976 and 1980, when it introduced a program of social credit for underprivileged beneficiaries. Since then, PBSP (2000) has supported 4,193 projects, helping 1.9 million beneficiaries in the process. Recently, Philippine social enterprises have focused on the basic needs of housing in rural areas and sustainable livelihood. These social enterprises provide training to set up businesses that will not only generate employment but also move toward a humane society. Their focus is on addressing peace and political stability while ensuring development. The foremost example of these new social enterprises is Gawad Kalinga (its name means "to give care"), which presents itself as an alternative solution to the problem of poverty. Gawad Kalinga's vision for the Philippines is "a slum-free, squatter-free nation through a simple strategy of providing land for the landless, homes for the homeless, and food for the hungry" (Gawad Kalinga, 2008, n.p.).

The Global Knowledge Partnership and Vision 2020

Malaysia is also a colonized state, and its citizens, like those of the Philippines, relied on the state to provide social services to the people. The effective one-man rule of Dr. Mahathir resulted in a progressive and growing country that is responsive to the needs of the people. Charity organizations exist, and corporate philanthropy is practiced by some companies, but social enterprise is at a nascent stage.

Social efforts in Malaysia include the Global Knowledge Partnership's (GKP) launch of the annual Global Young Social Entrepreneurs' Competition to identify innovative young leaders who have set up businesses with a social component. GKP offers them knowledge, networking, mentorship, and financing, all crucial things that most young social entrepreneurs need. Additionally, the Malaysian government recently placed importance on social enterprise through the implementation of Vision 2020. The ultimate aim of Vision 2020 is to establish a nation that is united: a Malaysian society infused by strong moral and ethical values, democratic, liberal and tolerant, caring, economically just and equitable, progressive and prosperous (Razak, 2004).

Population and Community Development Association

Thailand was never a colony of a Western country, though it has a history of monarchal rule. After the end of absolute monarchy in 1932, Thailand went through sixty years of military rule before embracing a democratic system. Military rule and monarchy have resulted in the people's strong reliance on their leaders for their needs. However, private sector initiatives were also growing at a moderate pace during this time. Relatively fewer foreign influences may have caused the growth of social enterprises to move at a slower pace, but more and more of these groups are being formed today.

Sombat Boonngamanong exemplifies the energetic, savvy approach of Thailand's current generation of social entrepreneurs. Working with children from minority groups, Sombat (through the Mirror Foundation) organized a volunteer teacher corps to teach in mountainous areas, then built this teacher corps into an advocacy base to uplift minority people. Sombat used the Internet to solicit and gather donations of books and clothing. He also marketed the handicrafts made by project beneficiaries (Cunningham, 2007).

Another group of Thai social entrepreneurs is the husband-and-wife team of Payong Srithong and Raweewan. For over ten years, the Srithong couple has been promoting agroecological farming. In agroecological farming, farmers forgo the use of chemical fertilizers and insecticides and grow a variety of crops to ensure food security and maintain their farms' ecological balance. The couple's efforts have resulted in benefits for both low-income farmers and the environment (Growing Self Sufficiency, 2006).

Social Enterprise Fund

In Singapore, the Hegelian tradition holds a very strong influence on civil society. The tradition states that the very existence of civil society presumes the presence of the nation-state. The state was a necessary arbiter of competing interests and the reflection of dominant ones (Heng, 1990; Latif, 1990). The themes of a strong state, political legitimacy, and harmonious social relations, as well as the political impracticality of an equally powerful civil society and state, run through many of the descriptions of Koh and Ooi (2000). They introduced the concept of the "new ideology of active citizenship" as the response of the Singapore state. This proactive stance promotes volunteerism among the wealthy to tap community-based resources to help the needy and disadvantaged.

Conceptualizations of civil society in Singapore are dominated by the state and the middle class. Indeed, social enterprise movements in Singapore started out as, and continue to be, state-led. Since 2003, the Ministry of Community Development, Youth, and Sports (MCYS) has provided seed funding through the Social Enterprise Fund to catalyze the growth of the social enterprise sector. MCYS formed the Social Enterprise Committee in August 2006 to explore ways to take the social entrepreneurship and social enterprise sector to the next level. The Social Enterprise Committee includes members who are themselves recognized as social entrepreneurs. One such entrepreneur is Norma Sit, the founder of Youth Life Ownership Ltd., a social enterprise that teaches life skills to disadvantaged young people. Other members include Alfie Othman, director of Ikhlas Holdings, a catering company that hires ex-offenders and disadvantaged single mothers.

The River Ambulance Project and BRAC

An innovative social enterprise in Bangladesh is the River Ambulance Project. This project, started by a French citizen and his Bangladeshi wife,

Runa, consists of helping poor people in char areas[1] of Bangladesh gain access to healthcare services. The river ambulance provides medical services through a ship-turned-hospital called Lifebuoy Friendship Hospital. With the help of a cellular phone, the river ambulance staff receives medical emergency calls from local residents. Joyark, a British-based organization, provides financial assistance for the project. Runa feels guided in this effort by her Muslim religion (River Ambulance, 2006).

Another social enterprise effort is the Bangladesh Rural Advancement Committee (BRAC), founded by Fazle Hazan Abed, a British citizen born in 1936 in northeastern Bangladesh. BRAC was created in 1970 out of Abed's desire to aid cyclone victims in his homeland. With him were a group of volunteers who joined various rehabilitation efforts, initially giving aid, then providing livelihood and eventually functional education.

BRAC's efforts can be divided into three phases. Phase 1 consisted of relief efforts, including resettlement, medical care, and emergency food supplies until an effort could begin in order to sustain resettled communities. Phase 2 involved a sectoral approach, which included the construction of community centers, the formation of cooperatives, health and family planning, and vocational training. Phase 3, which is ongoing, involves a people approach where the population is organized into groups of twenty to thirty people with similar economic interests (such as fishermen, destitute women, and landless laborers). Education at this stage consists of adult literacy with practical, hands-on instruction that provides villagers with a means of discussing their problems and craft solutions. The groups are then given the necessary training and are encouraged to submit project proposals to BRAC. Following the approval of feasible projects, the groups are extended credit and provided with the resources to ensure their continuing development and success. This phase also necessitated the formation of a research group in BRAC as an independent arm, to ensure the equitable distribution of grants (BRAC, 2008).

Bina Swadaya Foundation

In Indonesia, as manifested in its language, Javan society is hierarchical and reflects three levels of society. The group orientation of the culture discourages competition, as the individual is supposed to have a lower profile than the group and to be obedient and cooperative. The society's cultural emphasis on striving for harmony and order for the common good further reinforces the "group" concept. The Indonesian concept of "group" is a cultural influence that promotes the spread of social enterprise in the country. Various social enterprises have been created in the country in recent years. However, as most pro-poor social enterprises have complained, the government will have to provide a more serious financial commitment to guarantee their survival.

Indonesian Bambang Imwasan started the Bina Swadaya Foundation in 1967 in order to help his poor countrymen through microfinance activities. The major projects of Bina Swadaya are extension services to about 2,500 self-help groups (SHGS), which are supported by twenty-one field offices offering training services for development leaders, consultant services for government projects, and microfinance development. Currently, the foundation has expanded its services to include civil society empowerment through training and education, agribusiness development, promotion of communication for development, and alternative tourism development. The latter encourages international exposure of the country's culture and development and provides assistance with ticketing, transportation, and travel documents (GDRC, 2008; BWTP, 2008).

The concept of the community fits well with the aspirations of the former French Indochina colonies of Laos, Vietnam, and Cambodia, whose members often see themselves as a group with bonds based on blood ties, spatial locality, and spiritual affinity. These elements allow for the establishment of communities based on kinship, neighborhood, and friendship. As in other Southeast Asian countries, the success of social entrepreneurs here will depend on how effectively the governments of these states address the needs of their people and how the spirit of initiative and empowerment spur the populace to start enterprises for themselves.

ORGANIZATIONAL AND LEGAL FRAMEWORKS FOR SOUTHEAST ASIAN SOCIAL ENTERPRISES

Asian social enterprises may be grouped into four major categories: cooperative enterprises, civic foundations of corporations, religious-based organizations, and associations started by key social entrepreneurs. Though almost all Southeast Asian countries have these categories, the impact of each organizational framework varies from country to country.

Cooperatives are usually organized by a strategic leader who takes the initiative. Examples are the Prae Phan Women's Weaving Group in Thailand, created for the development and benefit of rural women, and the

Foundation for the Development of Social Reliance in Indonesia, founded by Bina Swadaya. Cooperatives may also be formed as a business owned by the people who use its services. These cooperatives enable people to pool their available resources.

The second type of social enterprise is a civic foundation formed by a business corporation or by a government mandate as an extension of a government entity. Specific examples of this form include the Philippine Business for Social Progress, or PBSP, mentioned earlier in this chapter. It was intended as a medium that would initiate, assist, manage, or finance programs and projects for the social and economic improvement of the Filipino poor (Dacanay, 2004).

The third type of social enterprise includes the initiatives of religious-based organizations or individuals who apply their religious beliefs to their work. This type of social enterprise is particularly predominant in countries where one's religious orientation plays a major role in one's lifestyle. Examples of this type include the Gawad Kalinga project of Couples for Christ, which was initially a Catholic Marriage Encounter group in the Philippines, and the River Ambulance Project in Bangladesh.

The fourth form of social enterprise is the association. An association is a group of individuals who come together to carry out a shared vision. In some associations, key individuals create a social project to address a social need. These individuals may not previously share any common ties or affiliations but create a social project to address a social need that all perceive as worth answering. This association takes the form of a social enterprise when it becomes a profit-making venture for the purpose of financially supporting its social objectives. A good example of a social enterprise using this form is La Frutera Inc. in the Philippines.

La Frutera Inc. and Paglas Corporation were entities born out of the partnership between Datu Ibrahim Toto Paglas II and Senen Bacani. Paglas, the mayor of Datu Paglas, wanted to provide gainful employment to members of formerly warring rebel groups, with the eventual goal of securing peace. Senen Bacani, a former secretary of the Department of Agriculture, saw the autonomous region for Muslim Mindanao as a promising area for a banana plantation. Their partnership led to the creation of two successful companies and a deal to supply bananas to a multinational banana company. Although Bacani and Paglas both had the usual concepts of helping the poor, creating wealth, raising the standard of living in the locality, and orienting business strategies toward shared benefits, the success of their social endeavor goes far beyond those aims. The LFI and PagCorp enterprise defines a new arena of social enterprise: fostering peace and prosperity as a stable route to development.

The Population and Community Development Association (PDA) of Thailand was created by the Thai minister of health in 1974 with the initial aim of complementing the Thai government's efforts to promote family planning. One of its well-known and colorful projects is the Cabbages and Condoms Restaurants, whose earnings support the PDA. The PDA later expanded its activities to include primary health care, HIV/AIDS education and prevention, water resource development and sanitation, income generation, environmental conservation, promotion of small-scale rural enterprise programs, gender equality, youth development, and promotion of democracy.

SUPPORTING THE SOUTHEAST ASIAN SOCIAL ENTERPRISE

Support for social enterprise in the Philippines is provided by both the public and private sector. The Philippine government recognizes the key role that these enterprises play in the country. Indirectly, it has adopted policies and reforms that provide a more encouraging environment for social enterprises. These policies and reforms include decentralization, the empowerment of local government units, the promotion of microcredit, the strengthening of government financial institutions, and the creation of bodies such as the Cooperative Development Authority. Directly, it has provided technical training, education, and funding, albeit limited. One example of government support for a social enterprise is Kalinga Luzon, the Gawad Kalinga partnering model for the island of Luzon. In this project, the national government, through the National Disaster Coordinating Council and the Department of Social Welfare and Development, provided half of the funds needed for Gawad Kalinga's construction of homes. The local government secured land and provided site development and the use of heavy equipment. Gawad Kalinga provided full-time workers, caretaker teams, and volunteers, while local and multinational companies gave financial support (Gawad Kalinga, 2008).

Malaysian government support for social enterprises has been strengthened with the Vision 2020 program for businesses. Vision 2020 aims to go beyond just the attainment of material wealth and economic advancement. With Vision 2020, the government affirms its commitment to achieving economic progress that is consistent with good personal values and corporate ethics.

The institutional support for social enterprise in Singapore is weak. Although Singapore has established a government-led Social Enterprise Committee, the group has not yet made a determined effort to reach its goals. Some Singaporeans follow the charity model, not the social enterprise model. They believe that social work is an act of altruism and that people who perform that altruism should not be rewarded with pay that is similar to that of their counterparts in the private sector. According to this concept, most of the money donated to the charity has to be spent directly on the charity's clients, leaving very little to help the organization. Thus, most charity organizations are difficult to maintain in Singapore. Another aspect of the charity model is that the social enterprise is subject to audits from accounting firms and advisory boards. These organizations cannot invoke the traditional charity's privilege of nondisclosure, since the charity generates its funds from individual and corporate donors.

In Bangladesh, as illustrated by the River Ambulance and BRAC endeavors, the government's initial support was quite limited in scope or was not an adequate solution. The government's attempt to support BRAC in the mid-1970s through a national education program was not supported by Abed, BRAC's founder, who believed that "boosting literacy alone won't change the people and in no time they'll forget about it. . . . People won't read unless they want to. They won't do anything unless they can see some value in it" (Abed, 1980, p. 4).

In terms of institutional capacities, the governments of Indonesia, Laos, Vietnam, and Cambodia are still in the initial stages of assisting social enterprise. Government help takes the form of providing networking assistance by linking them with international donor institutions and nongovernmental organizations. Government policy on social enterprise in these countries is still in the formulation stage. Initial government responses to social enterprise efforts have been encouraging and positive. It is expected that in the future the government policy of these countries will be finalized and implemented in order to assist private sector and civil society efforts.

According to best practices, the role of government is vital in determining the operating environment of social enterprises. Some governments promote entrepreneurship while failing to offer entrepreneurs an enabling environment. Most governments still need to reduce barriers to starting and staying in business or creating and sustaining a nonprofit venture. Some governments still overregulate the business and social sectors (Davis, 2002).

ASSESSING SOUTHEAST ASIAN SOCIAL ENTERPRISES

To assess Southeast Asian social enterprises one must consider how these enterprises have contributed through the social benefits they have provided the immediate society. These benefits include the alleviation of poverty, the provision of social services such as education and health, the creation of financial and credit facilities, the development of women, capacity building, catastrophe rehabilitation, rural development, and political stability.

Southeast Asian social enterprises have helped address Asia's burgeoning problem of mass poverty. Currently, 40 to 50 percent of Asians live below the poverty line. In Asia, 650 million people still live on less than one dollar a day. Here the problem of poverty has traditionally been addressed through state-controlled policies and interventions. However, inept and corrupt governments and bureaucracies in some countries have hampered economic growth and continued the prevailing situation of unjust distribution of wealth. The latest trends in poverty alleviation have moved toward market-oriented approaches. Mass-based responses have been the most effective. These responses have been in the form of and have originated from nongovernmental organizations working alongside the private sector, aided at times by the public sector. Social enterprises have taken the form of profit or not-for-profit social venture funds investing in small to medium-sized enterprises. They have adopted an enterprise approach to poverty alleviation, endeavoring to build commercially sustainable companies that can create jobs and empower the poor to improve their livelihoods (Tan, 2003).

Social enterprises that have contributed to poverty alleviation include La Frutera Corporation, which operates a banana plantation, and Paglas Corporation, which provides logistics services. Both organizations operate in the Philippines and work to raise the standard of living in rural Mindanao and orient business strategies toward shared benefits. The Maireang Farmers' Group brings together poor, indebted, and landless rubber farmers in Thailand and has created a successful rubber processing and trading enterprise that is owned and managed by the farmers. As a result, farmers' annual incomes have increased, and farmer-members are assured sustained incomes from selling their products. With membership, they are able to sell their latex at a higher price compared to the normal market rate and are also given dividends based on their number of shares (Anukansai, 2004).

Social enterprises also contribute to society by delivering social services. The Entrepreneurs School of Asia (ESA) in the Philippines and the Mirror Foundation in Thailand are two examples in the field of education. ESA promotes entrepreneurship and provides a unique entrepreneurial education, where its students train to become social entrepreneurs. Through action learning, students are given opportunities to experience entrepreneurship on a firsthand basis, taking them beyond strategy formulation and directly into new venture creation, implementation, and operation in order to bring about for-profit success as well as positive social change in their immediate communities. The school's college students bring entrepreneurship to secondary schools in the Philippines through an annual competition called the Teenpreneur Challenge. High school students partner with residents of various Gawad Kalinga communities, helping them to improve the production, packaging, marketing, and sales of the products they create (Entrepreneurs School of Asia, 2008).

The Mirror Foundation brings education to remote mountain areas and advocates for the improvement of minority groups by financing various social enterprises. In the health sector, the River Ambulance Project of Bangladesh reaches out to provide medical services to outlying areas. Several financial institutions have arisen to provide credit and loan services to marginalized groups that often did not receive them from Western banks. Examples of these social enterprises include the pioneering Grameen Bank of Bangladesh, the Mutra Usahi Mandiri (Self-Reliant Business Partner) of Indonesia, and the Bina Swadaya Foundation, also of Indonesia.

The development of women is another focus of some social enterprises, such as the Prae Phan Womens' Weaving Group in Thailand, which harnesses the weaving skills and traditional handicrafts of rural women. The Digital Divide Data provides employment to the disadvantaged women of Cambodia. Additionally, Datamation Consultants hires marginalized, non-English–speaking women of India to work in information technology jobs.

Disaster rehabilitation and rural development have also been addressed by certain social enterprises. The Gawad Kalinga in the Philippines provides relief to rural and disaster areas in the wake of typhoons, landslides, and earthquakes. The relief begins by providing assistance with rebuilding houses and subsequently helps develop economic opportunities for catastrophe victims and rural residents. Gawad Kalinga's practice of involving the household owners and families has also helped develop a sense of pride and contentment, as in the case of BRAC in Bangladesh. The latest BRAC efforts at organizing people and letting them take the initiative in continuing development has enabled BRAC to move beyond the original cyclone-torn area of Sylhet.

Another contribution of social enterprises has been to create and maintain political stability in war-afflicted areas. The foremost examples include the La Frutera Corporation and the Paglas Corporation, which allowed warring Muslim rebels to lay down their arms and take up farming. Also, peaceful and harmonious working relationships are realities among formerly feuding Christians and Muslims.

A BRIGHT AND CHALLENGING FUTURE FOR SOUTHEAST ASIAN SOCIAL ENTERPRISES

In Southeast Asia, social enterprises have advanced to the forefront of the development discourse. Their ability to strengthen and enhance the fiduciary relationship within and around the organizations and to generate resources from both individuals and the local community in this region makes their development and growth inevitable and indispensable. These social enterprises must continue to represent the interests of stakeholders while pursuing goals of democratic governance and volunteerism. The continuing support for social enterprise in the region represents the renewed interest of the public and private sectors in civil society. Social enterprise is the best response to the poverty, economic problems, and government neglect experienced by the Southeast Asian citizens of these developing economies.

While a bright future awaits social entrepreneurship in Southeast Asia, Professor Marie Lisa Dacanay (2006) explains that several looming challenges may deter or slow down its progress. An example of one social marketing issue is the development sector's lack of understanding that this market is an arena for change. Capacity building may also pose a problem because of the low capacity for building and scaling up social enterprises among civil society actors. Dacanay states that scaling up and mainstreaming may be difficult due to three factors: "1) the lack of access to financial capital for scaling up, 2) limited involvement of the business sector, and 3) the absence of a supportive policy environment" (Dacanay, 2006, p. 1).

Despite these drawbacks, social entrepreneurship is on the rise in this part of the world, and the efforts to foster its growth from both public and private sectors will increase its understanding and acceptance among individuals and institutions. Social entrepreneurs in the region squarely confront the task of delivering lasting social benefits and providing solutions to the many problems communities face. With their hands-on, can-do attitude and with the assurance of a paradigm that truly works, social entrepreneurs lead the way to socioeconomic progress.

EXAMPLE 1: GAWAD KALINGA: SOCIAL ENTERPRISE
IN HOUSING AND DEVELOPMENT

The Gawad Kalinga (GK) movement began both as a response to and an initiative of Couples for Christ (CFC), a Christian lay community established in Manila in 1981. Originally the group tried a new approach that involved evangelizing married couples. In December 1995, a group led by CFC member Tony Meloto was inspired by the call of Christ to serve the poor by starting a youth program at one of the biggest squatter relocation areas in metro Manila: Bagong Silang and Caloocan City. Meloto and his friends initiated a weekend camp for the youth with the hope of rehabilitating gang members and drug addicts raised in the slum areas to transform them into productive young citizens before they become criminals. Due to their constant interaction with the youths and the community where they lived, the group members realized that no matter how well they were able to rehabilitate the youths, the improvements were not sustainable if these adolescents went back to live within the same slum communities. The group then realized that the solution must involve the entire community. Thus, they raised the mandate to transform the slum environment, community after community, town after town (Meloto, 2006).

To achieve its vision of transforming slums, Gawad Kalinga has mapped out a five-point strategy of development:

1. *Land for the landless.* The urban and rural poor are driven to squatting because they do not own land on which they can build their own homes. GK aims to provide each poor family with land security.

2. *Homes for the homeless.* Decent homes and communities are GK's first intervention because they contribute to decreasing the incidence of sickness and crime. Bright, sturdy homes lift human beings from their primal state as shelter-seeking animals and allows them to begin their "journey of aspiration."

3. *Food for the hungry.* GK intends to guide communities toward producing food for consumption. Growing food effectively builds human capacity and is the first step toward self-reliance.

4. *Water for the thirsty.* GK works with the local government and its other partners to provide its community with a dependable water system. This system becomes an integral part of the community health program, which eradicates tuberculosis and the waterborne diseases that commonly plague poor areas.

5. *Light for those in darkness.* GK communities are built on this adage, which is both a practical and a pastoral tenet. Adequate physical lighting transforms living conditions—children can study properly at home, and people can walk the streets without fear. This concept also sums up a community-based child and youth development program where children are prioritized as the key to a bright future. (Meloto, 2006)

Beneficiaries and Partners

In GK, everyone is welcomed not as a donor but as a key stakeholder, defined as a committed and passionate partner in rebuilding the nation. Through a creative formula of counterparting,[2] GK has been able to forge strong multisectoral partnerships that bring together individual resources to effectively fill in gaps. Following the model of Gawad Kalinga in Luzon, the national government (through the National Disaster Coordinating Council and the Department of Social Welfare and Development) provided half of the funds needed for the construction of homes; GK itself provided the other half. The local government secured the land and provided site development and the use of heavy equipment.

Beneficiaries of a GK home are selected upon their agreement to certain rules and regulations, which include participating in and attending a values formation program. Also, the men provide a counterpart of "sweat equity" by helping build their homes and abiding by the rules of the neighborhood. The sustainability and success of the GK programs are predominantly due to its caretaker teams, its community organization, and its program volunteers who are on site almost every day. Each G K community has a strong community of caretakers, consisting of teams of volunteers who provide three years of service and are committed to supporting the recipient community in its struggle to rebuild its members' lives. The sustained presence of the caretaker team provides the backbone for the implementation of G K programs.

Development Programs and a Radical Culture
Sustainability and capacity building are established through programs such as Shelter and Site Development, which provides physical structures like paths and drainage systems, water and toilet facilities, a school, a livelihood center, a multipurpose hall, and a clinic. Through Gawad Kabuhayan ("to give livelihood"), G K conducts livelihood and skills training, provides start-up capital and materials for microfinance and microenterprise, and assists in the marketing of the G K communities' products.

The very act of building homes and common facilities teaches new masonry and carpentry skills, since the poor "pay" for their homes through "sweat equity." This both builds community spirit and contributes to greater peace. After all, how can a G K homeowner fight the neighbor who helped him build his house?

The program of development set by G K is supported by the culture and value system that inspires its workforce of caretaker teams, volunteers, and full-time workers. Guided by values that are primarily rooted in Christianity, the people of G K fuel the growing movement by leading with integrity and inspiration. Some components of this culture are:

1. *Bayanihan.* This is inherent, though a bit forgotten in the current Filipino culture. It means working together for the common good; it has now been renewed in G K, demonstrated literally through *bayanihan* chains during builds.
2. *Servant leadership.* G K aims to serve the poorest of the poor. Even in the Kapiitbahayan (the neighborhood association in every G K village), the type of leadership passed on to the community is best captured by the tenet "Una sa serbisyo, huli sa benepisyo" ("First to serve, last to benefit").
3. *Padugo.* Literally meaning "to bleed," this unique value requires one to give of oneself until it hurts.
4. *Heroism.* G K believes in the inherent heroism and nobility in

everyone. Its battle cry is "Bawat Pilipino bayani!" ("Every Filipino a hero!").

5. *Honoring and engaging the good in others.* Instead of being caught up in a vicious cycle of blaming each other, GK suggests a new culture of honoring.

6. *Stewardship and excellence.* GK calls for a new culture of caring and sharing: a culture driven by a sense of responsibility and accountability.

The Impact of GK Today

Gawad Kalinga has evolved into a movement for nation building. Together with its partners, GK is now in the process of transforming poverty-stricken areas, with the goal of building 700,000 homes in 7,000 villages in 7 years (2003–2010). To date, around 1,400 GK communities (each made up of sixty to one hundred families) have been built all over the country, in partnership with over three hundred local government units and one hundred corporations. Other communities have also been built and developed in other countries, such as Papua New Guinea, Indonesia, Cambodia, India, and Timor-Leste.

Working toward community empowerment, the recruitment of mass volunteers, and nation building, Gawad Kalinga is an example and model of social enterprise and innovation, one that gives back dignity to those who have lost hope. GK builds up homes, people, and hope.

EXAMPLE 2: MITRA USAHA MANDIRI

The Mitra Usaha Mandiri or MUM (Self-Reliant Business Partner) is a financial lending institution in Indonesia that mirrors the principles of the highly successful Grameen Bank.[3] It was founded by the Yayasan Mitra Usaha (YMU), a Business Partner Foundation. The YMU was established in 1993 by leaders from the business and NGO community in Jakarta with the aim of developing NGOs' ability to run business enterprises professionally. In its first five years of existence, YMU devoted its energies to training NGOs to learn business management, but it had limited success. In 1998, it changed its direction and goals to get directly involved in the development of what it called the "people's economy." YMU's founders believed that people at the grassroots level who had microbusinesses should be the primary recipients of their foundation, as they would grow with the infu-

sion of additional resources and access to production assets. YMU generated a new vision: "The economic growth of the poor community who are
able to compete and are free of exploitation" (Dacanay, 2004, p. 107).

YMU decided to provide microcredit services and sent some its staff to
study the Grameen Bank model. It decided to establish the Mitra Usaha
Mandiri (MUM) as a financial institution that provides savings and loans /
credit. MUM has two types of savings: obligatory savings and voluntary
savings. Loans and credit are also of two types: productive loans and consumption loans. Members are required to pay loans back on a weekly basis
at an interest rate that is slightly higher than those charged by traditional
banks but much lower than those charged by usurers.

After almost five years in operation, MUM has accumulated 10,993
members or customers, with a total distributed credit of Rupiah 9.98
billion. MUM members and customers are found across Indonesia, from
West Java to DKI Jakarta and Central Java.

MUM shares the same vision as the Grameen Bank: to reach the poorest
of the poor. Indeed, MUM founders were convinced of the ideals and
principles of operations of the Grameen Bank and carefully followed the
concepts and operations of the bank's founder, Dr. Muhammed Yunus of
Bangladesh. For instance, the five steps or phases that an institution had to
take in applying the Grameen Bank system were painstakingly followed:
assets study, general meetings, compulsory training, housing studies using housing indexes, and forming the central unit.

A great deal of the success of MUM was due to the leadership of Muchtar Abbas. Previous to founding YMU, he had acquired extensive experience in both business and community development, and he leveraged
that experience successfully in MUM. Abbas, however, gives credit to the
members of YMU, from board members to field workers, for their single-
minded work on carrying out the goals of the foundation. He further
identifies discipline in abiding to the Grameen Bank concept and the
constant recruiting and retraining of high-quality staff members as factors
that contributed to their success.

After five years of existence, MUM has successfully done a great deal in
providing financial services to the poorest of the poor. It aims to expand its
services in order to reach more of the entrepreneurial poor in Indonesia.
Looking toward the future, MUM faces many challenges, such as the need
for a computerized system, external financing, and resources; the need for

a "post-program for the poor"; and the need to resolve difficulties with government policies and programs. The "post-program for the poor" is intended to be an intervention to guide the progress of people who have successfully taken part in the credit program. However, if early success can be a predictor of things to come, MUM faces a promising future of providing financial services to Indonesia's poor in order to improve their plight and condition.

NOTES

1. The char areas are riverine tracts of land that frequently undergo erosion because of inundation by overflowing rivers. The environment and livelihoods of the people in the area are characterized by instability and insecurity due to the removal of soil as well as the emergence of new land due to silt deposits.
2. Counterparting is where beneficiaries provide an equity of "sweat" or labor as their contribution in return for their home; also, corporate or private partners and their employees are encouraged to go to the area and help build or paint homes.
3. Adapted from Nugroho and Saidi, 2004.

REFERENCES

Abed, F. H. (1980). Approaches to mobilizing villagers' latent capabilities. Presentation made to Group Discussion. Ramon Magsaysay Award Foundation, Manila, September 2.

Anukansai, K. (2004). Maireang farmers' group: Social enterprise in agribusiness. In M. Dacanay (Ed.), *Creating space in the market: Social enterprise stories in Asia* (pp. 73–86). Makati City, Philippines: Asian Institute of Management and Conference of Asian Foundations and Organizations.

BRAC. (2008). Founder and Chairperson—Fazle Hasan Abed. Retrieved July 2, 2008, from www.brac.net/index.php?nid=104.

BWTP (Banking with the Poor). (2008). Bina Swadaya. Retrieved July 5, 2008, from www.bwtp.org/arcm/indonesia/II—Organisations/MF—Providers/Bina—Swadaya.htm.

Cunningham, S. J. (2007). The serial fixer: Sombat Boonngamanong takes an entrepreneurial approach to curing Thailand's social ills. *Forbes Asia Philanthropy*, March 12, pp. 1–3.

Dacanay, M. L. (Ed). (2004). *Creating space in the market: Social enterprise stories in Asia*. Makati City, Philippines: Asian Institute of Management and Conference of Asian Foundations and Organizations.

———. (2006). Social entrepreneurship: An Asian perspective. Speech given at the Civil Society Forum, IMF-WB Annual Meeting, Singapore, September 14.

Davis, S. (2002). Social entrepreneurship: Towards an entrepreneurial culture for social and economic development. Retrieved July 21, 2008, from www.ashoka .org/files/yespaper.pdf.

Entrepreneurs School of Asia. (2008). Entrepreneurs for society. Retrieved July 23, 2008, from www.entrepreneur.edu.ph.

Gawad Kalinga. (2008). What is GK? Retrieved July 31, 2008, from www .gawadkalinga.org.

Gillis, E. K. (2005). *Singapore civil society and British power*. Singapore: Talisman Publishing.

Global Development Research Center (GDRC). (2008). Bina Swadaya. Retrieved July 5, 2008, from www.gdrc.org/icm/bina-swadaya.html.

Grameen Bank. (2006). Breaking the vicious cycle of poverty through microcredit. Retrieved July 1, 2008, from www.grameen-info.org/index.php? option=com— content&task=view&id=25&Itemid=128.

Growing self sufficiency: A husband and wife's mission to heal the environment and free poor farmers from debt. (2006). *Employee Volunteering Newsletter*, October 19. Retrieved July 24, 2008, from www.kiasia.org/En/ShowImages .asp?status=ShowSubGroupTierPDF&PDF—ID=208.

Heng, R. (1990). This is the year of civil society . . . *Straits Times*, December 30.

Kobayashi, K. (2006). What does social enterprise mean to civil society organizations? Ongoing efforts and discussion in Asia. Presentation for panel session Global Emergence of Social Enterprise at ISTR 7th International Conference, Bangkok, Thailand, July 10.

Koh, G., & Ooi, G. (Eds.). (2000). *State-society relations in Singapore*. Singapore: Oxford University Press.

Latif, A. (1990). . . . but how many Singaporeans are members? *Straits Times*, December 30.

Meloto, A. (2006). Building a nation from the ground up: The Gawad Kalinga Initiative. Presented at the Leadership Enhancement and Advancement Program, Asian Development Bank Headquarters, Manila, Philippines, May 9–10.

Mercado, E. (1974). *Elements of Filipino philosophy*. Tacloban City: Divine Word University Publications.

Morato, E. (1994). *Social entrepreneurship and enterprise development: Text and cases*. Makati: AIM.

Nugroho, A., & Saidi, Z. (2004). Mitra Usaha Mandiri replicating Grameen Bank.

In M. Dacanay (Ed.), *Creating space in the market: Social enterprise stories in Asia.*
Makati City, Philippines: Asian Institute of Management and Conference of
Asian Foundations and Organizations.

PBSP. (2000). *Our legacy.* Manila: Philippine Business for Social Progress.

Razak, Najib Abdul, Dato' Seri Tun, Deputy Prime Minister of Malaysia. (2004).
The role of CSR in achieving Vision 2020. Keynote Address at Corporate Social
Responsibility Conference—CSR: Creating Greater Competitive Advantage,
Securities Commission, Kuala Lumpur, Malaysia, June 21. Retrieved from
www.sc.com.my/ENG/HTML/resources/speech/sp—20040621DPM.html.

River ambulance to provide medical services to char people of North Bengal.
(2006). *Financial Express*, August 22, p. 1.

Santos, J. N. (2002). Entrepreneurs School of Asia and the Ten Inspiring
Entrepreneurial Students (TIES). Speech given at the Awarding Ceremony
of TIES.

Tan, K. (2003). Enterprise against poverty: The case for social venture capital.
Retrieved July 22, 2008, from www.tbnetwork.org/documents/Enterprise%
20against%20poverty%20v3.pdf.

Wongpanit. (2006). Wongpanit garbage recycling separation plant. Retrieved
June 25, 2008, from www.3rkh.net/3rkh/files/05%20WONGPANIT%20GA
RBAGE%20RECYCLING%20SEPARATION%20PLANT.pdf.

WorldAware. (2004). The P&O Nedlloyd Award for Infrastructure. Retrieved
June 24, 2008, from www.worldaware.org.uk/awards/awards2004/
wongpanit.html.

JANELLE A. KERLIN & KIRSTEN GAGNAIRE

United States

Social enterprise in the United States is becoming a watchword in both nonprofit and business communities as a way of coupling the resources generated by market activities with the social ambitions of nonprofit organizations. While not a new concept, social enterprise labeled as such has grown dramatically since the first use of the term in the late 1960s (Alter, 2007). New forms continue to emerge, and the concept has come to mean, broadly, the joining of a social cause and a business activity. A new set of actors and organizations largely working outside of government are supporting the movement, including foundations, consultants, university departments, and membership organizations. The rise in social enterprise has generated important questions about its conceptualization, development, and scope, as well as its potential and its limitations. This chapter examines the recent social enterprise movement in the United States and provides a starting point for understanding the movement and the questions it has raised.

THE CONCEPT OF SOCIAL ENTERPRISE

In the United States there are a number of different definitions associated with the term "social enterprise." Until recently, one of the largest divides was between academic groups that combined nonprofit and business forms of social enterprise and some practitioner-oriented groups that focused solely on social enterprise as a nonprofit activity. Recently, however, the different groups interested in social enterprise from an organizational perspective have coalesced around the broader definition of social enterprise that includes both nonprofit and business forms. Social enterprise is, therefore, increasingly understood to include a variety of forms along a continuum, from profit-oriented businesses engaged in sizable social commitments (corporate philanthropies) to dual-purpose businesses that mediate profit goals with social objectives (hybrids) to nonprofit organizations engaged in mission-supporting commercial activity (social purpose organizations, for-profit subsidiaries of nonprofits, nonprofit-business partnerships, etc.) (Young, 2006). For some, corporate philanthropy and dual-purpose businesses fall under the broader label of corporate social responsibility (csr) as well as social enterprise, though csr has carved out a larger business discourse that goes beyond these two social enterprise forms.

Actual definitions of social enterprise used by academics and practitioners show this convergence of thought. Dennis Young, a nonprofit academic, defines social enterprise as "activity intended to address social goals through the operation of private organizations in the marketplace" (2008, p. 23). This definition is consistent with how business schools at leading American universities understand social enterprise (Dees, 1994, 1996, 1998).[1] It is also closely aligned with the definition used by many social enterprise consulting firms who advise both nonprofit organizations and for-profit firms on social enterprise development.[2] Jerr Boschee, a leading social enterprise consultant and executive director of the Institute for Social Entrepreneurs, defines social enterprise as "any organization, in any sector, that uses earned income strategies to pursue a double bottom line or a triple bottom line, either alone (as a social sector business) or as a part of a mixed revenue stream that includes charitable contributions and public sector subsidies" (2006, p. 87). Similarly, Virtue Ventures defines social enterprise as "any business venture created for a social purpose—mitigating/reducing a social problem or a market failure—and to generate social value while operating with the financial discipline, innovation and determination of a private sector business" (Alter, 2007, p. 18).[3]

One of the most important changes that facilitated convergence on the definition occurred when the Social Enterprise Alliance, a professional association for social enterprise practitioners, removed the nonprofit focus from its definition. It now defines a social enterprise as "an organization or venture that achieves its primary social or environmental mission using business methods" (Social Enterprise Alliance, 2009, n.p.). However, the vast majority of its members remain nonprofit practitioners involved in nonprofit social enterprise.[4] Thus, though there has not been consensus around a single definition of social enterprise in the United States, there is increasing agreement that social enterprise involves socially beneficial, market-based activities undertaken by both nonprofits and for-profits.

However, other, more minor divisions in the conceptualization of social enterprise in the United States continue to exist. For instance, at times a new understanding of the term "social entrepreneur" becomes associated with the term "social enterprise," lending the latter an alternate meaning. Specifically, the foundation community in the United States[5] has recently promoted the following definition of "social entrepreneur": an individual that takes an exceptional, innovative approach to addressing social problems on a large scale, regardless of whether the approach involves the generation of earned income (Bornstein, 2004; Martin & Osberg, 2007). "Social entrepreneurship" thus describes the socially innovative action undertaken by the "social entrepreneur," and "social enterprise" becomes by extension the vehicle by which he or she accomplishes the action. Thus, some aligned with this approach to "social entrepreneur" understand "social enterprise" as an organization involved in exceptional social innovation regardless of whether or not it includes earned income. In many other cases, however, the earned income idea of "social enterprise" dominates, and the idea of earned income generation for social benefit remains consistent across the meaning of "social entrepreneur" and "social entrepreneurship" (Boschee, 2006; Alter, 2007; Wexler, 2006; Brooks, 2008). Indeed, Light (2008) states that historically these terms have been used interchangeably around this meaning.

Light (2008), however, notes a third path emerging in this discourse in the United States. Given the increasing popularity of the foundation definition for social entrepreneur, he identifies a clear distinction between "social entrepreneurship" and "social enterprise." He states, "Whereas social entrepreneurship seeks tipping points for innovation and change, social enterprise seeks profits for reinvestment and growth" (2008, p. 5). Citing Dees (2003), he argues that on an academic level there is increasing agreement that "social enterprise" is distinct from the foundation definition of "social entrepreneurship" due to its connection with revenue generation.

Where the focus is on nonprofit social enterprise, there is another minor divide between advocates who promote earned income as a viable strategy for all nonprofits (Boschee, 2006)[6] and those who caution that earned income may not be appropriate for certain types of nonprofit activities and circumstances or even at all (Dees, 1998; Foster & Bradach, 2005; Seedco, 2007; Weisbrod, 2004). More often than not, however, nonprofit social enterprise in the United States is acknowledged as being more appropriate for some nonprofits and activities than others (Young, 2007).

To summarize, the term "social enterprise" in the United States is generally understood to mean a nonprofit or for-profit organization focused on a double bottom line of both earned income and social benefit. Unlike social enterprise in other countries, it is tied to no single type of income generation or social benefit, though sometimes the concept of environmental sustainability is added to social benefit. Likewise, there is no prevalent type of governance structure. There are, however, a number of common organizational arrangements for social enterprise, which we discuss in the next section.

Organizational Arrangements for Nonprofit Social Enterprise

Nonprofit social enterprise has been cited as the most common form of social enterprise in the United States (Young, 2006). Recently it has expanded to include a number of organizational arrangements that in some way connect a nonprofit to commercial activity. These arrangements can either directly involve clients in a revenue-making activity as a part of client programming or exist solely as a revenue-generating vehicle with no client involvement. Sealey et al. (2000) identifies several main nonprofit earned income strategies, including sales of mission-related or non-mission-related products, the formation of for-profit subsidiaries by nonprofits, partnerships with for-profit companies, and cause-related marketing (co-branding of for-profit products), among others. Examples of these four more common types of nonprofit social enterprise arrangements are organized in table 5.1 according to location and extent of nonprofit commercial involvement and then discussed in more detail below.

The first arrangement, the internal commercial venture or *social purpose organization*, involves the generation of earned income through the in-house sale of products or services. Examples include the Girl Scout's annual cookie sale and recreational services provided by the Young Men's Christian Association (YMCA). Also included are sheltered workshops for those with disabilities and job-training initiatives where the commercial activity provides both social programming and revenue for the nonprofit. Nonprofit-owned franchises are also included in this category. One example includes the Latin American Youth Center that owns and operates a Ben and Jerry's ice cream franchise shop to provide on-the-job training for youth.

Sales of products or services can also be arranged through a *nonprofit or for-profit subsidiary*. The creation of subsidiaries allows a nonprofit to en-

TABLE 5.1. *Common Types of Nonprofit Social Enterprises and the Extent of Nonprofit Involvement in Commercial Activity*

	Location of Commercial Activity	Extent of Nonprofit Involvement in Commercial Activity
Social purpose organization	Whole organization / Internal program	Full
Trade intermediary	Enveloping	Partial
Nonprofit / For-profit subsidiary	External connected	Partial
Nonprofit-business partnerships	External dis / connected	Partial / minor

Informed in part by Alter (2007); Young (2006, 2007)

gage in activities that may only be peripherally related to its mission or to reduce its risk as it experiments with new program or business ideas. In particular, nonprofits create nonprofit subsidiaries when a parent nonprofit seeks to establish a large-scale program that differs from its parent organization's main operations. These subsidiaries are considered social enterprises when they include an earned income component. For example, a comprehensive social service provider might establish an employment agency for hard-to-place inner-city residents as a separate nonprofit subsidiary. While the parent organization may provide start-up funding and administrative services, the subsidiary is able to adopt its own structure and create a businesslike culture (Cordes, Steuerle, & Poletz, 2002).

The for-profit subsidiary tends to be chosen when a nonprofit wants to protect its tax-exempt status while engaging in substantial business activity that is not related to its charitable exempt purpose. Profits from the for-profit subsidiary are taxed at normal corporate income tax rates even though they support the charitable activities of the nonprofit. Examples include Sustainable Community Initiatives' establishment of a for-profit subsidiary called Community Forklift (a recovered building materials store) and the Nature Conservancy's for-profit Eastern Shore Sustainable Development Corporation.

At times nonprofits may establish a network of nonprofit and for-profit subsidiaries, creating a nonprofit conglomerate. The loose and fluid organizational structure that results allows for resources to easily flow between affiliates while administrative components often remain centralized, creating a highly cost-effective structure. Keeping administrative costs in a separate organization also allows image-conscious organizations to "hide" the administrative overhead of its affiliates and divide high executive salaries across several organizations. Examples of nonprofit conglomerates include the New Community Corporation, a community development corporation; Housing Works, which serves the homeless with HIV/AIDS in New York City; and the Manchester-Bidwell Corporation, which provides vocational and other educational services (Cordes, Steuerle, & Poletz, 2002).

Nonprofits in the U.S. also form partnerships with for-profits acting as *trade intermediaries* between small, local producers and markets for their products. These organizations either sell the locally acquired goods themselves or link local producers directly with buyers in distant markets. One example is Ten Thousand Villages, a nonprofit that sells products from artisans in over thirty countries in Asia, Africa, Latin America, and the Middle East in its 150 stores in North America and online. Another is Peoplink, Inc., an Internet-based service that connects artisan groups in developing countries directly with buyers in the United States. As a "trust broker" they handle promotion, payment, and returns for a 7 percent commission and direct expenses.

On the periphery of nonprofit social enterprise are *nonprofit-business partnerships*, exemplified most commonly by cause-related marketing. This marketing partnership is defined as "the public association of a for-profit company with a nonprofit organization, intended to promote the company's product or service and to raise money for the nonprofit" (Foundation Center, 2006). Also called co-branding, relationships commonly include a temporary collaboration where a portion of a company's product sales is returned to the nonprofit in exchange for the use of its name or cause in marketing. One of the first to use this strategy was American Express, which in 1983 donated one cent to the restoration of the Statue of Liberty every time one of its cards was charged. Innovative variations of this strategy have multiplied over the years. In a more recent example, City of Hope, a cancer research and treatment nonprofit, teamed with the 3M Company to introduce Post-It Super Sticky Notes with a pink ribbon. The company gave the nonprofit fifty cents for every three-unit pack and twenty cents for every single-unit pack sold.

A few nonprofits have become what are called *quid pro quo organizations*: a large portion of their revenue is generated through cause-related marketing in close partnership with a corporation. For example, City Year provides a year-long youth service experience for teenagers in thirteen cities across the U.S. In 2001, four corporate sponsors each contributed at least $1 million in cash or in-kind contributions, providing almost 30 percent of the total revenue for City Year. In return, these corporations actively market their involvement with City Year as a way to boost sales through increased public awareness of their civic-mindedness (Cordes, Steuerle, & Poletz, 2002).

Other forms of nonprofit-business partnerships include supplier and distributor relationships. In a supplier relationship either the nonprofit or the business provides products or services to the other. As an example, Ben and Jerry's has a "values-led sourcing" initiative through which it purchases brownies from Greyston Bakery, a nonprofit that employs ex-prisoners. In a distributor relationship, either the nonprofit or the business directs the other's products and services to its own customer network (Boschee, 2006). The corporations involved in nonprofit-business partnerships can also be viewed as practicing "business" social enterprise, discussed in the next section.

Organizational Arrangements for Business Social Enterprise

In the United States, businesses are increasingly an integral part of the contemporary social enterprise movement (Boschee, 2006; Dees, 1994, 1996, 1998). More and more, CEOs and their boards are investing in social values, in ways that are both related and unrelated to their missions. Such social enterprise activities fall under the label of corporate social responsibility (CSR), a growing phenomenon in the U.S. that includes any socially beneficial activity undertaken by business. "Business" social enterprise, however, involves a narrower list of activities than CSR. It includes the more common forms of corporate philanthropy, dual-purpose business, and nonprofit-business partnerships (discussed above). As with nonprofits, some businesses may make use of more than one social enterprise arrangement. Table 5.2 organizes the three forms around the degree of corporate involvement in social activity.

Dual-purpose businesses (hybrids) are for-profit businesses that mediate profit goals with internally realized social objectives to achieve either a double bottom line (financial and social returns) or a triple bottom line (financial, social, and environmental returns). An example is Puravida Coffee's mission, which calls for providing living wages to farmers and producers in Latin America through the sale of fair trade coffee, the educa-

TABLE 5.2. *Common Types of Business Social Enterprise and the Extent of Business Involvement in Social Activity*

	Location of Social Activity	Extent of Business Involvement in Social Activity
Dual-purpose business (hybrid)	Whole organization / Internal program	Full
Corporate philanthropy	External disconnected	Partial
Nonprofit-business partnerships	External dis/connected	Partial/minor

Informed in part by Young (2006)

tion of consumers and business leaders to take action toward social good, and serving at-risk children and families in Latin American communities (the latter is a form of corporate philanthropy). Other examples include Patagonia, a clothing maker; Stonyfield Farms, a yogurt company; and Ben and Jerry's.

Corporate philanthropy involves businesses that maintain a for-profit orientation while becoming involved in sizable outside commitments for social causes. One example is Cisco Systems, whose philanthropic efforts focus on three main objectives: human needs, access to education, and responsible citizenship. The corporation provides nonprofits with support in these areas through the donation of employee time, equipment, and finances (Chambers, 2006). Other examples include Home Depot, HSBC USA, and JP Morgan Chase.

Nonprofit-business partnerships under business social enterprise are the same as those discussed under nonprofit social enterprise, though the perspective is from the business's point of view.

HISTORICAL FACTORS PROMOTING AND
SHAPING SOCIAL ENTERPRISE

Social enterprise in the United States has been practiced since the founding of the country, though the actual term did not come into usage until much later.[7] Within the active civil society of the United States there is a long tradition of religious and community groups holding bazaars and selling homemade goods to supplement voluntary donations (Crimmins & Keil, 1983). Indeed, the commercial activities of nonprofits were the first to become associated with the term "social enterprise" at the end of the 1960s, when nonprofits created programs to generate employment (Alter, 2007). However, the term did not become widespread until the 1980s, with the start of the contemporary social enterprise movement.

In the United States, the initial expansion of social enterprise has been linked to a downturn in the economy in the 1970s that led to cutbacks in government funding for nonprofits in the late 1970s and 1980s. Increases in public funding in earlier decades set the stage for the large impact these government cuts had on nonprofits later on. Starting with the Great Society programs of the 1960s, the federal government invested billions of dollars in poverty programs, education, health care, community development, the environment, and the arts. To avoid the creation of a large bureaucracy, many of these funds were channeled through nonprofit programs, spurring the expansion and creation of these organizations in diverse arenas (Hodgkinson et al., 1992; Salamon, 1995; Young, 2003). However, Salamon (1997) estimates that social welfare cuts in the 1970s and 1980s resulted in the loss of $38 billion for nonprofits outside the health care field. Hopes that private contributions would fill the gap were not realized: private contributions dropped from 26 percent of nonprofit revenue in 1977 to 18 percent in 1992 (Hodgkinson & Weitzman, 2001).

Scholars have attempted to show that nonprofits relying on government funding turned to commercial activities and thus social enterprise as a way to fill the gap left by cutbacks (Crimmins & Keil, 1983; Eikenberry & Kluver, 2004; Young, 2003). Salamon (1993) states, "Fees and charges accounted for nearly half of the growth in nonprofit revenue between 1977 and 1997—more than any other source" (p. 24). Foster and Bradach (2005), however, are critical of Salamon's work; they contend that his statistics are taken out of context. They argue, "Fees and charges grew no faster in that 20-year period than other sources of revenue; they represented nearly half of the sector's total revenue in 1997, just as they had in 1977" (Foster & Bradach, 2005, p. 93).

To shed light on this dilemma, a new study using twenty years' worth of data from nonprofit organizations registered with the Internal Revenue Service (IRS), indicates that there was and continues to be an increase in nonprofit commercial activity among larger nonprofits.[8] These same findings also suggest, however, that social enterprise was not spurred on by declines in government grants or private contributions (see figure 5.1). Findings showed that from 1982 to 2002, the commercial revenue of

FIGURE 5.1. *Selected Sources of Revenue for All Nonprofits (Excluding Hospitals and Higher Education Institutions), 1982–2002, in 2003 Dollars*

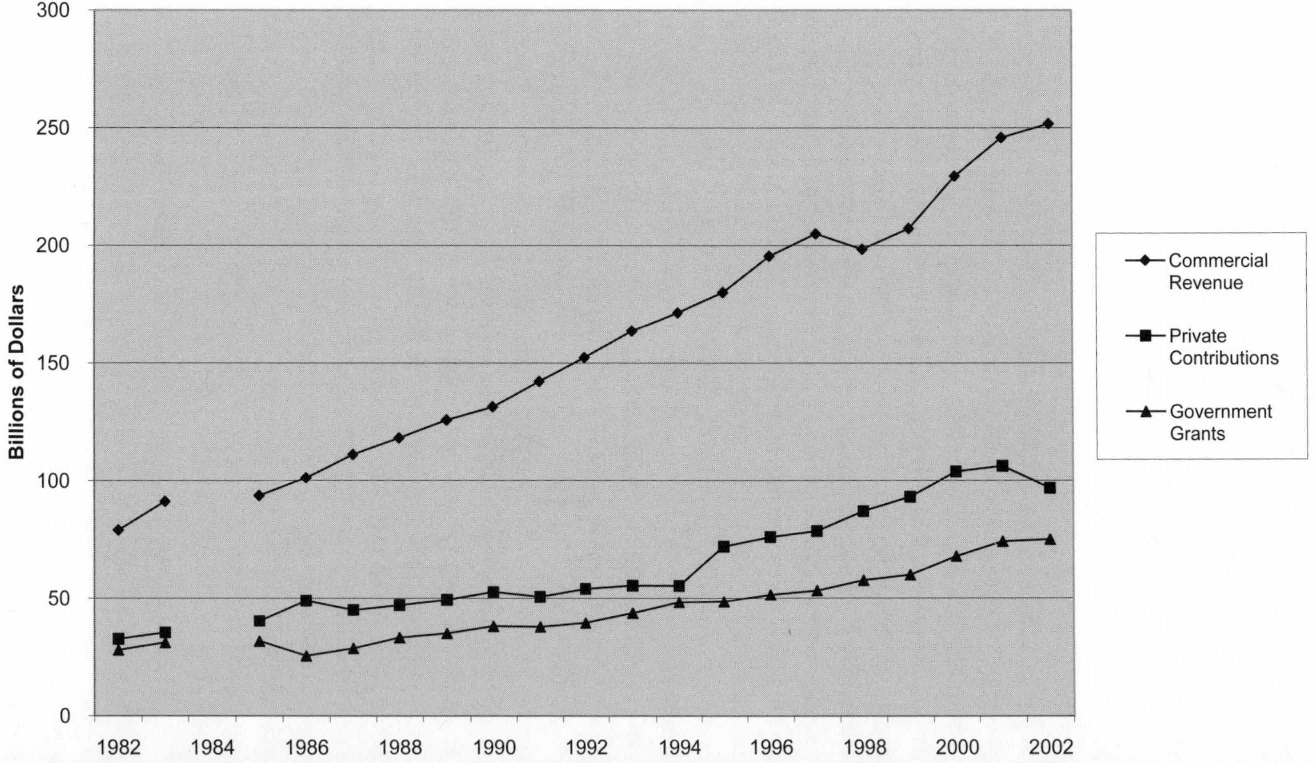

nonprofits increased by 219 percent, private revenue increased by 197 percent, while government grants increased by 169 percent.[9] Moreover, analysis showed that the increase in commercial revenue held true even as a percentage of total nonprofit revenue over time.[10] In 1982, commercial income made up 48.1 percent of nonprofit total revenue, but by 2002 it accounted for 57.6 percent. Meanwhile, private contributions only grew from 19.9 to 22.2 percent and government grants from 17.0 to 17.2 percent during this twenty-year time period (Kerlin & Pollak, 2006).[11]

Data from the Kerlin and Pollak (2006) study also showed that there was little or no association between declines in government grants (or private contributions) and increases in commercial revenue. While the aggregate data do not reveal trends in small categories of nonprofits nor account for the large number of small nonprofits (those with less than $25,000 in annual revenue), the data suggest that a drop in government grants and private contributions did not spur on the increase in commercial activity found in the nonprofit sector as a whole. An alternative explanation may be that the large growth in the number of nonprofits and rising social needs may have increased the competition for government grants and private contributions and, though such contributions were still rising, they were not able to keep up with the new demand. Thus, nonprofits increasingly turned to commercial revenue as competition grew for government grants and private contributions.

Unfortunately, there is no similar historical data on the rise of business social enterprise in the United States. Social enterprise operating out of a for-profit framework appears to be spurred on by a relatively new focus at leading business schools on social enterprise and social entrepreneurship. This focus is further supported by the efforts of business students involved in the association, Net Impact. We discuss these institutions in the next section.

INSTITUTIONAL SUPPORT FOR SOCIAL ENTERPRISE

The environment for social enterprise in the United States tends to reflect a private/business focus. Thus, the supportive institutional context largely consists of private organizations that provide financial support, education, training, and research and consulting services for social enterprise. Indeed, one of the most significant characteristics of social enterprise in the U.S. is that most outside financial support for the strategic development of social enterprise comes from private foundations as opposed to government (Paton, 2003).

Private foundation support for the development of social enterprise began in the 1980s and 1990s by a number of organizations. Some focused on basic information collection and the creation of networks (the Kellogg Foundation, the Kauffman Foundation, the Surdna Foundation, and the Rockefeller Foundation). Others turned their support toward social enterprise start-ups (the Roberts Enterprise Development Fund), social enterprise business competitions (the Goldman Sachs Foundation, the Pew Charitable Trusts), and increasingly toward individual social entrepreneurs through intensive education programs and/or grants (the Draper Richards Foundation, the Skoll Foundation, Echoing Green, Ashoka, and the Schwab Foundation).

One growing trend was the choice by some foundations to sponsor specifically nonprofit social enterprise projects. Such projects included the Venture Fund Initiative of the Rockefeller Foundation, the *Powering Social Change* report funded by Atlantic Philanthropies, initiatives by the David and Lucille Packard Foundation, projects pursued by the Roberts Enterprise Development Fund (a philanthropic program of the Roberts Foundation), and the *Enterprising Nonprofits* report commissioned by the Pew Charitable Trusts, among others.

Also largely backed by foundations are so-called "social enterprise accelerators." Though there are few such organizations, one of the best-known is the Pittsburgh Social Innovation Accelerator in Pennsylvania (formerly the Pittsburgh Social Enterprise Accelerator). It was started and initially funded by two large foundations to support the development of emerging nonprofit ventures in the Pittsburgh area, at no cost to the nonprofit. For a small portfolio of nonprofits, it provides one-on-one consulting, seed funding, business tools, and connections with key stakeholders in the community, such as service providers, funding sources, corporations, public agencies, and university programs. The diverse backgrounds of staff and advisory board members help facilitate connections in the community (Pittsburgh Social Innovation Accelerator, 2009). For those nonprofits and businesses willing to pay, a number of consulting firms have also sprung up that assist social enterprises on the operational and business side.[12]

In the United States, some limited, mostly indirect government support for social enterprise is found on local, state, and federal levels. For example, while community development programs sponsored by different levels of government are not directly aimed at the development of social enterprise, they can and do provide substantial support.[13] One of the few examples of direct support on the local level was the Social Enterprise Initiative (1998–2001) undertaken by the City of Seattle, Washington. It sponsored, often jointly with various foundations, such events as entrepreneurial training for nonprofits and the Seattle Social Enterprise Expo, one of the first social venture fairs in the United States. The Expo led to the development of the Seattle Social Investor's Forum, which the city subsidized for its first two years. It was later funded by corporate and philanthropic grants (Pomerantz, 2003).

There are also state and federal set-aside programs for social enterprise community rehabilitation programs that employ people with disabilities. Twenty-seven states set aside funds to buy state supplies and services from such rehabilitation programs. For example, Washington's rehabilitation programs sell about $3 million in goods and services to the state (Pomerantz, 2003). The Javits-Wagner-O'Day (JWOD) Act established a similar program, AbilityOne, on the federal level. This mandatory federal purchasing program "provides employment opportunities for over 45,000 Americans who are blind or have other severe disabilities by orchestrating government purchases of products and services provided by nonprofit agencies employing such individuals throughout the country" (JWOD, 2008, n.p.).

More recently, there has been a new effort to bring social enterprise and its need for support to the awareness of state and federal governments. In a 2008 report, Andrew Wolk identifies several new state and local government initiatives designed to promote and facilitate social enterprise. Most significantly, in February 2007, Louisiana's lieutenant governor, Mitch Landrieu, launched the country's first government-run Office of Social Entrepreneurship in response to social problems remaining in the wake of Hurricane Katrina in 2005. Wolk's report encourages policy makers and government leaders to support social enterprise toward the goal of generating "transformative, cost-effective solutions" to social problems. His specific recommendations for government officials include: "(1) encourage social innovation; (2) create an enabling environment for social entrepreneurship; (3) develop standards and produce knowledge for understanding performance; (4) reward social-entrepreneurial initiatives for exceptional performance, and (5) scale successful approaches" (Wolk, 2008, p. 8).

In the United States, institutions supporting social enterprise teaching and research include both business schools and social science departments. Since the early 1990s many leading business schools have either created centers on social entrepreneurship or started offering courses on the subject. By 2006, at least sixteen business schools across the U.S. had one or both (Nicholls, 2006). Business school research focuses on the practical knowledge needed by business and nonprofit managers to develop social enterprise activities in their organizations (Boschee, 1998, 2001; Brinckerhoff, 2000; Dees, Emerson, & Economy, 2001; Emerson & Twersky, 1996; Paton, 2003).

On the social science side, nonprofit centers and course offerings at universities have been on the rise as well. At least forty-seven universities now house a nonprofit center or program (NACC, 2004), and the nonprofit course work offered often includes discussion of nonprofit commercial revenue (Young, 2006). Nonprofit researchers have also published path-breaking books and articles on nonprofit commercial revenue with a more theoretical approach to the topic (Ben-Ner & Gui, 1993; Hansmann, 1980; Rose-Ackerman, 1986; Weisbrod, 1988, 1998; Young, 1983, 2006; Anheier & Ben-Ner, 2003).

In the United States, membership organizations have also formed around the idea of social enterprise and social entrepreneurship. One of the fastest-growing organizations is the aforementioned Social Enterprise Alliance, which describes itself as "the only member organization in North America to bring together the diverse field of social enterprise. It serves as advocate for the field, hub of information and education, and builder of a vibrant and growing community of social enterprises" (Social Enterprise Alliance, 2009, n.p.). It is run by and for lenders, investors, grantmakers, practitioners, consultants, researchers, and educators. The Social Enterprise Alliance is the result of a 2002 merger of two groups: the National Gathering for Social Entrepreneurs (founded in 1998) and SeaChange (founded in 2000). At the root of these groups are initiatives funded by foundations, including, among others, the Kellogg, Kauffman, and Echoing Green foundations and the Northland Institute (Ford Foundation) (Social Enterprise Alliance, 2004). Current funders include the Louis & Harold Price, Skoll, Surdna, and UPS (United Parcel Service) Foundations.

Established in 1993, Net Impact is another membership association that has emerged on the business side of social enterprise. Its stated mission is "to make a positive impact on society by growing and strengthening a community of leaders who use business to improve the world" (Net Impact, 2009). The association involves more than 10,000 young entrepreneurs and has created an innovative network of MBAs, graduate students, and young professionals.Increasingly international in its scope, Net Impact operates through a central office in San Francisco and has members on six continents.

LEGAL STRUCTURES FOR SOCIAL ENTERPRISE

Social enterprises in the United States generally make use of a number of legal structures. These include nonprofit, tax-exempt organizations; for-profit corporations; and limited liability companies. Social enterprise practitioners may choose to run a social enterprise out of a single organization or use a combination of organizations with different legal structures to advance their purposes (as discussed in the section on organizational arrangements). Ideally, practitioners will use the legal structures that best accommodate their specific purposes, including expectations for type of activity, raising funds, tax benefits, amount of control, and financial return (Wexler, 2006).

Among the different types of nonprofit, tax-exempt organizations used for social enterprise purposes, the most common is the 501(c)(3) charity, which can provide donors with a tax deduction on the contributions they make to the charity. The other is the 501(c)(4) social welfare organization, which allows for more advocacy activity by the organization but does not offer the benefit of tax deductions for donors. For both of these types of tax-exempt organizations, business income is allowed, and is taxed only if the business activity is unrelated to the mission of the organization. The major drawback of these nonprofit, tax-exempt organizations is that they do not allow social enterprise practitioners the ability to raise investment capital for their business activities by offering outside investors a return on their investment (Wexler, 2006). In other words, they are limited by the nonprofit nondistribution constraint.

In circumstances where practitioners desire more control over the organization (including the ability to attract outside investors) and can do without the charitable contribution tax deduction for donors, they may opt to form a for-profit corporation or limited liability company (LLC). The

LLC is preferable to the for-profit corporation when practitioners desire limited liability to the owner, more flexibility, and partnership income tax treatment.

In the United States virtually no new policy has been created to accommodate the business activities of the growing number of nonprofits involved in social enterprise. Since the 1950s the federal government has used the loosely defined Unrelated Business Income Tax (UBIT) to tax nonprofit revenue that is not related to the organization's exempt purposes (Cordes & Weisbrod, 1998).[14] State governments that collect corporate income tax have created similar UBIT taxes for nonprofits. Though the different levels of U.S. government attempt to regulate the for-profit activities of nonprofits, critics point out that "in practice . . . it has proved administratively difficult for federal, state, and local taxing authorities to differentiate taxable and nontaxable commercial activities" (Cordes & Weisbrod, 1998, p. 85; see also Simon, 1987). This situation has left nonprofits wary of engaging in certain types of revenue-generating activities for fear of compromising their charitable tax-exempt status. When nonprofits do engage in business activity, it has for-profit businesses claiming that nonprofit enterprises have an unfair competitive edge because they do not always pay taxes on the same services and products that for-profits do (Crimmins & Keil, 1983; Leavins & Wadhwa, 1998).

Over the past few years, social enterprise practitioners and lawyers have come together to explore new legal structures for social enterprise that would combine the access to capital that businesses enjoy with the legal advantages of a charitable organization. Since 2006, the Aspen Institute in Washington, D.C., and the Social Enterprise Alliance have hosted forums with leading social enterprise figures to explore concrete proposals for legal reform in this area, as well as standards for performance and accountability.[15]

One of the most promising advancements is legislation passed by the state of Vermont in April 2008 that created the low-profit limited liability company (the L3c). This "for-profit with a nonprofit soul" allows foundations more freedom to use program related investments (PRIS) as low-cost, high-risk capital in an L3c whose primary goal must be a socially beneficial cause. Although this new legal entity was enacted in the state of Vermont, the L3c is now legal in all fifty states if incorporated in Vermont or other states that have passed similar initiatives, including Michigan, Wyoming, Utah, and North Dakota (Americans for Community Development, 2009).

CHALLENGES AND BENEFITS

In the United States, though social enterprise is experiencing healthy growth, several challenges of the movement have been identified, including the exclusion of specific groups, the weakening of civil society, and the lack of government involvement. In relation to the first, specific types of social enterprise may have the unintended side effect of leading to the further exclusion of already marginalized groups. For example, revenue generated through a fee-for-service strategy is a popular type of social enterprise activity. However, when this strategy is applied in social service nonprofits, the concern is that potential, low-income clients are automatically excluded from receiving services because they are unable to pay for them (Salamon, 1993). Vulnerable groups may also become excluded when profit-making activities encroach on the focus of a nonprofit's mission or, worse, when revenue-generating activities become preferred over mission-related programs because they are more profitable (Eikenberry & Kluver, 2004; Weisbrod, 1998). Moreover, there is evidence that nonprofits engaged in market activities grow increasingly focused on meeting the needs of individual clients rather than those of the neighborhood or community through the provision of public goods (Alexander, Nank, & Stivers, 1999). Exacerbating the situation is the new competition nonprofit providers are feeling from for-profits that offer similar services (Young & Salamon, 2002).

Social enterprise also has some observers in the United States worried that the growing market orientation of nonprofits will put civil society at risk (Alexander, Nank, & Stivers, 1999; Eikenberry & Kluver, 2004). One of nonprofits' contributions to civil society is their ability to strengthen social capital.[16] However, a growing focus on a financial bottom line may lead organizations to abandon less efficient practices that strengthen social capital, such as running a volunteer program. Nonprofits engaged in social enterprise may also find they have less need to rely on traditional stakeholders and networks such as private donors, members, community volunteers, and other community organizations, with the result that opportunities to promote social capital are lost (Aspen Institute, 2001; Eikenberry & Kluver, 2004). Finally, nonprofit interest in market strategies may be leading to a shift in board membership: from board members connected to the community to those connected to business (Backman & Smith, 2000). As addressed above, other challenges in the

United States include the need for clearer legal definitions for nonprofits engaged in revenue-generating activities. Indeed, a comparison with Western Europe highlights the comparative lack of U.S. government involvement with social enterprise, revealing it as another area for possible improvement.

Notwithstanding these challenges, social enterprise in the United States provides some very important benefits. In terms of the nonprofit field, commercial revenue has become the nonprofit sector's main source of funding. As the Kerlin and Pollak (2006) study shows, since the 1980s nonprofit commercial revenue has consistently provided about half of all revenue received by nonprofits. This proportion continues to grow, providing nonprofits with a replacement for scarce charitable and government funding. On the organizational level, increased commercial revenue provides nonprofits with the opportunity to move toward self-sustainability due to their reduced reliance on other funding streams (Boschee, 2006).

Cause-related marketing in particular has the potential to bring in large amounts of money without the involvement of running a commercial venture. These partnerships with business also offer nonprofits more control over funding, as well as increased name recognition and access to new business knowledge, including marketing skills. The downside is that cause-related marketing is often limited to nonprofits with existing name recognition that makes them attractive candidates for marketing partners (Andreasen, 2008).

Organizations involved in social enterprise also find they have a freedom in operating that is not found with restricted funds from private contributions and government grants. Such organizations have the flexibility to change a program that is not working, expand programs that are working, and experiment with new ideas. They are also not bound by funders' reporting requirements, measurement tools, or definition of success, which nonprofits often find are not in line with the work they do. Some even find that with social enterprise they can be more responsive to the needs of the people they serve than when they are tied to the funding restrictions of traditional charitable sources (Burns, 2003).

Social enterprise can also help create a more entrepreneurial spirit that extends to the entire nonprofit. This shift in the culture of the organization can enhance the quality of programs by making them more consumer/beneficiary-oriented as well as efficient ·and effective. Some nonprofits have also found that social enterprise activities help attract and retain staff as well as donors. Indeed, nonprofits with earned-income strategies project an image of self-sufficiency that can be attractive to foundations looking to avoid grantee dependence (Foster & Bradach, 2005).

EXAMPLE I: HOUSING WORKS

Housing Works is the largest community-based AIDS service organization in the United States. It is a minority-operated, nonprofit corporation that provides housing, health care, drug treatment, advocacy, job training, and support services to homeless and low-income people living with HIV and AIDS in New York City. Housing Works was founded in June 1990, initially to address the city's lack of supportive housing for the HIV/AIDS homeless. At that time there were fewer than 350 housing units for the estimated 30,000 homeless in this situation. Housing Works now serves 20,000 New York City residents affected by HIV/AIDS. The organization developed out of the Housing Committee of the AIDS Coalition to Unleash Power (ACT UP) in response to the growing double crises of homelessness and AIDS. Its basic mission is to reestablish the fundamental human rights of this population through direct service programs, employment opportunities, and advocacy (Housing Works, 2009). To facilitate its work, "Housing Works has pioneered the use of entrepreneurial ventures both to underwrite programs and help clients achieve economic self-sufficiency" (Housing Works, 2009, n.p.).

Social enterprise at Housing Works has steadily evolved over the years to include a successful chain of thrift stores, a café bookstore, a food catering business, and the organization's own building maintenance service. The social enterprises help spread awareness of the Housing Works mission and provide jobs to graduates of its job-training programs (Housing Works, 2009). Moreover, Housing Works businesses contribute millions of dollars annually to the organization. For its fiscal year ending in June 2008, Housing Works business ventures generated over $13 million in revenue, 34 percent of total annual revenue (Housing Works, 2008, p. 34). This allows Housing Works an "unusual degree of flexibility and independence to pilot new business ideas and to engage in bold political advocacy" (Housing Works, 2009, n.p.). Housing Works social enterprises include the Housing Works Bookstore Café, The Works, and the Housing Works Thrift Shops.

Housing Works Bookstore Café

The Housing Works Bookstore Café is a well-established downtown New York institution and tourist destination. The bookstore has one of the best book, movie, and music selections in New York City and often holds readings and concerts. Its in-store café also draws in customers. The store is run almost exclusively by volunteers, and all merchandise in the bookstore is donated, making it possible for 100 percent of the profits to go to Housing Works, Inc. The bookstore, with its wooden staircases and balconies, is also often rented out for parties and other events to bring in additional income (Housing Works, 2009).

The Works

Founded in 1997, The Works is a nonprofit catering and events firm. It specializes in catering corporate parties, wedding receptions, and other events for large and small groups. Clients have included ABC Networks, MAC Cosmetics, and the United Way. The Works contributes all the profit it generates to Housing Works, Inc. (Housing Works, 2009).

Housing Works Thrift Shops

The Housing Works Thrift Shops consist of seven stores in the New York City area that sell high-end and other donated items. The stores provide Housing Works, Inc., with more than $12 million in funding per year and also ensure a steady supply of clothing and basic essentials for Housing Works clients. ShopHousingWorks.com, an outgrowth of the Thrift Shops, is an online auction shop for high-end, often vintage, merchandise. Online sales have raised more than $2,894,470 since 2002 (Housing Works, 2009).

EXAMPLE 2: GEORGIA JUSTICE PROJECT

The Georgia Justice Project (GJP), in Atlanta, Georgia, is a nonprofit organization established in 1986 to provide people accused of crimes with legal defense, social services, and employment. Its mission is "to eliminate injustices in the criminal justice system experienced by poor people who are the most often accused and to provide them with resources to advance their human potential, proving that the cycle of poverty and crime can be broken" (Georgia Justice Project, 2009, n.p.). To accomplish its goals GJP brings together lawyers, social workers, and a social enterprise venture (Georgia Justice Project, 2009).

GJP most often works with clients who cannot afford a lawyer, have a criminal case pending, and are committed to changing their lives. Clients are provided with high-level legal representation, counseling, substance abuse intervention, educational assistance, and job training and placement. If clients are convicted, GJP advocates for their needs while they are in prison and provides support after their release. GJP is funded by private foundations, corporations, individuals, religious congregations, and its business venture. By not accepting government funding, GJP has the flexibility to develop its own programming and select the clients it will work with. In addition, GJP is able to maintain its independence from the court system (Georgia Justice Project, 2009). Thus, it has "total control of [its] caseloads and can reverse the way legal services have been traditionally available to the poor" (Georgia Justice Project, 2009, n.p.).

GJP's social enterprise is a landscape company, New Horizon Landscaping. Established in 1993, the company provides quality lawn care services as well as job training and steady employment for GJP clients. The company also provides many other benefits, as its director, Christopher Hayes, explains:

> New Horizon Landscaping . . . provides an opportunity for clients to acquire the skills necessary to progress from their current situations and assimilate into the work force. With a management team of landscape professionals, we are able to model the mechanics of operating a business for our employee-clients. In addition, the fellowship and mentoring provided by our managers and supervisors—some of whom are former clients themselves—have repeatedly proven invaluable to our younger more recent additions to our mission-focused team. (Georgia Justice Project, 2009, n.p.)

Statistics show that GJP has found the right mix of assistance, opportunity, and dedication. The incarceration rate for GJP clients is only 7.3 percent, compared to urban public defender offices that average 71.3 percent. Similarly, only 18.8 percent of GJP clients return to prison, compared to an average national prison recidivism rate of over 60 percent (Georgia Justice Project, 2009).

NOTES

1. Examples include the Social Enterprise Initiative at Harvard Business School, the Center for the Advancement of Social Entrepreneurship at Duke Univer-

sity's Fuqua School of Business, and the Research Initiative on Social Entre-preneurship at Columbia Business School.

2. For consultant examples, see Community Wealth Ventures, the Social Enter-prise Group, and Origo Social Enterprise Partners.

3. Virtue Ventures is a U.S.-based international social enterprise consulting firm.

4. Increasingly, the nonprofit type of social enterprise is distinguished by use of the following terms: "nonprofit social enterprise," "nonprofit enterprise," "nonprofit ventures," and "enterprising nonprofits."

5. Foundations include among others Ashoka, Echoing Green, and the Skoll Foundation.

6. Either as the sole income generator or in combination with donated revenue.

7. Parts of this section are from Kerlin and Pollak (2006).

8. The study tracks the commercial revenue of nonprofits over twenty years using 990 financials that 501(c)(3) organizations (with $25,000 and over in annual revenue) filed with the U.S. Internal Revenue Service (IRS) (Kerlin & Pollak, 2006). Commercial revenue includes program service revenue (including gov-ernment contracts), dues and assessments, income from special events, and funds from third-party payers.

9. To account for year-to-year fluctuations, the average annual increase was also calculated showing that from 1982 to 2002 the average annual increase was 9.87 percent for commercial revenue, 9.08 percent for private contributions, and 9.13 percent for government grants.

10. In figure 5.1, the apparent drop in commercial revenue in the year 1998 is in part attributed to the fact that two large organizations lost their tax-exempt status in 1997: the Teachers Insurance Annuity Association and the College Retirement Equities Fund (together known as TIAA-CREF) (Arnsberger, 2001). No data was collected in 1984.

11. The total of the percentages for these three sources is more in 2002 than in 1982 because these sources were steadily increasing in real dollars, while other revenues such as income from rent, investments, and assets remained rela-tively stable.

12. See notes 1 and 2.

13. Dennis Young, Professor, Georgia State University, personal communication, May 16, 2004.

14. According to the IRS, an "activity is an unrelated business if it meets three requirements: 1) It is a *trade or business*, 2) It is *regularly carried on*, and 3) It is not *substantially related* to furthering the exempt purpose of the organization" (IRS, 2009, n.p.).

15. Rachel Mosher-Williams, Project Director, Nonprofit Sector and Philanthropy Program, the Aspen Institute, personal communication, October 12, 2006.
16. Social capital includes the social norms of trust, cooperation, and reciprocity, which develop through positive citizen interaction and undergird the effective functioning of democracy and a market economy (see Salamon, 1997; Backman & Smith, 2000).

REFERENCES

Alexander, J., Nank, R., & Stivers, C. (1999). Implications of welfare reform: Do nonprofit survival strategies threaten civil society? *Nonprofit and Voluntary Sector Quarterly, 28*(4), pp. 452–475.

Alter, K. (2007). *Social enterprise typology.* Retrieved January 2009 from www.virtueventures.com/files/setypology.pdf.

Americans for Community Development. (2009). Introducing the new, socially responsible limited liability company. Retrieved January 19, 2009, from www.americansforcommunitydevelopment.org/supporting.html.

Andreasen, A. (2008). Partnerships, sponsorships and cause-related marketing. In J. Cordes & E. Steuerle (Eds.), *Nonprofits and Business.* Washington, DC: Urban Institute Press.

Anheier, H. K., & Ben-Ner, A. (Eds.). (2003). *The study of nonprofit enterprise: Theories and approaches.* New York: Kluwer Academic/Plenum Publishers.

Arnsberger, P. (2001). *Charities and other tax-exempt organizations, 1998.* Retrieved April 2006 from www.irs.gov/taxstats/charitablestats/article/0,,id=97176,00.html.

Aspen Institute. (2001). *The nonprofit sector and the market: Opportunities and challenges.* Publication 01-013. Washington, DC: Aspen Institute.

Backman, E., & Smith, S. R. (2000). Healthy organizations, unhealthy communities? *Nonprofit Management and Leadership,10*(4), pp. 355–373.

Ben-Ner, A., & Gui, B. (Eds.). (1993). *The nonprofit sector in the mixed economy.* Ann Arbor: University of Michigan Press.

Bornstein, D. (2004). *How to change the world: Social entrepreneurs and the power of new ideas.* New York: Oxford University Press U.S.A.

Boschee, J. (1998). *Merging mission and money: A board member's guide to social entrepreneurship.* Washington, DC: National Center for Nonprofit Boards.

———. (2001). *The social enterprise sourcebook: Profiles of social purpose businesses operated by nonprofit organizations.* Minneapolis: Northland Institute.

———. (2006). *Migrating from innovation to entrepreneurship.* Minneapolis: Encore! Press.

Brinckerhoff, P. (2000). *Social entrepreneurship: The art of mission-based venture development*. New York: John Wiley & Sons.

Brooks, A. C. (2008). *Social entrepreneurship: A modern approach to social value creation*. Upper Saddle River, NJ: Pearson/Prentice Hall.

Burns, M. (2003). Self-sufficiency: How important is it? In Community Wealth Ventures (Ed.), *Powering Social Change* (pp. 30–33). Washington, DC: Community Wealth Ventures.

Chambers, J. (2006). Cisco: Giving back is good business. *CECP New Century Philanthropy, 6*(2), p. 4.

Cordes, J., Steuerle, E., & Poletz, Z. (2002). Examples of nonprofit/for-profit hybrid business models. Unpublished paper, Urban Institute.

Cordes, J., & Weisbrod, B. (1998). Differential taxation of nonprofits and the commercialization of nonprofit revenues. In B. Weisbrod (Ed.), *To profit or not to profit: The commercial transformation of the nonprofit sector* (pp. 83–104). Cambridge: Cambridge University Press.

Crimmins, J. C., & Keil, M. (1983). *Enterprise in the nonprofit sector*. New York: Rockefeller Brothers Fund.

Dees, J. G. (1994). *Social enterprise: Private initiatives for the common good*. Harvard Business School Note. Cambridge, MA: Harvard Business School Press.

——. (1996). *Social enterprise spectrum: Philanthropy to commerce*. Harvard Business School Note. Cambridge, MA: Harvard Business School Press.

——. (1998). Enterprising nonprofits. *Harvard Business Review, 76*(1), pp. 55–67.

——. (2003). *Social entrepreneurship is about innovation and impact, not income*. Retrieved from www.caseatduke.org/articles/1004/corner.htm.

Dees, J. G., Emerson, J., & Economy, P. (2001). *Enterprising nonprofits: A toolkit for social entrepreneurs*. New York: John Wiley & Sons.

Eikenberry, A., & Kluver, J. (2004). The marketization of the nonprofit sector: Civil society at risk? *Public Administration Review, 64*(2), pp. 132–140.

Emerson, J., & Twersky, F. (Eds.). (1996). *New social entrepreneurs: The success, challenge and lessons of non-profit enterprise creation*. San Francisco: Roberts Foundation.

Foster, W., & Bradach, J. (2005). Should nonprofits seek profits? *Harvard Business Review, 83*(2), pp. 92–100.

Foundation Center. (2006). *What is cause-related marketing?* Retrieved from http://fdncenter.org/learn/faqs/html/cause—marketing.html.

Georgia Justice Project. (2009). About Georgia Justice Project. Retrieved January 23, 2009, from www.gjp.org/about.

Hansmann, H. (1980). The role of nonprofit enterprise. *Yale Law Journal, 89*(5), pp. 835–901.

Hodgkinson, V. A., & Weitzman, M. (2001). Overview: The state of the independent sector. In J. S. Ott (Ed.), *The Nature of the Nonprofit Sector* (pp. 9–22). Boulder, CO: Westview Press.

Hodgkinson, V. A., Weitzman, M., Toppe, C., & Noga, S. (1992). *Non-profit almanac, 1992–1993.* San Francisco: Jossey Bass.

Housing Works. (2008). *Housing Works 2008 Annual Report.* Retrieved January 23, 2009, from www.housingworks.org/i/page-media/housingworks—AR08.pdf.

——. (2009). About. Retrieved January 23, 2009, from www.housingworks.org.

Internal Revenue Service (IRS). (2009). Unrelated business income defined. Retrieved January 28, 2009, from www.irs.gov/charities/article/0,,id=96104,00.html.

JWOD. (2008). *A brief history of the AbilityOne Program.* Retrieved January 2009 from www.jwod.gov/jwod/about—us/about—us.html.

Kerlin, J., & Pollak, T. (2006). Nonprofit commercial revenue: A replacement for declining government grants and private contributions? Paper presented at the Third Annual United Kingdom Social Enterprise Research Conference, London, U.K., June 22–23.

Leavins, J., & Wadhwa, D. (1998). Are your activities safe from UBIT? *Nonprofit World, 16*(September–October), pp. 49–51.

Light, P. C. (2008). *The search for social entrepreneurship.* Washington, DC: Brookings Institution Press.

Martin, R., & Osberg, S. (2007). Social entrepreneurship: The case for definition. *Stanford Social Innovation Review.* Spring.

NACC (Nonprofit Academic Centers Council). (2004). Member centers. Retrieved January 2008 from www.naccouncil.org/members.asp.

Net Impact. (2009). About Net Impact. Retrieved January 28, 2009, from www .netimpact.org/displaycommon.cfm?an=1.

Nicholls, A. (2006). Introduction. In A. Nicholls (Ed.), *Social entrepreneurship: New models of sustainable change* (pp. 1–36). Oxford: Oxford University Press.

Paton, R. (2003). *Managing and measuring social enterprises.* Thousand Oaks: Sage Publications.

Pittsburgh Social Innovation Accelerator. (2009). Retrieved January 28, 2009, from www.acceleratenow.org/content/how-we-work.aspx.

Pomerantz, M. (2003). *Social entrepreneurship in the northwest.* Communication to the Coleman Symposium on Social Entrepreneurship, United States Association for Small Business and Entrepreneurship Annual Conference. Hilton Head, South Carolina, January 23–25.

Rose-Ackerman, S. (1986). *The economics of nonprofit institutions*. New York: Oxford University Press.

Salamon, L. (1993). The marketization of welfare: Changing nonprofit and for-profit roles in the American welfare state. *Social Service Review, 67*(1), pp. 16–39.

——. (1995). *Partners in public service*. Baltimore: Johns Hopkins University Press.

——. (1997). *Holding the center: America's nonprofit sector at a crossroads*. New York: Nathan Cummings Foundation.

Sealey, K., Boschee, J., Emerson, J., & Sealey, W. (Eds.). (2000). *A reader in social enterprise*. Boston: Pearson Custom Publishing.

Seedco. (2007). *The limits of social enterprise: A field study and case analysis*. New York: Seedco Policy Center.

Simon, J. (1987). The tax treatment of nonprofit organizations: A review of federal and state policies. In W. Powell (Ed.), *The nonprofit sector: A research handbook*. New Haven: Yale University Press.

Social Enterprise Alliance. (2009). About us. Retrieved January 19, 2009, from www.se-alliance.org.

Weisbrod, B. (1988). *The non-profit economy*. Cambridge, MA: Harvard University Press.

—— (Ed.). (1998). *To profit or not to profit: The commercial transformation of the nonprofit sector*. Cambridge: Cambridge University Press.

——. (2004). The pitfalls of profits. *Stanford Social Innovation Review, 2*(3), pp. 40–47.

Wexler, R. A. (2006). Social enterprise: A legal context. *Exempt Organization Tax Review, 54*(3), pp. 233–244.

Wolk, A. (2008). Advancing social entrepreneurship: Recommendations for policy makers and government agencies. Report prepared for the Aspen Institute & Root Cause.

Young, D. (1983). *If not for profit, for what?* Lexington, MA: Lexington Books.

——. (2003). New trends in the US non-profit sector: Towards market integration? In OECD (Ed.), *The nonprofit sector in a changing economy* (pp. 61–77). Paris: OECD.

——. (2006). Social enterprise in community and economic development in the USA: Theory, corporate form and purpose. *International Journal of Entrepreneurship and Innovation Management, 6*(3), pp. 241–255.

—— (Ed.). (2007). *Financing nonprofits: Putting theory into practice.* Lanham, MD: AltaMira Press.

——. (2008). Alternative perspectives on social enterprise. In J. Cordes & E. Steuerle (Eds.), *Nonprofits and business.* Washington, DC: Urban Institute Press.

Young, D., & Salamon, L. (2002). Commercialization, social ventures, and for-profit competition. In L. Salamon (Ed.), *The state of nonprofit America* (pp. 423–446). Washington, DC: Brookings Institution Press.

ABSOLOM MASENDEKE & ALEX MUGOVA

Zimbabwe and Zambia

THE CONCEPT OF SOCIAL ENTERPRISE

Nongovernmental organizations (NGOS) have become universally recognized in African societies as key development actors. For NGOS, social enterprise is a core strategy for social and economic development, and this is often evident in their mission statements. Some NGOS work in partnership with government, the private sector, and other donors in order to realize their social enterprise objectives. NGOS also act as intermediaries in delivering microfinance packages targeted to the poor, mainly because of their experience working with communities. When working in this capacity, NGOS are known as social enterprises. Recently, NGOS operating in some countries in southern Africa, especially Zimbabwe, have experienced serious funding challenges that make it difficult for them to sustain their activities. As a result of this resource squeeze, there is now a trend toward cost recovery and commercialization of some services in local and international NGOS, and these activities make them social enterprises. Returns from commercialized services are used to support and expand activities of the organization. The quest for organizational viability and sustainability has been one of the prime motivations behind this phenomenon.

Examples of social enterprises in southern Africa are varied. They include:

- Enterprises set up by NGOS to generate income meant to sustain their activities
- Organizations set up to provide goods and services to the poor on a commercial basis
- Cooperatives set up by members to pool resources and skills and to provide goods and services for sale

- Associations set up by members to facilitate working together and speaking with a collective voice and to facilitate access to inputs and services that enhance the viability of the members' businesses

Individual perspectives on social enterprises are varied. Some view social enterprises as self-empowerment mechanisms. Some look at social enterprises as a coping strategy for enhancing economic survival at the individual and household levels. For some, especially those in societies molded around cooperative approaches/models of development, social enterprises refer to collective enterprises. This view of social enterprises often leads to cooperative and group-based initiatives for the attainment of social and economic objectives. Some people define social enterprises as social gifts. These people normally adopt attitudes that undermine their ability to benefit from social enterprises. Viability and long-term sustainability are keys to the success of individually run social enterprises.

Social enterprises in Africa exhibit seven key features, but not every social enterprise has all these characteristics. They are:

- Delivery of goods and services to the public for a fee
- Viability and sustainability considerations
- Financial sponsorship
- Community empowerment
- Partnerships
- Social accountability
- Social and economic value creation

These common characteristics provide a good basis for conceptualizing the social enterprise phenomenon in Africa. While many definitions of social enterprises have been brought forward, the one by Kim Alter (2007) best applies to the African context: A social enterprise is any nonprofit-owned revenue-generating venture created for the purpose of contributing to a social cause while operating with the discipline, innovation, and determination of a for-profit business.

Care needs to be taken to avoid confusing social enterprises with public social services and utilities. The key distinction is that social enterprises seek to generate revenues for further investment in charitable activities, whereas public utilities and social services are not driven by this motive. Social enterprises should also not be confused with NGOS. Many social enterprises are created by NGOS, but not all NGOS create social enterprises. NGOS create social enterprises when they are driven by the need to create additional income to sustain their operations and/or to expand the charitable services they provide to communities with whom they work.

When one looks at the common features identified above, one may see very little separating social enterprises from business enterprises. Kim Alter (2007) acknowledges this dilemma and singles out purpose as the key factor distinguishing the two. According to Alter, profit is the primary purpose of socially responsible businesses and corporations practicing social responsibility, whereas social impact is the primary purpose of social enterprises and nonprofits with income-generating activities. Hence, the common features between social enterprises and business enterprises may be due to the fact that nonprofits, although founded on the basis of social value creation, need external or self-generated funds for financial sustainability. On the other hand, although for-profit enterprises are primarily focused on economic value creation, they need to make social contributions to remain relevant and to survive in the marketplace. Therefore, the social and economic imperatives of for-profit and nonprofit organizations may not be mutually exclusive in nature.

In an African context with high levels of poverty and unemployment, it is very common to find nonprofit enterprises with a focus on both social and economic value creation. According to Moyo, Makumbe, and Raftopoulos (2000), the debate over NGOS in Zimbabwe centers on funding mechanisms that can lead to self-financing, sustainable, and productive institutions and programs that have internally driven impetuses and capacities to pursue development. Now many nonprofit organizations in Africa incorporate some form of revenue generation through commercial means into their operations. One example is Development Aid from People to People (DAPP), which is operating in most southern African countries with its secondhand clothing enterprise. In figure 6.1, DAPP's managing director in Zambia, Jane Broen Jensen (e-mail correspondence, November 20, 2005), explains the origin and public conception of their clothing and shoes venture in Zambia.

Most social enterprises in Africa were created as social welfare concerns with very limited roles to play in the economic development process; there were initially very few mission-related social enterprises after the era of structural adjustment. Due to donor withdrawal and the rolling back of state funding, most NGOS began incorporating social enterprise activities to increase their financial sustainability so that they could continue to deliver goods and services to the public. A new breed of NGOs began to emerge, with missions explicitly targeting social enterprise development as a key strategy. Thus, since the 1990s, Africa's nonprofits have had some form of embedded social enterprise. Kim Alter (2007) identified five different forms of embedded social enterprises that can be applied to help understand the different operational models of social enterprises in Africa. These forms are the entrepreneur support model, the market intermediation model, the employment model, the fee-for-service model, and the market linkage model.

The entrepreneur support model is common in organizations that focus on creating economic opportunities for the poor. In Zimbabwe, these organizations include the Zimbabwe Opportunities Investment Centre and the Entrepreneurial Development Trust. These organizations explicitly target the development of small enterprises that are run by the local population. Self-identified entrepreneurs are trained in enterprise development and management skills mostly through a "learning by doing" approach.

The major bottleneck for most small producers is access to markets for their goods and services, as they fail to compete in terms of quality and price with businesses that are well established and have many resources. Most NGOs in southern Africa that have been promoting small enterprises have been struggling to make markets work for poor producers. Market intermediation has now become a key model of social enterprise support by some organizations, especially those that seek to add value to products that are produced by resource-poor communities. Field observations for some Practical Action projects have shown that market intermediation becomes imperative because of the very low prices for commodities, such as raw honey, paid to the poor by unscrupulous middlemen. After processing and packaging the honey, they later sell the same product at five times the producer price. The production and marketing of natural products and other high-value commodities by small producers has attracted market intermediation interventions from NGOs.

Unemployment is a major problem in Africa. In southern Africa the unemployment rates vary from about 40 to 80 percent. The high rates of unemployment stem from the early 1990s, when Structural Adjustment Programmes (SAPS) were implemented in most southern African countries. It was at this time that employment-oriented social enterprises

FIGURE 6.1. DAPP *Operations in Zambia*

DAPP started operations in Zambia in 1986. DAPP is a cofounder and member of the Federation Humana People to People, which has its headquarters in Zimbabwe. Some member organizations of the federation are implementing projects in various countries in Africa, Central America, and Asia, while other member organizations in Europe and North America are collecting used clothing for resale. Some of the clothes are sold in Europe and North America to raise funds for projects in Africa, Central America, and Asia. Most of the clothes and shoes are donated to the organizations in Africa. Here the clothes are again sorted and sold to raise funds for the projects.

DAPP in Zambia pays the freight and import costs as well as a small collection fee. As part of the agreement to receive the clothes and shoes, DAPP in Zambia commits to using the income to contribute toward the basic running costs of the projects in Zambia. This is after paying all freight, import duty, VAT, and sales costs.

DAPP in Zambia sells the clothes and shoes in retail shops throughout the country. The customers include individuals who buy clothes for themselves and their families, as well as marketers who make a living selling items from small market stalls.

Thus, for DAPP in Zambia, the value of the clothes is being transformed from a small value at the moment of delivery into the collection containers to considerable value—in other words, from small value for those who no longer need the clothes, to considerable value for others, expressing itself in the form of employment for some, quality and affordable clothing for many, and ultimately support to projects that improve the life, health, and education of many people in Zambia.

This way of raising funds for the projects has been very instrumental in starting and building up new projects. It is often difficult to get partners for new projects. Most partners want to see something on the ground before committing support. By raising funds through clothing and shoe sales, we have been able to start projects, show results, lay the foundation for other partners to join in, and sometimes pay for the staff cost when partners do not want to pay such an expense.

FIGURE 6.1. *Continued*

In Zambia, the sale of secondhand clothes and shoes is regarded as business in line with any other commercial business, regardless of how the proceeds are used. As a development organization we have the same conditions as private commercial importers. The duty is approximately US$0.50 per kg that has to be paid up front on import. DAPP in Zambia has less than 2 percent of the whole secondhand clothes market.

The Zambian government does to some extent support these kinds of ventures but is sometimes also bound by international and regional trade agreements, such as WTO agreements, World Bank agreements, and COMESA.

Source: E-mail correspondence, November 20, 2005

emerged. There are many organizations promoting employment-focused social enterprises in southern Africa. A key example of this model is the promotion of technical service centers by Practical Action Southern Africa in peri-urban areas meant to increase employment opportunities for small-scale artisans. Technically oriented NGOs are increasingly attaching a fee to the services they provide to communities. The fee-for-service social enterprise model is mainly justified as a measure for enhancing the viability and sustainability of the organization.

The market linkage model is also common in southern Africa. The organization in this model acts as a broker that connects producers to markets or vice versa, whereas in the intermediary model, the organization facilitates the selling of client products into the different markets.

HISTORY OF THE RECENT SOCIAL ENTERPRISE MOVEMENT

Social enterprises, in their varied forms, are increasingly becoming recognized by governments, donors, and the public as a key aspect of development in Africa. However, political, social, economic, and cultural forces in Africa have influenced the form, character, and behavior of most social enterprises. The effects of natural calamities such as droughts have also influenced the social enterprise development agenda, in that relief may become a focus for alleviating the suffering of people. The impact of

TABLE 6.1. *Evolution of Social Enterprises in Zimbabwe*

Phase	Main Activities of Social Enterprises	Type(s) of Social Enterprise Models
Pre-independence (before 1980)	• Relief • Donations	• Welfare
Immediate postindependence (1980–1986)	• Relief • Donations	• Welfare
Pre-economic structural adjustment program (1987–1990/1)	• Small enterprise support • Skills training	• Market intermediati∢
Economic structural adjustment program (1992–2000)	• Income and employment generation	• Fee for service
Poststructural adjustment program (2000–2005)	• Value addition support • Market access for the poor	• Market intermediati∢ • Market linkages
Post-2005	• Self-reliance initiatives • Social protection for vulnerable people	• Entrepreneur suppo⟩ model • Social safety net mo⟩

politics and economics on social enterprises emerges vividly when one examines the historical evolution of social enterprises in Zimbabwe.

The struggles for democratic transition in southern Africa had a huge impact on the nature of social enterprises. Before independence, the colonial environment was highly restrictive of the emergence of social enterprises, as there was a tendency for any social and economic initiatives to turn political and challenge the status quo. However, strictly regulated relief initiatives for old people, children, and social support were common. Soon after independence, the social enterprise sector became predominantly relief focused as governments assumed a more commanding role in the economy. Gradually, NGOs and community groups started to redefine both their constituency base and their linkages with the state and the private sector. In Zimbabwe, most of the early independence social enterprise initiatives focused on women's enterprise and savings clubs, which were formed under umbrella organizations such as Voluntary Organizations in Community Enterprises, the Zimbabwe Women's Bureau, the Federation of Women's Institutes, and the Association of Women's Clubs (Moyo, Makumbe, & Raftopoulos, 2000).

As national governments focused more on national reconstruction and rehabilitation processes, the immediate postindependence social enterprise effort was directed at social relief and development that worked closely with relevant government departments. In Zimbabwe, the Ministry of Community Development and Women's Affairs was actively involved in promoting social enterprise work. For example, as the profile of NGOs and their social enterprise work grew, they started linking with external donors.

The second generation of social enterprises focused on income generation and productive enterprises. Such initiatives included market gardening, sewing, milling, poultry, piggery, and soap-making projects. These social enterprises were motivated by the need for local employment and cash income in poor communities. This concept of social enterprise was also driven by a widespread belief among government and NGO practitioners that pooling labor through cooperative approaches was viable in underdeveloped rural economies. It was also believed that there was a huge pool of unexploited raw materials that could be used to produce inexpensive products that could compete with large suppliers, including multinational corporations.

A closer analysis of the above trend shows that most of the social enterprises that were promoted soon after independence, such as cooperatives and unions, were based on socialist principles. These groups were not founded on strong economic principles, and most folded as fast as they were created. There was accelerated degradation of these social enterprises during the period of structural adjustment, which saw the rolling back of the state and the full influence of market forces.

The introduction of SAPs in Africa was widely seen as a way of enabling developing countries to adjust their economies to make them more efficient and stable. The countries could then promote sustainable development and improve the lives of their populations. The reform package required the countries borrowing from the IMF and the World Bank to restructure their economies by managing demand, devaluing currency, liberalizing trade, eliminating price controls, reducing budget deficits, removing government subsidies on goods and services, and increasing interest rates to their natural market levels to discourage capital flight. Other requirements were that the borrowing country should reduce state investment in the economy, privatize public corporations such as public utilities, and open the local economy up to foreign investment. Although the impact of SAPS on social enterprises has not been fully evaluated, a number of issues must be discussed. First, there is no doubt that state withdrawal from direct economic management had a negative impact on public social enterprises that emerged in the immediate postindependence era. Liberalization of trade led to the progressive destruction of fledgling locally owned enterprises by creating room for the dominance of multinational businesses, which can supply goods and services at relatively lower costs. Commenting on the negative impact of trade liberalization on fragile local economies, a 1993 OXFAM study noted that SAPS can lead to disinvestments and deindustrialization rather than recovery (Renfrew, 1992).

The call by NGOS for "adjustment with a human face" during the SAP era created a new wave of social enterprise development, with the explicit goal of protecting poor and vulnerable communities. Massive resources were mobilized for enhancing the productive capacity of the poorest producers, especially women, and targeting the most marginalized areas.

On the other hand, SAPS created a pluralistic environment in which the state was no longer regarded as the main actor in socioeconomic development processes. The nonstate sector grew rapidly as a result of worsening socioeconomic conditions in many southern African countries. As the capacity of state institutions in Africa to manage their economies became constrained, the growing nonstate sector began to attract international aid. Faced with declining resources, a contracting economy, and growing poverty levels, governments were forced to forge complementary relationships with the nonstate sector. However, the state had an upper hand in defining the conditions of the relationship. The focus on nonstate actors as recipients of international aid has been identified by Chabal and Daloz (1999) as the single most important factor leading to the proliferation of NGOS as key agents of social enterprise development in Africa.

Despite the rapid expansion of the nonstate sector, the success in social enterprise initiatives remained constrained due to a number of macroeconomic and structural factors that needed reform by the state. As a result of pressures by international aid agencies to show impact on the ground, the nonstate sector grew impatient with state reforms, and a more confrontational relationship between the state and nonstate actors became inevitable. This is clearly seen in Zimbabwe, where legislative and political surveillance mechanisms over nonstate actors have been developed and vigorously implemented. Confrontational approaches toward state policies were advocated through pressure groups such as the Zimbabwe Congress of Trade Unions, students, and other professional NGO bodies in Zimbabwe.

Toward the end of the 1990s, NGOs began confronting the state more explicitly about the need for reforms to address the poverty crisis. A group of NGOs formed the Lobbying and Advocacy Group (LAG) under the leadership of the Ecumenical Support Services (ESS) to facilitate the involvement of nonstate actors in socioeconomic development processes. This initiative did not succeed in creating a breakthrough for nonstate actors to participate in socioeconomic reforms. Meanwhile, the state was increasingly concerned with the level of socioeconomic activism within the nonstate sector. In 1995 the government passed the Private Voluntary Organisations (PVO) Act, which superseded the Welfare Organisations Act (1967). The act tightened the definition of organizations falling under the act and their activities, laid down the legal procedures for registering NGOs, and clarified the selection and respective functions of the minister, the PVO board, and the PVO registrar for registering, monitoring, and deregistering NGOs. This act gave extensive powers to the minister and signaled the state's keen interest in controlling the growing NGO sector.

The climate of state restriction and surveillance complicated the funding situation for NGOs and the social enterprise development initiatives that were emerging. As a result of this scenario, a more radical wing of NGOs has emerged in Zimbabwe advocating for the protection of human rights, the autonomy of socioeconomic development initiatives, and the need for constitutional reforms. Most of the advocacy work in Zimbabwe is now being executed through the National Association of Non-Governmental Organisations (NANGO), Mwengo, and the National Constitutional Assembly (NCA). Individual organizations and community groups are members of these umbrella organizations.

In the post-SAP era, the economic crisis facing African states worsened due to their failed attempts to unhook themselves from the global economic system. Zimbabwe is a typical example. As it introduced more indigenous-oriented economic policies, such as land reform and redistribution in 2002, the flight of international capital has triggered massive

FIGURE 6.2. *Crisis Situation for Social Enterprise in Zimbabwe*

There are many signs that Zimbabwe's current economy is a crisis economy, and this has a bearing on the growth and development of social enterprises. A recent UNDP discussion paper (2008) highlighted the following crisis dimensions:

- Gross Domestic Product (GDP) fell from 9.7 percent in 1996 to as low as 1.4 percent in 1997. Since 1997, GDP growth rate has been declining from 0 percent in 1998 to −7.4 percent in 2000 and −10.4 percent in 2003. The real growth rate has averaged −5.7 percent in a period when other African states (Angola, Democratic Republic of Congo, Madagascar, Malawi, Mauritius, Namibia, Swaziland, Tanzania, and Zambia) were experiencing an average positive growth rate of 4.8 percent.
- The impact of HIV and AIDS is likely to further reduce growth rates by between 1 and 2 percentage points in Africa. Zimbabwe is one of the worst-hit countries: there, 1.6 million adults below the age of fifty are already living with HIV and AIDS.
- The country's fiscal deficit averaged −6.5 percent during the 2000–2006 period.
- Business confidence has been seriously undermined by the uneasy relationship between the state and the business community. The introduction of the Indigenization and Economic Empowerment Act (No. 14 of 2007), which requires businesses to sell 51 percent of their shares to indigenous Zimbabweans, has created uncertainty in the business sector.
- Employment growth declined to just above 0 percent in the 1990s and has remained negative since 2000. There has generally been a significant decline in the major sectors of agriculture, mining, and manufacturing.

The poor performance of public and private sectors negatively affects social sector expansion in Zimbabwe. A stable middle class, which is necessary for development of social enterprises, has unfortunately been wiped out by the economic crisis in Zimbabwe. As a result, the informal sector is rapidly expanding as more middle-class people join the ranks of poor people. Under such conditions, the growth of the social enterprise sector is seriously constrained.

unemployment (now estimated at 85 percent), rising levels of inflation (which is over 300 percent and the highest in the world), and increased state control of civil society and social enterprise initiatives, mainly to get rid of any politically oriented initiatives. The situation that has prevailed in Zimbabwe since 2002 has not been conducive to viable social enterprise development on a significant scale. In a survival economy, individual en-trepreneurship and money-laundering activities are a threat to the functioning of the social enterprise sector. Access to loans and microfinance is facing major problems because the amount of risk for the lender and the recipient is too high when the local currency is unstable. Therefore, the new types of social enterprises in Zimbabwe tend to be individualistic, short-term, and greedy, which violates the universally accepted norms of social enterprises. However, there is a type of social enterprise associated with fragile situations that is based on the need for social protection. The number of such social protection initiatives, meant to protect vulnerable people from the effects of a harsh economic environment, has grown, mainly driven by the NGO sector.

As a result of the conflicts and confrontations between the state and civil society in Zimbabwe and the region at large, social enterprise development initiatives lack clear definition and coordination. These state-NGO conflicts create an unfavorable environment for the nurturing and growth of social enterprises. With most countries in the region grappling with the effects of social and economic crisis, social enterprises are on the decline. Most of the surviving social enterprises are the result of the creativity of NGOs, donors, and the private sector that are eager to respond to the worsening socioeconomic conditions in Zimbabwe.

LEGAL FRAMEWORKS FOR SOCIAL ENTERPRISE

Socioeconomic and political factors have largely shaped the evolution and development of the legal forms for social enterprises in southern Africa. In the pre-independence era, social enterprises tended to be very temporary and ephemeral despite the harsh economic environment that prevailed then. With continued migration of Africans into cities, many convenient social welfare clubs or associations were formed as part of mutual support systems for supporting each other in a harsh economic environment. As the numbers of Africans in urban areas continued to increase in the late 1930s, the state became more interested in monitoring social activities. As a result, the Native Welfare Society was formed in 1930 to supervise the activities of associations. According to Yoshikuni (1996), many welfare clubs such as dance, tennis, cricket, and sewing clubs were formed under the auspices of the Welfare Society.

In the post–World War II period, continued labor migration and a crisis in labor reproduction led to the formation of trade union organizations, some of which were vocal and militant. This militancy resulted in a clamp-down on social activities by the state in colonial Zimbabwe and led to legislation that outlawed politically oriented social groups. J. Moyo (1993) laments this type of legislative regime because it led to an underdeveloped civil society. He further observes that most postindependence govern-ments in Africa simply took advantage of this weak civil society to establish state dominance and patronage over people's local initiatives.

Beyond the social and political unions that experienced tighter regula-tions, there were also production-oriented associational activities that were based on cooperative principles. In most former British colonies, coopera-tives modeled on the British pattern were formed as early as 1900. The Cooperative Agricultural Societies Act was passed in 1909, and African cooperatives only started being registered in 1954, when a Registrar of African Cooperatives was appointed. In 1956, the Cooperative Societies Act was introduced, and the first African Cooperative Society was regis-tered the same year. Three similar societies were formed and registered within nine months (Mararike, 1995). Complementing the 1956 Coopera-tive Societies Act was the 1926 Cooperative Companies Act, which dealt with limited liability cooperatives. This act was repealed in 1977 by an amendment that allowed registration of cooperative companies with lim-ited liability. Informal and unregistered groups such as master farmers' associations, savings clubs, and cooperative groups existed in addition to formal cooperatives, and these informal groups still remain voluntary to date. The main reason for not formally registering was to evade taxes.

Soon after independence, most governments in Africa recognized the role of cooperatives in fueling socioeconomic development processes. In 1994, a policy paper on cooperatives was released by the ruling party in Zimbabwe, and a cooperative was defined as "a voluntary social organiza-tion of economic units, based on equality, carrying out allocated or self-given economic objectives aimed at uplifting human living standards" (Republic of Zimbabwe, 1994, p. 1).

The paper referred to socialist cooperatives in which all the means of production, distribution, and social services are organized collectively

(Mararike, 1995, p. 21). However, the experience of cooperatives in Africa has not been very positive. King (1976), who examined cooperative policy and development in northern Nigeria, observed that the general approach to cooperatives, as expressed in Nigeria's cooperative laws of 1956, originated before the country's independence in 1960. When the cooperatives expanded, "the period of expansion was also a period of carelessness and political corruption in which societies were sometimes formed in order to distribute bribes on behalf of a political party under the guise of agricultural credit" (King, 1976, pp. 259–260).

King's observations hold for many cooperative initiatives in Africa. In the case of cooperatives, legislation is deliberately left loose to allow local and/or national political figures to manipulate the social enterprise agenda. It is interesting to observe the following legislative trend toward social enterprise development: for more radically oriented social groups, legislation is made tight, and for loosely organized cooperative ventures, legislation is made looser to allow local elites to benefit. Weak legislation has resulted in corrupt leaders who do not understand the business requirements of the cooperative, and this, in turn, has caused many people to lose their hard-earned contributions.

Although legislative changes have been made since Zimbabwe gained independence, there has been continuity in terms of the law's spirit and purpose. A clear example is the replacement of the Welfare Organisation Act of 1967 by the Private Voluntary Organization (PVO) Act (1995) in Zimbabwe. In terms of the PVO Act, the registrar and board have marginal roles to play; the minister of social welfare assumes a more central and defining role in the running of social enterprises. The minister is now empowered to take action against NGOs in breach of the act. The "minister has powers to suspend all or any of the members of the executive committee of a registered private voluntary organisation from exercising all or any of their functions in running the affairs of the organisation" (Section 21.1).

The PVO Act was a major drawback to the nonstate actor because it made registration difficult and cumbersome. As a result of the difficulties, many organizations resorted to registering as trusts. The legislation for trusts in Zimbabwe allows for fast and open formation and registration. In terms of the law, a deed of trust is prepared by a legal practitioner with a list of the trustees who protect the public interest. Once the deed of trust is registered, a certificate of registration is issued, and the trust is legally obliged to respect the terms specified in the deed of trust. However, the

FIGURE 6.3. *NGO Operational Requirements in Zimbabwe (2008)*

1. Only NGOS or PVOS with a PVO number and registered under the PVO Act Chapter 17:5 are allowed to operate.
2. To reenter into the provinces and districts, a copy of the registration certificate must be surrendered to the Department of Social Welfare, the local authority, provincial or district office, and police.
3. Guidelines for all PVOS must be followed in full.
4. MoUs (Memorandum of Understanding) must be in place for all districts and provinces of operation.
5. No meetings should be held at low levels without clearance from the DA or province.
6. An M&E (Monitoring and Evaluation report) form must be filed within two weeks and submitted to the Department of Social Welfare; the form is to be distributed by OCHA or NANGO or placed on their respective Web sites.

Source: Minutes from meeting between NGOS and Ministry of Public Service, Labour and Social Welfare, September 1, 2008

state is closely monitoring this avenue of social enterprise creation, as evidenced by the recent gazetting of a code of conduct for NGOS operating in Zimbabwe.

Activities of international NGOS are normally regulated through Technical Cooperation Agreements. These are facilitated through the Ministry of Foreign Affairs in consultation with the host ministry. The host ministry is responsible for verifying the proposed activities of the international organization and providing a recommendation letter. A cooperation agreement is then produced stating the terms of the cooperation. Monitoring adherence to these terms is done by the host ministry. Given the conditions of the technical cooperation agreements, it is very difficult for international NGOS to drive a radical social enterprise development agenda.

Private social enterprise initiatives still do not have clear legislation. Many of these are ephemeral, are home based, or occur in informal markets. Because of the need to access financing from banks, some of the enterprises register as sole traders under the Company Law of Zimbabwe. But only one in ten enterprises of this nature attempts to register; the

FIGURE 6.4. *The Rise and Fall of Informal Sector Social Enterprises in Zimbabwe*

Zimbabwe's informal sector is rapidly expanding, and its size and scope cannot be precisely measured. In 2000, the informal sector was estimated to contribute 59 percent of GNP, which was found to be the largest among twenty-three countries for which calculations were made (Schneider, 2002). The average in Africa was 42 percent. In 1998, a USAID survey found that there were 860,000 informal sector business establishments employing 1.6 million people, which represented a quarter of the working population at the time (MacPherson, 1998). In 2003, Ayyagari, Beck, and Demirguc-Kunt (2003) estimated that 15 percent of the workforce was engaged in formal SME activity and 34 percent in the informal sector.

Informal sector enterprises tend to use low-input technologies and low-productivity activities with very little capital and have no access to formal banking facilities. The majority (67 percent) of those employed are own-account workers; only 14 percent are permanent paid workers.

There has always been a love-hate relationship between the informal sector and the state. A number of politicians tend to get their support from informal sector traders and are therefore not keen to close the door on them. However, the hate dimension clearly emerged in Zimbabwe with the launch of the Murambatsvina Operation "Restore Order" in 2005, in which 32,500 SMEs were ruthlessly demolished and 700,000 people lost their shelter and sources of livelihood (United Nations, 2005, p. 32).

The lack of a clear policy environment for the informal sector remains a major challenge for the growth and development of informal sector–based social enterprises. Hence, they always rise and fall.

others fear taxation. Profitability margins for these enterprises are variable and unpredictable. In Africa, however, a lot of attention is directed toward informal sector activities because they generate a lot of employment and income. For this reason governments have come up with operational rules for informal traders, mainly through bylaws produced and administered by local authorities.

The increasing interest in the informal sector is also evident in some microfinance initiatives promoted by the private, public, and NGO sectors in Africa. The regulation of microfinance institutions (MFIS) is through the Ministry of Finance, which stipulates the conditions for the microfinance operation. Private sector–based microfinance institutions tend to use commercial lending rates for prospective borrowers, whereas the government and NGO microfinance initiatives tend to be subsidized and targeted at reaching the poorest communities. In some cases, lending is done through established private sector finance organizations. The prime motive of MFIS is to reduce the dependence syndrome in local communities.

Although there have been some initiatives to strengthen legislation for the various types of social enterprises, overriding concerns have been overfocused on control, management, and manipulation by local and national political elites. Legislation has not been informed by a clear vision for social enterprises because most of it tends to have been driven by moments of crisis. Laws are made when there is an actual or perceived problem in controlling the activities of the nonstate sector. A lot still needs to be done to create strong legislation for promoting social enterprises as an integral part of socioeconomic development in southern Africa.

INSTITUTIONAL SUPPORT FOR SOCIAL ENTERPRISE

Both in Zimbabwe and in other countries in southern Africa, social enterprise has largely been supported by international donors, government, and the private sector, with donors being the most prominent. Donors that have been active in supporting social enterprises in Zimbabwe and other countries in the region include NGOs and bilateral and multilateral funding agencies. Among those funding NGOs, the Humanist Institute for Cooperation with Developing Countries (Hivos) has been one of the most active. It has provided initial investment capital to a wide range of organizations, including MFIS, NGOS, and trusts. One of the earliest MFIS to benefit from Hivos's investment was the Collective Self-Finance Scheme (CSFS). The money was instrumental in enabling CSFS to set up a viable capital base for lending to micro and small enterprises. The whole idea behind the provision of financial support to CSFS was to enable the institution to eventually build an adequate capital base to ensure continued growth and viability of its lending activities to micro and small enterprises.

Bilateral donors that have provided funding support to social enterprise in Zimbabwe and the region include the British Government's Department for International Development (DFID) and USAID. In Zimbabwe, DFID has funded the Zimbabwe Association of Micro Finance Institutions (ZAMFI), the apex institutions for all MFIS operating in the country. The typical problem confronting all MFIS is building a capital base that is large enough for both continuous lending and the ability to recover money lent out with a sufficient margin to cover costs and realize a profit. ZAMFI is playing an important part in articulating the needs of MFIS and influencing the development and implementation of policies that are favorable to the operation and viability of MFIS.

In southern Africa, USAID has supported sustainable management of local resources by communities through the Communal Areas Management Program for Indigenous Resources (CAMPFIRE) Program. Under the program, funding has been provided to communities to manage and utilize locally available resources in a sustainable manner. The program has been hailed as an effective approach to empowering communities to build and operate sustainable social enterprises for local economic development. It has been successful for the following reasons:

- Communities have been involved in the design and execution of activities.
- Communities have realized immediate and tangible benefits from improved management and utilization of local resources.
- Management and utilization of local resources have been integrated with local economic activities.
- Sufficient income has been generated to enable the program to expand.

Support for social enterprise from the private sector has mainly come from funds set aside by companies under their corporate social responsibility programs. In the majority of cases, funds are allocated to charities to assist them in setting up and running viable social enterprises. The overriding idea behind providing financial support to charities to start and run enterprises is to reduce continued dependence on external funding and create conditions for medium- and long-term sustainability.

ASSESSMENT OF SOCIAL ENTERPRISES

Assessment of the performance of social enterprises set up in the region presents mixed results. There are cases where initial external funding support has been effectively used by NGOS and other charitable institutions to set up viable and sustainable social enterprises that are now making significant contributions to economic development and income generation. There are other cases, however, where the created enterprises have failed to perform and the goal of creating incomes to sustain operations has not been realized. In such cases, dependence on external donor support has continued.

Broadly speaking, MFIS appear to have been more successful in making use of initial donor support to create sufficiently strong capital bases in order to continue lending activities beyond the donor-funding phase. In Zimbabwe, CSFS and Zambuko Trust stand out among some of the MFIS that started their microcredit programs with donor support but are now standing on their own feet. In South Africa, the Mine Workers Development Agency (MDA) is also making significant progress on the road to financial sustainability in its operations. MDA started off with donor (mainly DFID) funding to finance its activities. It focuses on helping retired and retrenched mine workers in South Africa, Lesotho, and Swaziland to use their retrenchment/retirement packages to set up group businesses that subsequently enable them to continue to earn incomes and enjoy decent standards of living. Starting in the early 1990s with donor funding, MDA has now put in place an arrangement where they charge a fee for the training, business advisory, and extension support they provide to retired and retrenched miners participating in their empowerment programs.

In Zimbabwe, Environmental Development Agency (ENDA) and Practical Action also received donor support to set up small-scale light engineering workshops for the benefit of small-scale and marginalized artisans. The two institutions followed slightly different approaches in the management and ownership of the workshops. ENDA facilitated the creation of an association of artisans that took over ownership and management of the workshops at the end of the donor-funding phase. Unfortunately, artisans possessed neither the business management skills nor the organizational capabilities required to run the centers successfully, and the centers collapsed soon after the donor-funding phase.

Based on lessons learned from the ENDA experience, Practical Action decided to set up a private company to take over the ownership and management of its light engineering workshops at the end of the donor-funding phase. Although the service centers demonstrated their value by empowering artisans to improve their production skills and produce high-quality, small-scale capital goods for sale to micro and small enterprises, the centers failed to sustain their operations much beyond the donor-funding phase. The company experienced serious viability difficulties and went into voluntary liquidation in April 2005.

The picture presented in the foregoing assessment is one of modest success for social enterprises set up by MFIS and of nonsustainability for those set up by NGOS focusing on the provision of nonfinancial business development services. This raises the following question: what can we learn from these contrasting outcomes with respect to the viability and long-term sustainability of social enterprises? The following appear to be the most critical and pertinent lessons.

1. *The beginning has a strong bearing on end results.* The point of departure for all microlending programs by MFIS is a strong belief that lending to the poor is a viable and sustainable business. No MFI is set up to give free funds to borrowers. Even in cases where funds for lending are provided by donors, the message to borrowers is crystal clear: namely, the funds are accessible only as loans that have to be paid back. As a result, both MFIS and borrowers pay particular attention to the viability of the business that takes the loan. In an effort to depart from traditionally stringent requirements for collateral from borrowers by commercial banks, MFIS have largely relied on lending to solidarity groups to circumvent the absence of collateral among most microcredit borrowers.

On the other hand, a key reason that nonfinancial interventions often fail is that commercial and development objectives are often indistinguishable, at least in the early stages of the intervention. Because the initial capital required to set up and operate the business is provided by donors, the services and products offered are often priced unrealistically. The signal conveyed to users is that donor support will continue to be available in perpetuity. An unfortunate and undesirable consequence is that innovation and drive among the users of services and products provided may even be undermined. Consequently, the foundation for long-term viability and sustainability of the intervention is weak.

2. *Interventions that distort markets are difficult to sustain.* Loans provided by MFIS predominantly have interest rates that are set at least 5 to 10 percent above the prime lending rate. Again, the message sent out is clear: it is worthwhile to borrow from an MFI only if the returns from the business are sufficiently high to repay the loan and leave the business with a profit. On the other hand, if providers of subsidized nonfinancial services charge unrealistically low prices, this distorts the market for the goods and ser-

vices provided. In the worst case, marginal businesses may fail to compete against the subsidized businesses and get pushed out of the market. However, as soon as the subsidy comes to an end, the underlying weaknesses of the subsidized business are exposed, hence the subsequent collapse.

3. *The poor are willing and able to pay for products and services that make a difference.* Interventions by both MFIS and providers of nonfinancial business development services have shown beyond any reasonable doubt that the poor are willing, and indeed able, to pay for products and services that make a difference in their lives. Although lending rates charged by MFIS are invariably higher than those charged by commercial banks, demand for the loans and repayment rates have been consistently high. In most cases, repayment rates have exceeded 90 percent. Clearly, this happens because of good credit assessment and loan performance monitoring. Borrowers also pay the loans back because access to the loans makes the difference between remaining in poverty and making the first step out of poverty.

In the case of subsidized nonfinancial services, users have equally demonstrated their willingness and ability to pay for the services and products offered. The drawback has been the charging of unrealistic prices, which in many cases has undermined innovation and drive among those buying the services and products offered.

EXAMPLE 1: PRACTICAL ACTION'S LIGHT
ENGINEERING WORKSHOPS

Practical Action's Light Engineering Workshops were set up in 1996 in an effort to improve access to precision engineering equipment for small-scale artisans and to build their capacity to produce and supply a diversified range of high-quality, small-scale capital goods to small and medium enterprises (SMES). By 2004, three workshops had been successfully established in three major towns. Artisans were actively utilizing the facilities provided to produce and sell a diversified range of high-quality, small-scale capital goods. Goods produced and sold by artisans included grinding mills, peanut butter processors, maize dehullers, grain threshers, and roofing tile–making equipment. The business was realizing an average monthly turnover of US$4,000 by December 2003, and indications were that the business was poised for further growth when donor funding ended in March 2004.

However, by November 2004 it was evident that the business was under financial stress and would not be able to continue to meet its financial obligations much longer. Project staff inherited from the donor-funded phase continued to work on the project. In hindsight, this was a mistake because it became increasingly difficult to instill a new management approach and work culture that the business desperately needed. For example, no timely adjustments to fees charged for use of equipment by artisans were made, even though competitor businesses were charging prices that were often two to three times higher.

Two key lessons emerge from Practical Action's efforts to set up and run a social enterprise. First, a transaction-based approach must be adopted right at project inception. Although artisans were informed that that they would pay fees for the products and services offered by the project, staff behavior and practices conveyed the message that this was a donor-funded project for which profit was not a top priority. As late as one month before the termination of donor funding, artisans continued to think that more donor funding would be available to the project. The second lesson is that prices charged must be market-related right from project inception. It became increasingly difficult to raise prices paid by artisans for goods and services, since they had been set at unrealistically low prices at the beginning. When project staff made the case for raising prices, artisans felt that project staff were deviating from the poverty alleviation objective of the project.

EXAMPLE 2: COLLECTIVE SELF-FINANCE'S
MICROLENDING PROGRAM

Collective Self-Finance Scheme (CSFS) has established itself as one of the leading MFIS on the Zimbabwean microcredit landscape. Established in 1989, the scheme started as an association of SMES eager to pool savings for purposes of lending to members. Hivos and the European Commission were among the donors who provided critical funding that enabled the scheme to set up infrastructure and systems during the early years of its existence.

By 2000, CSFS had established six branch offices around the country and was arguably one of the largest MFIS in Zimbabwe. Beginning in the same year, access to donor funding by MFIS drastically decreased due to a number of factors. Rapidly deteriorating socioeconomic conditions led to a massive reduction of funding assistance by donors to Zimbabwe. Rising inflation (estimated at 613 percent in February 2006) led donors to

TABLE 6.2. *Performance by CSFS on Key Indicators, 2004–2005*

	2004	2005
Resources mobilized locally	US$20,000	US$67,000
Loans disbursed	US$12,416	US$15,125
Repayment rate	85%	89%
Profitability	5%	15%
Outreach	Countrywide	Countrywide

Source: Collective Self-Finance Scheme, quarterly and annual reports, various issues, 2004–2006

conclude that sustainable microlending was almost impossible under conditions of hyperinflation. Consequently, it was concluded that little would be achieved by allocating scarce resources to support microlending activities. There was also the strong belief among donors that MFIS must work toward making their lending programs self-sustaining if they were to be relevant and play a useful role in enterprise development and poverty alleviation.

Because of these challenges, in 2004 CSFS transformed itself from an NGO into a private company. Soon after the transformation, it embarked on an aggressive mobilization of financial resources from the local community. Table 6.2 summarizes the performance of CSFS over the last two years on key indicators.

EXAMPLE 3: IDE ZAMBIA'S AGRICULTURAL SUPPORT
TO SMALLHOLDER FARMERS

International Development Enterprises (IDE) has achieved phenomenal success in Asia, especially India and Nepal, promoting the adoption and utilization of treadle pumps and drip irrigation kits by smallholder farmers. IDE Zambia was set up in the mid-1990s in an effort to replicate the Asian experience in Africa. Funding for IDE Zambia activities has been provided mainly by Canadian International Development Agency (CIDA) and USAID.

One of the fundamental approaches adopted by IDE is to provide drip irrigation kits and other inputs required by smallholder farmers at cost. In this way, the organization recovers some of its costs and enhances its

capacity to gradually move toward self-sustainability of its assistance programs to smallholder farmers. At present, it is difficult to confidently
assess whether the organization is on its way to long-term sustainability because the organization continues to receive donor funding for its
activities.

REFERENCES

Alter, K. (2007). Social enterprise typology. Discussion paper. Retrieved from
www.virtueventures.com/setypology.pdf.

Ayyagari, M., Beck, T., & Demirguc-Kunt, A. (2003). Small and medium
enterprises across the globe: A new database. World Bank Policy Research
Working Paper 3127.

Chabal, P., & Daloz, J. (1999). *Africa works: Disorder as political instrument.* Oxford:
James Curry.

Collective Self Finance Scheme. Quarterly and annual reports, various issues,
2004–2005. Unpublished report.

King, R. (1976). *Farmers' cooperatives in northern Nigeria.* Reading, Berkshire:
University of Reading.

MacPherson, M. (1998). Zimbabwe: A nationwide survey of micro and small
enterprises. United States Agency for International Development, Harare.

Mararike, C. G. (1995). *Grassroots leadership: The process of rural development in
Zimbabwe.* Harare, Zimbabwe: University of Zimbabwe Publications.

Moyo, J. (1993). Civil society in Zimbabwe. *Zambezia, 20*(1), 1–13.

Moyo, S., Makumbe, J., & Raftopoulos, B. (2000). *NGOs, the state and politics in
Zimbabwe.* Harare, Zimbabwe: SAPES Books.

Renfrew, A. (1992). *ESAP and health.* Gweru, Zimbabwe: Mambo Press.

Republic of Zimbabwe. (1994). The policy paper on cooperatives: Part one.
Republic of Zimbabwe.

Schneider, Friedrich. (2002). Size and measurement of the informal economy in
110 countries around the world. Presented at Workshop of Australian National
Tax Centre, Australian National University, Canberra, Australia, July 17.

United Nations. (2005). *Report of the fact-finding mission to Zimbabwe to assess the
scope and impact of Operation Murambatsvina by the UN Special Envoy on
Human Settlements Issues in Zimbabwe, Mrs. Anna Kajumulo Tibaijuka.* New
York: United Nations.

United Nations Development Programme (UNDP). (2008). Comprehensive
economic recovery in Zimbabwe. Discussion document. Retrieved December

2008, from www.internal-displacement.org/8025708F004CE90B/(http Documents)/E42604ADF4D93C4DC12574CD002AD961/$file/UNDP+-+ Comprehensive+Economic+Recovery+in+Zimbabwe+-+A+Discussion+Docu ment+2008+170908.pdf

Yoshikuni, T. (1996). Before the stormy years: Native welfare, community centralisation and urban protest in the Harare Township, 1935 to 1947. Unpublished paper.

MARIO M. ROITTER & ALEJANDRA VIVAS

 Argentina

This chapter describes and analyzes some characteristics of social enterprises that have appeared in Argentina over the last few years in response to social concerns that have affected the country. Broadly speaking, social enterprise, as used in this chapter, refers to any private activity that is conducted by some form of organizational management that seeks to benefit a collective interest. The principal objective is not to obtain the highest possible profit but, rather, to fulfill certain economic and social objectives and to provide innovative solutions to the questions of social exclusion and unemployment through the production of goods and services.

The initial section of the chapter provides an overview of both the appearance of these various organizational experiences at different historical moments and the criteria by which these experiences are defined. The second section examines the long history of cooperatives in Argentina and their development through time. The third and final section analyzes one particular form of organization: enterprises recovered and managed by their workers, known in Argentina as recuperated companies. Although most of these enterprises have the legal status of cooperatives, the process by which they emerge has its own particular characteristics as well as its own operating rules and, on occasion, its own forms of distributing profit.

SOCIAL ENTERPRISES IN ARGENTINA

The first examples of social enterprise organizations in Argentina appeared in the nineteenth century. These organizations took on the following two institutional forms: cooperatives, which emerged in rural areas at the end of that century to support initiatives by European immigrants; and mutual benefit societies, which developed based on the values of solidarity, self-help, and mutual help. The development of mutual benefit societies in Argentina during the twentieth century was tied to the working sectors of the population, who were mainly immigrants and brought with them the influence of the European tradition (unions, Roman collegia, guilds, etc.). The best-known mutual benefit societies were those that provided insurance, burial and health services, and other forms of economic assistance. Cooperatives and mutual benefit societies have common roots and are manifestations of the same concept, which is based on voluntary commitment, democratic organization, collective effort, and institutional neutrality.

Having acknowledged that these organizations are foundational to the social economy,[1] the so-called "new social economy" must now also be included in the analysis. Social enterprises are a central component of the social economy. Their growth has been particularly strong since the 1990s, and new kinds of social enterprises have appeared in recent years. This constellation of organizations is made up of many heterogeneous enterprises, ranging from small-scale collective manufacturing businesses, microcredit programs, and sports and cultural organizations to companies managed by their workers and market-oriented initiatives managed by nonprofit organizations, generally in association with corporations.[2] This extensive group of organizations is the result of strategies based on cooperation, solidarity, and self-management that have been adopted with varying impacts by different groups. To a large extent, the space occupied today by social enterprises appeared and grew as an alternative to unemployment and social exclusion in Argentina. Their activities highlight problems related to poverty, income inequalities, and production conditions that were no longer being addressed by the economic sphere and the public sector.

Regarding this, Defourny (1992) proposes that political conditions favoring the recognition of these social enterprises appeared as a result of both the crisis in the welfare state of developed capitalist economies and the failure of centralized socialism. For decades the management of social affairs had been thought of and organized within the framework of an ever-growing intervention by public powers. But because of the latter's lack of concern and the impossibility of referring to existing socialist systems with any real credibility, an ideological vacuum was left that simultaneously opened up areas of activity where the social economy, already present for some time, has been able to make a contribution and be better understood.

Social enterprises have several main characteristics that differentiate them from other economic sectors. First, most social enterprises tend to be undertaken by a group of citizens with some collective interest, such as a group of unemployed persons, neighbors, or workers who take over the enterprise at which they once worked. Second, although their principal activity is the production of market goods and services and they carry out commercial operations, their rationale proposes a vision different from that of a capitalist company. This difference in vision is that power is not based on the accumulation of capital. Instead, better conditions are created (in matters related to company management) that allow for broader democratic participation in the "one worker, one vote" decision-making process. According to Defourny (1992), the objective of these efforts is the investigation of a new and original way of doing business, one that is different from both the so-called "capitalist management system" and the economic initiatives of public power; it is one based on the values of solidarity and democracy.

There are many other characteristics that describe this sector and testify to the existence of a new social commitment. Social enterprise is motivated not by profit or return on investment capital but rather by the objective of satisfying a general or mutual interest (Laville, 2004). Because it does not pursue a profit objective, the concept of salary for paid workers is replaced by an advance payment on future profit, which in turn is determined according to the criteria of each company. These criteria might be equal withdrawals for all workers or proportional withdrawals based on merit or the kind of work done. Logically, this designation will vary according to the company's income.

The purpose of social enterprise is to provide a service to the community either as a result of its positive externalities or through assurance of equal rights to access the service it renders. Its main objective is to confront ever-growing social exclusion through job creation and recovery, which in turn restores employment as the pillar of the social structure. Many of these social enterprises are not an option but rather a last resort in the face of unemployment. It is for this reason that those who form part of these organizations are in many cases the ones most negatively affected by the existing socioeconomic matrix. These are the unemployed, marginalized people, young people, and the handicapped. To this effect, Vilanova and Vilanova (1996) say that the birth of these collectives is the confirmation that poverty, social exclusion, and the progressive degradation of the most vulnerable sectors have become generalized.

Additionally, social enterprises tend to be difficult to implement due mainly to deficiencies in policies and the existing regulatory framework. In Argentina, the widest-ranging legislation governing the exercise of free association is the National Constitution, which in article 14 establishes the right of all its citizens to "associate for useful purposes." These associations are formally recognized in the civil code under two types of legal status: civil associations and foundations. Jurisprudence, on the other hand, admits other nonprofit organizations, which are regulated by special legislation, although these can be considered civil associations when taken in a broader sense. Civil associations are cooperatives (regulated under Law 20.337), mutual benefit societies (Law 20.321), and medical and social welfare entities (Law 23.660).

There is no one specific legal framework under which the various social enterprises can be classified. These kinds of organizations operate mainly under the guise of cooperatives and associations, while a growing number confront a major obstacle: their own exclusion from the formal economy. This exclusion creates challenges for market insertion, invoicing systems, the impossibility of accessing sources of financing, and their ineligibility for public sector programs. The problem of legal status is undoubtedly one of the main issues facing the development of social enterprise in Argentina.

According to Cassano (2003), a bill of law fostering the promotion of the social economy and all its manifestations should be introduced by the government. Such a bill would apply to all economic activities undertaken by private persons or entities whose principal motivation is not profit-taking and who search for solutions to questions about how to gain access to the labor market that affects popular, low-income sectors. Social enterprises can be used as a tool to implement this plan. A bill of law would also make it easier for the public sector to review and develop better policies, not limited to specific interventions but instead as a way of approaching the question of social enterprise as a whole and organizing actions promoting social enterprise development.

In accordance with Federico Sabaté (2000), therefore, it would seem necessary that the public sector lay out an implementation strategy for the social economy that would allow budget-related and financial resources to be reoriented and reassigned. This strategy would replace traditional social policies, which are now considered anachronistic, with support for diverse social undertakings in general and social enterprise in particular.

RECENT INFLUENCES

Since the late 1980s, Argentina has carried out a series of structural reforms within the framework of the so-called "Washington Consensus," which encouraged Latin American countries to adopt policies of fiscal and monetary austerity in order to bring macroeconomic variables under control. In Argentina the stabilization plan was based on establishing a fixed exchange rate between the local currency and the U.S. dollar. The plan also included the privatization of most state companies, the deregulation of markets and the opening up of commercial and financial sectors. This forced the country to play by a new set of international rules marked by the consolidation of increasingly international productive and financial sectors as well as the rise of economic blocs.

Within the framework of these structural reforms, social policies began losing their universal nature, a featured characteristic of the welfare state systems that saw limited development in America until the 1980s. These once-universal social policies now focused on solving situations at the margins through the provision of basic goods and services. Indeed, under the neoclassical paradigm, the state minimizes economic intervention, leading to the formation of ever-larger areas of activity in the private sector, along with a simultaneous reduction in public expenditure. Contributing further to this objective, social policies become increasingly focused on fighting poverty and thus abandon their universal applicability.

The changes that resulted, once proposals made by international finance institutions were accepted, could be summarized in three ways. The first change implied that interventions should be targeted to groups "according to the need and urgency" of the support requested. The second change was that decentralization appeared as a mechanism to increase the efficiency and effectiveness of public spending allocation, while social plans began to be designed and executed by subnational and regional centers (provincial, municipal, or possibly civil organizations and NGOs) more familiar with the specific characteristics of each region. Finally, privatization developed in response to the fiscal restrictions of the public sector. That is to say, changes were made in how social policies were financed, how they were administered, how they provided access to benefits, and the types of benefits they offered. The ultimate objective of all these changes was to reduce public spending and to provide new areas of activity for the private sector (Hintze, 2003).

In a climate of growing unemployment and social conflict, this economic model spurred revitalization during the early 1990s, aided by massive foreign capital inflows (in the form of direct investments and portfolio investments, and accompanied by rising public debt) and a fall in inflation. In 1996, after the shock caused by the crisis in Mexico (which was basically financial in nature), the Argentine economy recovered its growth rate until mid-1998. It was at this point that a crisis began to emerge in Argentina. After three years of recession, this plan, considered a model of success by the international community, succumbed to one of the most violent crises ever to face the country. Devaluation of the currency at the end of 2001, foreign debt default, and a series of chaotic events in both the economic and political spheres resulted in a situation that left 53 percent of the population below the poverty line and 24 percent destitute.

In this context, the capacity to address ever-increasing unemployment, poverty, and marginalization exceeded the possibility of any social intervention based on pinpointed assistance; such extreme degrees of poverty required new tactics. Simultaneously, as pointed out by Abramovich et al. (2003), the informal economy[3] developed an "anomalous" behavior as it did away with manual labor during the latter years of the crisis. In other words, the informal economy in Argentina is of a procyclic nature and is thus incapable of providing shelter to the unemployed in the way it does in other countries. In other countries the existence of an informal economy is related not to crisis situations but to institutionalized structures of inequality and exclusion.

In Argentina, due to a relatively high capacity for self-organization and the existence of productive skills and capabilities in a large part of its population, the social strategies that appeared with the greatest force during this period were independent efforts driven by the popular economy. These strategies generated self-sustaining economic activities, and it is among these activities that we locate social enterprise.

At the federal government level, the National Institute of Activism and Social Economy (INAES), a branch of the Ministry of Social Development, brings together all cooperatives and mutual benefit societies in the country. For these entities to be officially recognized they must register with the INAES, which regulates and monitors their activity.

The INAES has developed a group of support programs for cooperatives and mutual benefit societies in an attempt to improve their capacities of commercialization and provide financial assistance. These programs include training for cooperative and mutual benefit society leaders, programs promoting businesses and commercial relationships among them, and initiatives that foster the collective purchase and sale of goods.

On another front, the National Institute of Industrial Technology (INTI) has developed an assistance program for cooperatives and recuperated companies. This program attempts to provide technical assistance for all different kinds of cooperatives and to support the reopening of recuperated companies by collaborating on installation and development. Activities include assisting cooperatives of an industrial nature, coordinating with corresponding ministries, searching for financing and institutional support for the cooperative, and promoting the concept of decent, hard work rather than mere philanthropic assistance. The objectives of the program are to achieve cost savings, to improve internal organization and supplier and client contacts, to support the effort to obtain legal status by drafting proposals to the courts and municipalities, to assist with environmental management, to diagnose security and labor conditions, and to help obtain certifications and develop products. It should be mentioned that these objectives have already been achieved in a significant number of cooperatives and recuperated companies.

With the help of tutors, the INTI also tries to facilitate the formulation of a business plan to cover all the cooperative's needs, including the search for financing. It also tries to help the cooperative get internally organized in an efficient way without setting aside the cooperative principles of internal democracy and the search for the well-being of all its members.

Finally, INTI fosters the organization of cooperative groups to improve, on the one hand, their opportunities with suppliers and clients and, on the other, the communal use of their physical resources and knowledge. In this way, social economy organizations are able to better administer their resources and improve their purchasing and selling skills.

THE CASE OF COOPERATIVES

The INAES, which is supported by the Ministry of Social Development, defines cooperatives the same way the International Cooperative Alliance defines them. In its Declaration on Cooperative Identity and Principle (adopted in Manchester in 1995), the INAES declared, "A Cooperative is an autonomous association of people that have voluntarily come together to confront their economic, social and common cultural needs and aspirations by means of a jointly owned and democratically controlled company"

(2009, n.p.). This means that their collective natures and democratically controlled frameworks are two characteristics that differentiate them from other types of organizations, such as companies controlled by capital or by the government.

Argentina is the Latin American country in which the cooperative movement first developed and where it most closely reflects the development of its European counterparts. Cooperativism along with mutualism (the activities related to mutual benefit societies) appeared in Argentina at the end of the nineteenth century, although it really began to take off during the first decades of the following century, principally in connection with the many waves of immigration at the time. As Campetella and Bombal (2000) point out, the activities of mutual benefit societies typically developed into an urban movement that provided immigrants and workers with health and social security services, while cooperatives began as a rural phenomenon around which settlers and farmers of different nationalities organized their agricultural and cattle-raising activities.

The first rural cooperative, El Progreso Agricola (Agricultural Progress), founded in the Province of Buenos Aires by a group of French settlers, appeared in 1898 and was organized to provide insurance against hail. Similar organizations were promoted by French, Dutch, and Jewish immigrants, concentrated mainly in the Pampa Humeda region (mostly in the provinces of Buenos Aires, Santa Fe, Cordoba, and Entre Rios) in response to the exploitation suffered by agricultural and cattle farmers at the hands of large general goods stores and stockpilers. As a result, these were originally established as multifunctional cooperatives intended to provide services for their members who were agricultural and cattle producers.[4]

The cooperative movement had developed among rural producers for fifteen years before the Entre Ríos Confederation of Cooperatives, the first second-degree cooperative (a cooperative of cooperatives, as they were known), was founded in the province of Entre Ríos, bringing together for the first time a group of first-degree cooperatives. Although short-lived (it was reestablished in 1930 bearing its current name, the Entre Ríos Federation of Cooperatives), it served as a model that led to an important integration process among the first-degree cooperatives, a movement that spread rapidly throughout the country after the creation of the Argentine Association of Cooperatives (ACA) in 1922.[5] Finally, in 1956, a third-degree cooperative entity called the Confederación Intercooperativa Agropecuaria

(CONINAGRO) appeared. This association resembled a union more than a second-degree cooperative (which was known for its commercial nature), and even today it is a symbol of the cooperative movement's union representation in Argentina.[6] Currently, the provision of supply, marketing, and transportation services are among the principal functions carried out by both first- and second-degree farm and cattle cooperatives.

Organized cooperativism received a big push during the second half of the twentieth century. Progressively, many of these immigrant associations began to open to everyone in the community and incorporated new members. As a result, the bonds of common trade interests became more important than those associated with questions of nationality. Slowly, the economic areas in which cooperatives operated also started to expand and spread to other spheres. For example, public services like electricity and communications, particularly in the interior of the country, were provided by cooperatives, and cooperatives that provided loans, work, and housing services appeared as well (Campetella & Bombal, 2000).

Another sector of the cooperative movement in Argentina that merits emphasis is the cooperative credit and loan unions. First appearing in 1958 with the creation of the Instituto Movilizador de Fondos Cooperativos (Institute for the Movement of Cooperative Funds), they were the result of the cooperative movement's strong conviction and belief that it could generate its own sources of financing. At the beginning of the 1970s, the cooperative credit and loan unions controlled 13 percent of the market. Its clientele was composed of small rural producers, industries, shopkeepers, artisans, professionals, and workers who had little or no access to bank loans and in some cases could not even rely on them when they did have access.

What is interesting about this type of financial structure is that in areas with no commercial banks, certain forms of banking developed that were able to accumulate residents' savings because they offered residents an alternative that was safer than keeping it themselves. This fostered the logical recirculation of these funds to finance productive projects in the region, making credit easily available to micro, small, and medium-sized companies in different areas. The agrarian, public services, and housing cooperatives were also very interested in setting up their own credit and loan unions as a way of using the money generated by their activities to promote their own development and that of the community.

Under the military regime that took power in 1976, led by Economy Minister Martinez de Hoz, actions aimed at reducing the presence of credit cooperativism forced the elimination of credit and loan unions. The objective was to eliminate the legal status of "cooperative" within the organization of banks, leaving only the credit and loan unions, which were forbidden from operating with current accounts. Within this framework, and solely as a result of pressure exerted by various groups that defended cooperativism, the legal status of "cooperative" was allowed exclusively for commercial banks. As a result, the credit and loan unions had to choose between disappearing or reorganizing themselves into banks.

There are currently eight different types of cooperatives, classified according to the kind of need they fill: housing, work, public services, insurance, supply, credit, consumer, and farming and cattle breeding. According to information provided by INAES (n.d.), there are currently more than 20,400 cooperatives in Argentina, of which 38 percent are concentrated in Capital Federal in the greater Buenos Aires area and 25 percent are found in Córdoba, Santa Fe, and Tucumán. The kind of activities they carry out include workers cooperatives (over half);[7] housing cooperatives (15 percent); and farming and cattle-breeding cooperatives (11 percent). Although this pattern is basically the same for the majority of the provinces, the relative importance of rural cooperatives is higher in the case of interior provinces, such as Santiago del Estero, Córdoba, and Entre Ríos, vis-à-vis their counterparts in Capital Federal and Buenos Aires.

On another front, in the middle of a profound economic crisis in the 1990s, new cooperatives emerged in a context characterized by a rationale that excluded large sectors of the population. Cooperativism took on new meaning as a strategy for survival, and as a consequence, an enormous variety of productive commercial undertakings were established and organized. These new efforts carried out a wide range of activities that, besides combining survival and resistance strategies, also led them to begin understanding cooperative action as a form of socioeconomic organization that could provide for the basic necessities of daily life. In other words, these new cooperative actions could generate a new way of achieving social integration.

It is important to highlight that these new cooperative forms were new modes of resistance born, at a fundamental level, out of need. "The double role of the cooperative as a company and as a social movement is the element which leads us to believe that these organizations are strategies with which to break away from profoundly asymmetrical social situations that in the long term are incompatible with the idea of democracy" (Giarraca, 1994, p. 18). Despite the long history of cooperatives, it is at this stage that they have taken on a new meaning. Moreover, this stage of development saw many of these cooperatives restricted to the area of marginal activities, making the state's active role in the promotion and strengthening of these activities so important. "Governments should promote the important role that cooperatives have in the transformation of what are often marginal, survival activities—often referred to as 'informal economy'—into work protected by legislation and fully integrated into the main currents of economic life" (International Labour Organization, 2002, n.p.).[8]

THE CASE OF COOPERATIVES

The cooperative is a legally sanctioned form that allows community organizations to offer fundamental public utilities in vast regions of Argentina. The case of telephone cooperatives is a good example of how social enterprises operate in relation to the supply of public utilities.

Telephone cooperatives first appeared in the first half of the twentieth century as part of the emergence of other public utility cooperatives. But contrary to what has happened to many other public utility cooperatives, most telephone cooperatives have been able to develop and grow in strength to the present time.

From the 1990s onward, telephone cooperatives have sustained a high level of growth, despite the fact that land phone lines were left in the hands of just two multinational companies due to privatization. Currently, these two companies operate in most large urban areas and are, in many ways, similar to monopolies.

Despite this context, telephone cooperatives have grown, extended their lines, and begun offering Internet services; they have even pioneered the installation of digital service. From a social point of view, they are less expensive and offer better quality services, which makes them stand out in relation to the two firms that control the phone business in Argentina. This is a particular accomplishment because they achieve these results in geographic areas where the large companies are not as profitable as they would like. Felipe Boccoli, president of the Federation of Telecommunication Cooperatives, has said, "Although we have no obligation to do so, the cooperatives are the only ones to universalize the service . . . because we go to those places where the population density is low and there is little or no profit" (Simonetti, 2006, n.p.).

EXAMPLE I: THE TELEPHONE COOPERATIVE OF EL CALAFETE
IN THE PROVINCE OF SANTA CRUZ

Similar to many other association experiences in Argentina, the needs of a community were what led the inhabitants of El Calafate, located in the extreme south of the country, to organize in 1969 in order to receive phone service. There were many obstacles to overcome, but because there was a lot of enthusiasm and they were already familiar with other experiences around the country, the citizens decided to formally set up a telephone cooperative.

In view of the fact that it would not be easy to carry the project out, it was necessary to collectively determine the first actions to be taken. The town decided that the idea should first be disseminated to attract possible future partners. Because it was difficult to get funding to cover the required costs of the project, the agreements and strategic alliances that this group of people created through great effort represented an important push toward achieving the final objective. In May 1970, approximately nine months after the project was inaugurated, it was granted legal status, and a few days later the governor of the province confirmed that the construction of the cooperative's headquarters would be completely paid for by the state.

Presently, in response to the important demographic growth the region has undergone and the increase in tourism, the cooperative has been incorporating state-of-the-art telecommunications technology, permanently training its personnel, and generating employment as need demands. Today, more than fifty people work for the cooperative, and investments of approximately US$200,000 are being made to build three more communication centers.

This is but one of many successful telephone cooperatives. According to the latest available statistics, Argentina had 311 of these organizations in the year 2002 (Finquelievich & Kisilevsky, 2005). At that time, they provided the nation with a total of 401,367 telephone lines, which represented 5.3 percent of lines in the entire country.

THE CASE OF RECUPERATED COMPANIES

When social enterprises in Argentina are analyzed, the paradigmatic case of the so-called "recuperated companies" must also be studied. The Movimiento Nacional de Empresas Recuperadas (National Movement of Recuperated Companies) (MNER) defines these companies as those which were abandoned by their owners due to either bankruptcy or administrative embezzlement and whose workers, organized predominantly into cooperatives, decided to continue production under a system of self-management.[9]

The process of recuperating these companies began at the end of the 1990s and reached a high point after the profound social and economic crisis of 2001, one of the most serious in the history of Argentina. Since then, more than 170 companies, employing over 12,000 workers and with an annual turnover of 300 million pesos,[10] have been recuperated. Most of these companies (72.3 percent) are concentrated in the Autonomous City of Buenos Aires and in the Province of Buenos Aires (Rebón & Saavedra, 2006, p. 15).

Although these companies represent diverse industries, they are concentrated to a great extent in the manufacturing sector, with some in the service sectors.[11] The manufacturing sector includes activities such as the metallurgic, textile, graphics, and foodstuffs industries, while the other sector includes health and education services along with the hotel and restaurant industry.

As has already been mentioned, recuperated companies appeared for the first time in the context of a grave economic, social, and political crisis in Argentina. During the 1990s, the decline of industrial activity, a process that had begun in the second half of the 1970s, worsened. This was accompanied by a sharp reduction in both wage-earning employment and real salaries and generated a large increase in unemployment that, even today, is still one of the most difficult structural problems to reverse. This is clearly evidenced by the unemployment index: at the beginning of 1990 it oscillated somewhere between 6 and 7 percent, but at the beginning of 2002, it peaked at 21.5 percent.

In 2001, the imminent financial crisis became reality due to the impossibility of maintaining the rate of exchange with the dollar. Although the devaluation of the Argentine peso allowed the recovery of gross domestic product levels and, to a lesser degree, employment, it was not sufficient to modify the distribution pattern. The crisis resulted in a society with high levels of social exclusion where employment is no longer the axis for social integration. Although some indicators have improved, 31.4 percent of the population continues to live below the poverty line, and 11.2 percent are still destitute (INDEC, 2006).

The recuperation of companies took place within this economic scenario. Recuperating companies was a way of resisting the closure of factories that were involved in insolvency or bankruptcy proceedings, were behind in salary payments, or had already been abandoned. At this point it is necessary to distinguish between two types of companies. The first are those that, as a result of the economic climate, found themselves on the verge of shutting down. They were unable to maintain profitable operations due to the indiscriminate commercial opening of the market, which at the time was becoming more and more depressed. The second type includes those companies that deliberately implemented a series of actions that led to their closing in what is called *vaciamiento*, or "the emptying of the company." This practice, which became popular during the 1990s, implies that in the absence of conditions permitting the cycle of accumulation and maximization of profit for reinvestment to take place, withdrawing from the company with the lowest possible costs is a morally acceptable capitalist alternative (Rebón & Saavedra, 2006).

Confronted with this situation and a context of increasing unemployment, the workers' principal objective was the preservation of the company and their jobs. As Fajn et al. (2003) explain, workers initially motivated by the need to defend their employment find a collective response to the problem of unemployment in the recuperation of their companies.

Although it was a heterogeneous group of companies and the manner in which each company was recuperated had its own particularities, the ways in which such reclamations were carried out can be classified into three categories, each with its own set of problems. The cases with the most conflict were those in which an agreement had not been reached with the owners and where the reclamation was achieved with a takeover in the strictest sense of the term, with the workers wresting control of a production unit in direct opposition to the owners (Rebón & Saavedra, 2006). In many cases the workers had to remain inside the factory for an extended period of time, taking care of the installations and machines, while they awaited some kind of resolution: either a favorable ruling by a judge or an expropriation law passed by the local or provincial legislature. Diametrically opposed to this situation are cases in which a degree of consensus was reached with the owners, allowing the company to continue working but under the workers' management.

Finally, there were also companies that were abandoned by the owners, in which case reclamation was accomplished not through force but rather by the workers themselves. Although few cases fall into this category, as Rebón (2004) points out, this does not make it any less significant, given that many recuperated companies started out as a result of workers merely remaining at their workstations after the owner abandoned the company, a process that later turned into an occupation. This occurred in cases where a process of response and resistance was triggered by the owners or the state trying to defend their rights as property owners once the workers had the company up and running again.

As the phenomenon of recuperated companies grew, other actors who felt committed to the situation started participating more actively. The occupation and holding of the installations in most cases had the support of neighborhood assemblies, students, professors, and other individuals who participated actively in solidarity events (Arévalo & Calello, 2003).

Once a company was recuperated, the fundamental objective became how to reorganize the work, production, and administration. With respect to this, it is important to point out that the workers had to start production as well as administrate, and it is precisely here that many inconveniences began to appear. In most cases, occupations were carried out by shop or factory workers who then suddenly also found themselves in administrative and management roles for which, in most cases, they had no experience.

As can be seen, workers face many obstacles when getting a company up and running again. Additional obstacles arise as the result of the disputes described above, including legal expropriation of the installations, rental of the factory from the owners, contracting for the loan, and restitution of use of the machinery, among others. Establishing legality was a key aspect in assuring the success of the process because not achieving legal stability raised the risk of being evicted and made productivity more difficult (Rebón & Saavedra, 2006).

To this effect, more than 90 percent of recuperated companies today operate as work cooperatives, while others claim state ownership but are run by the workers. Compared to those cooperatives established freely and voluntarily by their members, recuperated companies that have chosen this legal status break with traditional models of cooperative self-management. This situation led to the structuring of a hybrid form of cooperative, whose main features can be summarized as follows: the elimination of administrative organs in many cases; more frequent holding of assemblies; a higher degree of horizontality in the decision-making process (this particular factor tends to slow things down a bit or often does not allow activities to progress smoothly); and the election of representative bodies in order to comply with legal formalities without really considering their functions and responsibilities, as in the case of the legal figures of trustees or receivers (Meyer & Pons, 2003).[12]

These experiences occur under various guises, but all of them have as a common denominator the transformation of how things operate. They no longer operate under the rationale of a capitalist company but rather take on the characteristics of a social enterprise. In this sense, there are two outstanding features. The first is the way in which decisions are made: in recuperated factories this occurs within the framework of participative, democratic assemblies in which decisions are made by consensus. Second is the way in which income is distributed: in these organizations the figure of an "owner" that seeks to maximize profit does not exist; rather, there are systems of retribution for the workers that are set up according to different criteria and the rest is reinvested in the company. Although salaries tend to be low at first, this is considered a necessary effort until the company is running again.

With respect to production, difficulties are related to the precarious state of the companies, which in general are underfinanced, alienated from markets, and in debt to suppliers. As a result, initial strategies aim at reactivating the production of some of the company's more characteristic product lines and reconstructing links with former clients and suppliers. Another obstacle is the difficulty of obtaining financing to accumulate working capital in order to take advantage of the maximum production capacity. However, perhaps the greatest challenge is the company's management by its own workers, as it is shown in the cases presented below.

Although the legal situation of many of these companies must still be resolved, the growth and development they have undergone since recuperation is significant. Almost all of the companies continue working solidly, playing an active role in their communities—for example, setting up civic centers or establishing health services and education centers.

Many of these initiatives arose in the heat of the moment, when the entire community was participating in the company's recuperation; this was fundamental when it came to legitimizing the process.

The interesting thing about these companies is that they operate within a market economy, sell at market prices, and compete with other capitalist companies, but internally, they operate in a noncapitalist manner. Decisions are made collectively, income is redistributed more fairly, and the viability of the factory depends not on the rate of return on investment but rather on the level of well-being among the workers. Workers are undeniably the leading characters in this phenomenon. As the National Movement of Recuperated Companies (n.d.) explains, these organizations are reviving a "culture of living" in their work while at the same time becoming a viable alternative to the predominant corporate culture. This is a culture that is primarily oriented toward having at its disposal capital assets that it uses without considering the social and environmental consequences of its decisions.

EXAMPLE 2: BRUKMAN

"We, the men and women who work at Brukman, returned the way we wanted: backed by a COURT ORDER extended by a JUDGE of the Argentine Nation and breaking the chains on the entrance door because it was so authorized, we entered through the front door, covered in glory, because we deserved it and because our intention was always none other than to recover our jobs." This is how the workers of the 18th of December Work Cooperative, formerly the Brukman Company, described the moment they reentered the factory on December 29, 2003, after two years of intense struggles.

The ex–Brukman Company, located in Buenos Aires, makes clothing. On December 18, 2001, when the workers arrived at the factory to start a new day's work, they discovered to their surprise that the owners had abandoned the company installations. There had been an ongoing conflict between the owners and the workers, mainly due to a large debt the owners had incurred with their employees. The wages of the last few months had not been paid, and social security and ART (Health and Job Risk Insurance) payments had not been made.

The employees suddenly found themselves on their own, and from that moment they were confronted with a major challenge. Their principal objective was to keep their jobs, and this led them to a group consolidation process that would allow them to reach a consensus about the best way to regain and organize the company.

To achieve their objective it was essential to gain the support of other actors. Logic led them to first look for the support of the union, which in this case was the Garment Industry and Accessories Workers Union. However, the union was their first obstacle: it was both absolutely indifferent to their problem and supportive of the owner-solicited bankruptcy, which had left the workers totally unprotected. Despite this obstacle, they started to harvest support among university students, left-wing political parties, workers of other recuperated companies, and neighbors who became involved in the situation. A large support network developed—a phenomenon that has appeared in almost all experiences involving recuperated companies.

The company started producing again, and after a month of worker management, it was able to make its first sale. The first deals were important because the money from them was reinvested and led the company into full, productive activity once again.

The company's reestablishment process ran into various conflicts for about two years. The first conflicts occurred in the middle of March 2002, when, thanks to the strong support of the people, a very violent attempt to throw the workers out was halted. A month later, however, the second attempt to throw the workers out was successful; the police cleared them out. Given the situation, it would be logical to assume that the workers would give up, but because of the support they had, they tried to enter the factory again a few days later, accompanied by more than 10,000 people. Though this attempt also failed, the workers decided to set up camp and sleep in tents on the corner near the company while continuing the struggle to recover their jobs.

Things did not change for the next eight months as the dispute moved to the courts and to the Buenos Aires city government. In September, the workers began to consider the possibility of having the company expropriated, and accordingly, they presented an investment, production, and sales plan to the Buenos Aires city government in order to demonstrate the feasibility of their plan.

Finally, on October 20, 2003, the owners of Brukman were officially declared bankrupt, and ten days later, on October 30, the Buenos Aires legislature voted in favor of the Expropriation Law, which declared the company's assets to be of public utility. Thus, the management of the factory was passed to the hands of the workers, who were now united in a work cooperative called The 18th of December. The only remaining thing to do was to receive authorization to enter the factory. This was given on December 29, 2003. After a two-year-long struggle and eight months of resistance, the workers were finally able to enter the factory again.

FINAL CONSIDERATIONS

The question that arises, after reviewing the outstanding features of these new social enterprises in Argentina, is whether they can become agents of a development process that could be more socially inclusive than the existing process. We argue that this is possible by taking into account the importance of these new models of enterprises, most of all as relevant examples of people's self-organization. We acknowledge, however, the limited capacity of these new organizations to modify the current dynamics of an economy whose main characteristics are increasing inequality and social fragmentation. Indeed, even when social enterprises have placed the most pressing social needs at center stage or have turned them into fundamental objectives, these are, for the time being, just valuable defensive strategies used by working-class sectors who find an alternative to unemployment and marginalization in these recuperated companies.

Is this reason enough for these experiences to be underrated? In this case, we do not think so, because for those who undertake them, social enterprises represent an invaluable and an irreplaceable individual experience. Above all, they highlight in the social agenda the possibility and necessity of building an economy with multiple forms of property and new forms of management favorable to the empowerment of its members. Additionally, these types of enterprises can potentially be extremely positive because they reassert the long-standing Argentine tradition of creating different institutional models based on cooperation, democratic participation, and different forms of association. Last but not least, getting these recuperated companies under way has implied a long and admirable struggle, aimed at making them socially legitimate and, above all, legal.

To this effect, it is worth mentioning that there are many social enterprise initiatives that have acquired skills that make them, on the one hand, fully functioning agents for local development operating in a market economy and, on the other hand, models of working-class self-management based on democratic principles and equal participation. Social enterprise initiatives can be taken as examples of alternative forms of organizing production that can potentially become socially and economically sustainable. Despite this, as a whole, they have not yet become a superior dynamic organizational model because they are still isolated and disjointed initiatives. Therefore, what is needed is the creation of specialized institutions and the implementation of public policies aimed at promoting the growth and sustainability of such enterprises. This requires technologically innovative systems as well as adequate financial programs in order to generate new productive and managerial skills.

For this to occur, it is important to intensify and broaden the scope of the actions already undertaken that seek to implement joint initiatives with technical organizations that support small business, local and national authorities, and universities. These alliances and agreements should not be limited to making specific claims or solving specific problems. Instead, it would be most useful if they approached the question in a more integral way. Such an approach would contribute to the development and legal recognition of social enterprises and would also allow them to consolidate into an alternative sector, bearing the values of solidarity, reciprocity, and self-management within the framework of a pluralistic economy.

NOTES

1. The social economy includes cooperatives, nonprofit organizations, mutual benefit associations, and social enterprises, such as recuperated companies. These organizations produce goods and services predominantly but not exclusively for the market and manage their operations and redirect their surpluses toward social and environmental goals.

2. Being even more generous in defining the concept of social enterprise, business initiatives called *market-based poverty initiatives* (more commonly known as "business at the base of the pyramid") could also be included as social enterprises. Here the work and papers produced by the Social Enterprise Knowledge Network (SEKN), an academic initiative led by various Latin American and Spanish business schools and the Harvard Business School, are applicable (www.sekn.org/en/index.html).The definitions and points of view proposed by SEKN on occasion differ from ours.

3. Informal economy refers to the general market income category (or sector) wherein certain types of income and the means of their generation are unregu-

lated by the institutions of society, in a legal and social environment in which similar activities are regulated. It is a dynamic process that includes many aspects of economic and social theory, including exchange, regulation, and enforcement. By its nature, it is difficult to observe, study, define, and measure. No single source readily or authoritatively defines the informal economy as a unit of study.

4. According to Hirschman (1986), the cooperative efforts of the developing low-income sectors can easily be understood as a response to adverse situations, whether they are of natural origins or whether the "aggressor" is, for example, the state itself by means of its polices or lack thereof. There are also cases of collective action that have not been provoked by any previous or recent aggression. Be that as it may, in Argentina's case, the genesis of the association movement must be understood mainly as a reaction by an ever-growing sector of the population to the state's absence, in terms of social security and health services as well as other types of services required by the community— housing, recreation, canteens, etc.

5. In addition to these experiences, there are others we can mention: the Union of Agricultural Cotton Cooperatives (UCAL) founded in 1934 in the province of El Chaco that currently comprises sixteen first-degree cooperatives; the United SanCor Cooperatives Limited, which was set up in 1938 and presently brings together more than one hundred cooperatives with around five thousand dairy producers in the provinces of Santa Fe and Cordoba; and the Federation of Agricultural Cooperatives of Misiones, which appeared a year later and currently comprises twenty-nine cooperative members that bring together fifteen hundred producers.

6. The founding federations of the CONINAGRO were the UCAL, the Federation of Entre Rìos, the Federation of Misiones, the FACA, the Argentine Association of Agrarian Cooperatives Limited, Rosafè, and the Regional Federation of Cooperatives of Rio Negro and Neuquèn.

7. A worker cooperative is an association of people who gather to work together and pool everyone's efforts with the objective of improving their social and economic situation. These people forgo their status as salaried workers to become owners of their own destinies, putting capital and work at the service of humankind.

8. This recommendation for the promotion of cooperatives was approved by the International Labor Organization (ILO) at its 2002 conference.

9. The MNER brings together the majority of the recuperated companies and fosters the formation of work cooperatives.

10. Equivalent to approximately US$100 million.

11. According to numbers provided by Meyer and Pons (2003), 68 percent and 32 percent, respectively.

12. The assembly is the body that exercises the governance of the entity and can be considered in a complementary and auxiliary manner the highest in the hierarchy, as it is in charge of examining the internal administration and fiscal control. There are two types of assemblies: the ordinary ones, which meet once a year after the end of accounting exercises, and the extraordinary ones, which are convened randomly by the counselors, the receiver or the members. In addition, it has an administrative council made up of three members that occupy their posts for a term that must not exceed three years. Among their duties is the naming of the general manager. This person is not a member of the council and has no decision-making power: he or she only has executive functions in the administrative area. Finally, the body in charge of internal fiscal control is led by the trustee, who must be a member of the cooperative.

REFERENCES

Abramovich, A. L., Hintze, S., Montequín, A., & Vázquez, G. (2003). Empresas sociales: Características, problemas y perspectivas. Un estudio de casos de la Región Metropolitana de Buenos Aires. In A. L. Abramovich, D. Cassano, A. F. Sabaté, S. Hintze, A. Montequín, & G. Vázquez (Eds.), Empresas sociales y economía social: Una aproximación a sus rasgos fundamentales, Cartillas 6. Buenos Aires: Instituto del Conurbano, Universidad Nacional de General Sarmiento.

Arévalo, R., & Calello, T. (2003). Las empresas recuperadas en Argentina: Algunas dimensiones para su análisis. Presentation at the Segundo Congreso Argentino de Administración Pública, Sociedad, Estado y Administración, Córdoba, Argentina, November 27–29.

Campetella, A., & Bombal, I. G. (2000). Historia del sector sin fines de lucro en Argentina. In M. Roitter & I. Gonzalez Bombal (Eds.), Estudios sobre el sector sin fines de lucro en Argentina. Buenos Aires: EDIPUBLI.

Cassano, D. (2003). Aportes jurídico-institucionales para un proyecto de ley sobre la promoción de la economía social y las empresas sociales. In A. L. Abramovich, D. Cassano, A. F. Sabaté, S. Hintze, A. Montequín, & G. Vázquez (Eds.), Empresas sociales y economía social: Una aproximación a sus rasgos fundamentales, Cartillas 6. Buenos Aires: Instituto del Conurbano, Universidad Nacional de General Sarmiento.

Defourny, J. (1992). The origins, forms and roles of a third major sector. In

Jacques Defourny & José L. Monzón Campos (Eds.), *The third sector: Cooperative, mutual and nonprofit organizations*. Belgium: De Boeck Université.

Fajn, G., et al. (2003). *Fábricas y empresas recuperadas: Protesta social, autogestión y rupturas en la subjetividad*. Buenos Aires: Centro Cultural de la Cooperación.

Federico Sabaté, A. (2000). La economía del trabajo y las empresas sociales. Presentation at the ICO-UNGS seminar "Las Grandes Regiones Metropolitanas del MERCOSUR y México: Entre la competitividad y la complementariedad," Buenos Aires.

Finquelievich, S., & Kisilevsky, S. (2005). Community democratization of telecommunications community cooperatives in Argentina: The case of TELPIN. *The Journal of Community Informatics, 1*(3).

Giarraca, N. (1994). Introducción. In Giarraca Norma (Ed.), *Acciones colectivas y organización cooperativa: Reflexiones y estudios de caso*. Buenos Aires: Centro Editor de América Latina, Instituto de Investigaciones, Facultad de Ciencias Sociales, Universidad de Buenos Aires.

Hintze, S. (2003). Estado y políticas públicas: Acerca de la especificidad de la gestión de políticas para la economía social y solidaria. Presentation at the Segundo Congreso Argentino de Administración Pública. Sociedad, Estado y Administración, Córdoba, Argentina.

Hirschman, A. (1986). *El avance de la colectividad: Experimentos populares en la América Latina*. México: Serie de Economía, Fondo de Cultura Económica.

INAES. (2009). *¿Qué es una cooperativa?* Retrieved from www.inaes.gov.ar/es/articulo.asp?id=39.

———. (n.d.). Retrieved from www.inaes.gov.ar.

Instituto Nacional de Asociativismo y Economía Social, INAES. (2005). Congreso de la Alianza Cooperativa Internacional (ACI). Manchester.

Instituto Nacional de Estadísticas y Censos (National Statistics and Census Bureau), INDEC. (2006). Encuesta Permanente de Hogares, 2do semestre de 2006.

International Labour Organization (ILO). (2002). *The general conference: Promotion of cooperatives recommendation*. Retrieved from www.ilo.org/ilolex/cgi-lex/convds.pl?R193#Link.

Laville, J. L. (2004). *Economía social y solidaria: Una visón europea*. Buenos Aires: Fundación OSDE-Universidad Nacional de General Sarmiento Editorial Altamira.

Meyer, R., & Pons, J. (2003). La gestión de empresas recuperadas. Working Paper 42. Buenos Aires: Departamento de Cooperativismo, Centro Cultural de la Cooperación.

National Movement of Recuperated Companies (MNER). (n.d.). Retrieved from www.mner.com.ar.

Rebón, J. (2004). *Desobedeciendo al desempleo. La experiencia de las empresas recuperadas.* Buenos Aires: Ediciones Picaso/La Rosa Blindada.

Rebón, J., & Saavedra, I. (2006). *Empresas recuperadas: La autogestión de los trabajadores.* Buenos Aires: Claves Para Todos, Capital Intelectual.

Simonetti, F. (2006). Tirá una línea. *Pagina 12*, April 9.

Vilanova, E., & Vilanova, R. (1996). Las otras empresas: Experiencias de economía alternativa y solidaria en el Estado español. Madrid: Ediciones Talasa S.A.

ICHIRO TSUKAMOTO & MARIKO NISHIMURA

 Japan

Since the early 2000s, the concept of social enterprise has increasingly attracted public attention as an alternative business model for traditional nonprofit organizations, businesses, and public-private partnerships in Japan. Recently, the Japanese national government and some local authorities have become interested in the potential of this model, particularly for the regeneration of local communities and social integration, although their approaches are still ad hoc.

The purpose of this chapter is to explore the conceptualization, current state, and potential of social enterprises in Japan as well as challenges to their sustainable development. It begins with a discussion of the concept of social enterprise in Japan by reviewing previous studies on the topic by Japanese authors. This is followed by an analysis of the state of the current emerging social enterprise movement and its implications for traditional nonprofit organizations, businesses, and public-private partnerships. Next, we examine the legal framework and supportive environment for social enterprise development and the actual operations and social impacts of social enterprises. Finally, this chapter brings to light some challenges facing the sustainable development of social enterprises in Japan.

THE CONCEPT OF SOCIAL ENTERPRISE IN JAPAN

Although the approaches to social enterprise in Europe and the United States can be different (Kerlin, 2006a, 2006b), much of the literature from these regions has viewed social enterprises as socially innovative, entrepreneurial, hybrid organizations. Dees, Emerson, and Economy (2001) endorse the concept of social enterprises as organizations that have a social intent as their primary objective but that also blend social and commercial methods. Therefore, social enterprises can be considered hybrids of commercial and philanthropic approaches. EMES (Borzaga & Defourny, 2001) and other research networks (Nyssens, 2006) highlight their hybrid character as multigoal, multi-stakeholder, and multiple-resource enterprises.

Even in countries where a more supportive environment has been created, there is no universal and commonly accepted definition of social enterprises. This is also true in Japan. Social enterprise, or *shakaiteki kigyō*, has remained an ambiguous and relatively new term, even among scholars and practitioners who are involved in the third sector. The legal and organizational forms of social enterprises also tend to vary. Actually, the concept can cover different legal entities, such as the specified nonprofit corporation, also known as *NPO hōjin* (Tsukamoto & Nishimura, 2006), as well as cooperatives and business enterprises that take on the legal forms of limited liability companies and joint-stock companies.

Instead of "social enterprise," the term "community business" has been more commonly used in Japan to describe nonprofit organizations or businesses with a hybrid character. Since the late 1990s, the community business concept has become popular among nonprofit practitioners and policy makers and tends to be associated with the policies of local community regeneration. Hosouchi (1999) introduced successful cases of community businesses in the U.K. to Japanese society and applied this imported concept to similar activities in Japan. He defined community businesses as "local businesses by local community." However, proponents of community business do not necessarily stress their entrepreneurial character and approach to broader social issues beyond the locality.

Since the early 2000s, however, emerging innovative and hybrid organizations that have combined social and economic goals have increasingly utilized the concept of social enterprise or social entrepreneur instead of community business. These social enterprise concepts tend to be concepts imported from other European countries or the United States. Thus, their approaches to social enterprises have been influenced by European and U.S. social enterprise schools and practitioners such as the EMES Network (Borzaga & Defourny, 2001), Dees (Dees, Emerson, & Economy, 2001), CAN, and Social Enterprise London (SEL) (2001).

Four main social enterprise schools of thought have emerged in Japan. The first groups several approaches to social enterprise into what can be called the social innovation school. Machida (2000), an early influential proponent in the emergence of the concept of social enterprise in Japan, introduced the concept of social entrepreneur, or *shakai kigyōka*. He presented advanced cases of U.K. social enterprises that Leadbeater described in a DEMOS publication (1997). However, his concept of social enterprise has limited usefulness in Japan, since it is an imported concept from the U.K. and the United States and was not based on both theoretical and empirical work. By contrast, Tanimoto (2006) contributed an advanced approach to academic research on social enterprise in Japan. He has been engaged in defining social enterprises and examining their potential in more theoretical and empirical ways. His approach to social enterprises is influenced particularly by the social enterprise school in the United States. He considers social enterprise a vehicle for bringing about social innovation and defines social enterprise groups as hybrid organizations that have "three main characteristics such as social mission related, social businesses and social innovation" (Tanimoto, 2006). However, his definition is vague and hard to operationalize in research on actual organizations that can be quite diverse. More importantly, though his approach tends to highlight the purpose and mission of social enterprises, it neglects their governance and ownership structures. Both Machida and Tanimoto have been influenced by the social enterprise schools in the U.K. and the United States and thus employ broad concepts of social enterprise that include private companies with social missions as well as nonprofit organizations. However, as mentioned above, they tend to highlight social innovation accomplished by utilizing business methods but neglect the democratic, participative, and socially inclusive aspects of social enterprises that are evident in continental European social enterprise schools such as those to which EMES has often referred.

The second school of thought is the cooperative school. There is a strong cooperative tradition in Japan. Research groups such as the Consumer Cooperative Institute of Japan (CCIJ) and the Policy Research Institute for the Civil Sector tend to focus on the participative and democratic structure of social enterprises as exemplified by worker cooperatives and social cooperatives in Italy. Indeed, in recent years, researchers and practitioners of the cooperative movement in Japan have become interested in the European social economy tradition and the social enterprise concept of the cooperative as employed by EMES. A cooperative research group translated and published a work by EMES (Borzaga and Defourny, 2001) in 2004. They also contributed to the dissemination of a European social enterprise concept, although again it had limited usefulness because it has not been developed beyond an imported concept.

The third school of thought regarding social enterprise is the social work school. Some researchers and practitioners who are engaged in social work and social policies have come to employ a social enterprise concept that focuses on social inclusiveness. This concept can include both non-profit and for-profit organizations that operate for the purpose of the employment or social integration of disadvantaged people. Some work initiatives in Japan have been influenced by the European social policy tradition, which promotes social inclusion (Sumitani, Oyama, & Hosouchi, 2004).

The fourth school of thought is the third sector school. Some researchers (Tsukamoto, 2004, 2006; Tsukamoto & Nishimura, 2007) have been engaged in comparative research on social enterprises in the U.K., continental Europe, the United States, and Japan from the viewpoint that social enterprises can be considered an alternative to and sustainable business model of the third sector. This social enterprise concept can include nonprofit organizations, cooperative enterprises, and hybrid groups or networks composed of nonprofit and for-profit organizations. However, they tend to focus on the hybridization and commercialization of the third sector organizations and the potential of social enterprise to emerge from these contexts.

Needless to say, the divisions between these four schools (social innovation, cooperative, social work, and third sector) are not absolute but relative. What the schools have in common is that they view social enterprises as socially innovative, entrepreneurial, hybrid organizations with both social and economic goals. These goals distinguish them from traditional nonprofit organizations, which are overly dependent on nonmarket resources such as donations, government and philanthropic foundation grants, and volunteering. Social enterprises in the conceptual framework of all four schools can include nonprofit organizations, cooperatives, and business enterprises such as the limited liability company and the joint-stock company. However, the cooperative and third sector schools tend to focus on social enterprises rooted in the third sector.

THE HISTORY OF THE RECENT SOCIAL ENTERPRISE MOVEMENT

As we already noted, the concept of social enterprise in Japan has only begun to emerge since the early 2000s. In our view, however, the current social enterprise movement seems to be closely associated with the wider socioeconomic and political changes that began in the late 1990s. This new movement has been caused by the following five remarkable factors:

the launch of a new legal framework for the nonprofit sector; the commercialization of nonprofit organizations; a change in local government and
public policies; a strong tradition and new developments in the cooperative movement; and the emergence of corporate social responsibility (csr).

First, the social enterprise movement has emerged in part from social
and political changes related to the Japanese nonprofit sector that resulted
in the launch of a new legal framework for small and medium-sized nonprofit organizations and contributed to the emergence of a new kind of entrepreneur. Rapid growth in grassroots nonprofit organizations, which was
initially caused by the public's and then policy makers' interest in social
change, resulted from significant voluntary activity after the Hanshin-
Awaji Earthquake of 1995. This social change resulted in political changes,
such as the enactment of the Law to Promote Specified Nonprofit Activities
(the NPO Law) of 1998. This law created a new category of incorporated
organizations for small and medium-sized nonprofit and voluntary activities and enabled civic groups to acquire a legal status known as NPO
hōjin ("specified nonprofit corporation") (Pekkanen & Simon, 2003). For
many years Japan has had several categories of legal incorporation status
for large nonprofit organizations with sizable endowments, such as *shadan*
hōjin ("incorporated association") and *zaidan hōjin* ("incorporated foundation"). An NPO hōjin is much easier to incorporate than these traditional
nonprofit corporations because it does not require an endowment and
entails less government regulation. The total number of all categories of
incorporated nonprofit organizations in Japan can be estimated at over
250,000, while the total number of NPO hōjin established from 1998 to
January 2007 is estimated at 30,000. These numbers show that the growth
of NPO hōjin has been remarkable, especially when compared with the
growth of traditional nonprofit corporations. The new legal framework of
NPO hōjin has attracted a new kind of entrepreneur with a social purpose
by motivating the entrepreneur to create nonprofit and social ventures
through use of this legal entity with fewer government regulations. The
behavior of this new kind of entrepreneur tends to be associated with
socially beneficial objectives rather than material incentives, such as profit
maximizing. The so-called "supply side or entrepreneurial theory of nonprofits" used to explain the rise of the nonprofit sector (Young, 1986, 2003)
is helpful for understanding this phenomenon. As Frumkin noted, one of
the principal reasons the nonprofit sector is becoming an attractive vehicle

for entrepreneurship is that the barrier to entry is low (2002, p. 130). The NPO hōjin provides a much lower barrier to entry than the traditional forms of nonprofit incorporation in Japan.

The second factor that has influenced the emergence of a new kind of nonprofit entrepreneurship is the commercialization of nonprofit organizations due to economic and organizational change. According to the 2005 national survey on specified nonprofit corporations conducted by a government research institute (Keizai Sangyo Kenkyujo, 2005), 64.3 percent of their total income came from earned income,[1] 5.6 percent from membership fees, 9.5 percent from government and private grants, 7.7 percent from donations, and 12.9 percent from other sources. The high percentage of earned income in the data shows the tendency toward the commercialization of nonprofit organizations in Japan. Actually, this tendency has been strengthened by the expansion of contractual relationships with local authorities and "quasi-markets," such as the Long-Term Care Insurance System implemented under New Public Management (NPM)–oriented public service reforms since the late 1990s (Tsukamoto & Nishimura, 2006). As a result, nonprofit organizations have become critical players in the field of public services, especially the provision of social care services, under contractual relationships with local authorities. This shows that nonprofit organizations have increasingly relied on commercial revenues stemming from a quasi-market.

In addition to this trend, the institutional environment has also contributed to increasing nonprofit commercialization. For example, the Japanese system provides only a few nonprofit organizations with tax benefits, and Japanese society also has a weak tradition of charitable giving. This has led some nonprofit organizations to start income-generating activities in the marketplace. As the social enterprise examples in this chapter will show, some nonprofit organizations have launched business enterprises as their subsidiaries. In this context, social enterprises have emerged among commercializing nonprofit organizations as hybrids of nonprofit and for-profit activities. They tend to operate in a more self-sufficient way and rely on mixed nonmarket and market financial resources. For example, Florence is a nonprofit organization established as an NPO hōjin. It is a high-profile social enterprise that delivers child-care services for female workers who have difficulty balancing work and child care when their children become sick. Florence utilizes not only paid care workers and administrative staff but also some unpaid administrative staff called professional volunteers.

In addition, while it receives private donations and grants, a large part of its income is generated through its own businesses that provide care services. The third factor contributing to the increase in Japanese social enterprises involves changes in local government and public policies. The decline of the local economy; the revision of the Local Government Law of 2003, which led to a series of local government reforms known as decentralization; the fiscal crises of local authorities; and the decay of community cohesion in Japan have resulted in increased interest in nonprofit organizations and community-based businesses. They have been expected to play a significant role in local service provision and the regeneration of the local community without overdependence on government subsidies. In this context, most local governments have been interested in contracting out their services to local nonprofit organizations and community businesses. Some local governments have been engaged in building partnerships with them in order to promote community involvement. Under such partnerships, local governments tend to recognize nonprofit organizations and community businesses as interdependent and equal partners in addressing social problems, in improving the quality of public services, and in encouraging community involvement in local issues. In more recent years, elimination of social exclusion has been on the social policy agenda in Japan. Socially excluded groups include the unemployed, homeless, disadvantaged, and youth with difficulties in socializing, known as *hikikomori* ("shutting oneself indoors"). In this context, policy makers have increasingly paid attention to more sustainable and entrepreneurial nonprofit organizations or community businesses that can be strategically and successfully involved in local community regeneration and social and work integration.

The fourth factor is the strong tradition of cooperatives in Japan. Most large cooperatives such as consumer, farmer, and financial cooperatives have become increasingly commercialized and businesslike under competition with private rival firms despite their continued formal adherence to democratic governance structures. Some cooperatives have been supportive of the social enterprise movement, particularly those known as Seikatsu Club Seikyō (Seikatsu Club Consumers' Cooperative). They have been engaged in setting up and supporting social enterprises and worker collectives. For example, Seikatsu Club Seikyō Hokkaido supported the 2000 launch of an NPO hōjin called the Hokkaido Green Fund, which promotes the civic ecological movement and wind power owned and managed by citizens. This nonprofit organization set up a joint-stock company, Community Wind Power Co., Ltd., as its subsidiary in 2001. It is considered a social enterprise. Japan also has over 400 worker collectives in elderly- and child-care services and community cafes that together employ over 12,000 workers. These worker collectives began in the late 1980s with the purpose of creating more equal and participative workplaces run by women themselves. In recent years, these worker collective groups, such as Workers' Collective Network Japan (WNJ), have begun to be interested in the concept of social enterprise.

The fifth and final factor providing a supportive environment for the social enterprise movement in Japan since the early 2000s is the emergence of new business thinking known as corporate philanthropy and corporate social responsibility. For example, NEC, a leading company in the field of information technology and computer products, has been engaged in fostering social entrepreneurs in collaboration with a nonprofit organization. Additionally, Masao Ogura, former president of Yamato Transport Co., Ltd., who is well known in Japan as a business entrepreneur, set up a social enterprise chain of stores named Swan Bakery & Cafe in 1998 as a joint venture with the Yamato Welfare Foundation. Swan is a joint-stock company founded for the purpose of the social and work integration of disadvantaged people. Swan's formation involves the case of an entrepreneur of a large and established enterprise who became engaged in the launch of social enterprises. In addition to the increase in large businesses starting social enterprises, a more noteworthy increase, though there are only a few cases, is a new group of entrepreneurs with social missions who have incorporated their small businesses as joint-stock companies or limited liability companies from their start. For example, Atmark Learning Co., Ltd., was founded in 1999 as a joint-stock company and operates an Internet high school providing Internet-based education programs to students who choose not to study in school. Another example is The Big Issue Japan, which was set up as a limited liability company in 2003 for the purpose of helping the homeless through opportunities to work as street magazine vendors.

DIVERSITY IN SOCIAL ENTERPRISES IN JAPAN

The five factors described above are interrelated in their impact on the emergence of social enterprise in Japan. Scholars, supporters, and the mass media have been increasingly concerned with the social enterprise movement. Actually, many social enterprises operate in the different fields of welfare services, community cafes, bakeries, community transports, recycling, and so on. Their organizational forms are diversified as well, including nonprofit organizations such as NPO hōjin, cooperatives such as worker collectives, and business enterprises such as limited liability companies and joint-stock companies. Despite this diversity, the degree of actual social enterprise development has been low. More importantly, social enterprise has not necessarily become a widely and commonly accepted concept among practitioners of organizations in Japan in comparison with Europe and the Unites States. The definition of what qualifies as a social enterprise is still ambiguous. Thus, it may be difficult to categorize various social enterprises. However, five major types (A–E) of emerging social enterprises can be identified by focusing on their origins, as follows:

- Type A: Social enterprises that stem from commercializing nonprofit organizations
  - Nonprofit organizations that become social enterprises due to commercialization
  - Florence can be classified as Type A.
- Type B: Social enterprises that are spun off from existing nonprofit organizations
  - Subsidiaries of nonprofit organizations that become organizationally independent social enterprises
  - Funnybee, described in the following examples, can be classified as Type B.
- Type C: Social enterprises that stem from the cooperative movement
  - Cooperatives such as consumer cooperatives that are engaged in community and social businesses
  - Worker cooperatives can be viewed as social enterprises.
  - Community Wind Power can be classified as Type C.
- Type D: Social enterprises that stem from business enterprises
  - Business enterprises with social missions that are launched initially as social enterprises, or ones that change into social enterprises in the process of business development
  - Atmark Learning and The Big Issue Japan can be classified as Type D.

- Type E: Social enterprises that are spun off from business enterprises
  - Business enterprises such as joint-stock companies that set up social enterprises as subsidiaries or as independent organizations
  - Swan can be classified as Type E.

In addition to the categorization of types A through E, the following three major types of social enterprises can be identified from the perspective of organizational form.

- *Nonprofit Organizations (NPO type)*: Social enterprises that are legally incorporated as nonprofit corporations, such as NPO hōjin, or are not incorporated but employ the governance structure of a nonprofit organization (e.g., an unincorporated grassroots or community-based organization with a governing board that appoints a director)
- *Cooperatives (Cooperative type)*: Social enterprises that employ cooperative principles such as "one person, one vote" and democratic governance by members; but because there is no specified legal entity for worker cooperatives in Japan, many worker cooperatives are registered as NPO hōjin or other legal entities
- *Companies (Company type)*: Social enterprises that are incorporated as companies, such as joint-stock companies or limited liability corporations

The overall distribution of social enterprises among these categories cannot be precisely determined at this time. However, in our view the most common forms of social enterprises in Japan are "A-NPO" and "B-Company" types. A notable fact is that the former types of social enterprises have generated the latter types, and as the following examples show, they have managed both nonprofit organizations and companies jointly as a kind of group.

LEGAL FRAMEWORK AND INSTITUTIONAL SUPPORTS FOR SOCIAL ENTERPRISE

As we discussed earlier, there is no specified legal framework for social enterprises such as the Community Interest Company (CIC) in the U.K. Therefore, social enterprises tend to select the preferred legal entity that fits their objectives and business structure. In most cases, social enterprises are legally incorporated as NPO hōjin, joint-stock companies, or limited liability companies; the NPO hōjin form is the most common in Japan. As the examples show, some social enterprises utilize multiple legal entities. For example, an NPO hōjin may be used along with a joint-stock company.

In terms of institutional support by the public sector, in recent years national and local governments have become concerned with the economic and social impact of social enterprises. For example, the Ministry of Economy, Trade and Industry (METI) estimated the economic effect generated by the nonprofit sector and concluded that its economic impact on the economy in 2002 was large enough to be regarded as significant. In this context, social enterprise, when viewed as the commercial activities of nonprofit organizations, has been seen as a tool for tackling both economic and social problems. Since the early 2000s, one of the regional offices of METI has been engaged in the development of infrastructure for social enterprises by helping to build business networks among them. In 2003, when the concept of community business was more common among policy makers, the Kanto Bureau of METI established the Greater Kanto Community Business Promotion Association, a regional network for social enterprise. The association provides social enterprises and community businesses in the Kanto area with information, consulting services, and networking events in order to build business networks. In April 2007, METI launched a new initiative with government funding that supports intermediary organizations through specified training programs for social entrepreneurs. The total sum of its grant is 160 million yen (1 million Euros, £0.8 million, or US$1.5 million). This was the first time METI explicitly employed the concept of social enterprise in its policy.

Some local governments have also been engaged in fostering social enterprises and social entrepreneurs and their business networks through consultation, training programs, and government funding. For example, the Osaka prefectural government launched the Osaka Social Entrepreneurs Support Program in 2003 in order to foster social entrepreneurs and their networks. The program provides various services such as consulting for business support and building networks for social entrepreneurs.

Social enterprises also receive institutional support from the private sector. In recent years, private foundations have not been engaged in such support, but some intermediary organizations have been created especially to support social enterprises. These intermediary organizations include the Center for Active Community (CAC, 2001–), Social Innovation Japan (SIJ, 2005–), and some community banks. Both intermediary organizations have been strongly influenced by the concepts of social enterprise imported from the U.K. and the United States.

CAC is an independent research network that is dedicated to supporting social entrepreneurs and disseminating information about the role of social entrepreneurs. CAC is an unincorporated organization composed of researchers and consultants. However, practitioners of social enterprises are not involved in CAC's governance and management. CAC provides various services such as gatherings, symposiums, seminars, and research for social entrepreneurs and supporters.

SIJ is another intermediary organization that aims to promote social innovation, foster social entrepreneurs as core agents of that innovation, and build their networks. Professor Tanimoto of Hitotsubashi University played a significant role in founding this organization and has been engaged in its operation as president. SIJ was incorporated as an NPO hōjin and provides various services such as gatherings, symposiums, seminars, research consulting, and advocacy for social entrepreneurs and supporters. Researchers, consultants, supporters, and practitioners have been engaged in its governance and management. Its Social Business Award is a notable prize that recognizes social entrepreneurs' excellent businesses.

Both CAC and SIJ have contributed to disseminating the concepts of social entrepreneur and social enterprise in Japan. However, they are rather small organizations and are not necessarily able to represent the broad interests of social entrepreneurs in Japan.

With respect to research on social enterprise, there has been an increase in university and other institute-based research projects since the early 2000s. The Open Research Center Project (a five-year project subsidized by the Ministry of Education, 2004–2008) based at Meiji University has been engaged in international comparative research on social enterprises since 2004 in collaboration with SEL and overseas researchers from the U.K. and the United States (Tsukamoto & Nishimura, 2007). Additionally, the Consumer Cooperative Institute of Japan (CCIJ) has played a significant role in comparative research on social enterprises in European countries and Japan.

On the other hand, university-based specific education on social enterprises has been underdeveloped in Japan. The nonprofit-based organization ETIC (an NPO hōjin), however, does develop and deliver specific education programs for social entrepreneurs in collaboration with the NEC Corporation. In particular, ETIC supports social entrepreneurs in their businesses' start-up stages by offering lectures and consulting services.

In summary, legal frameworks and institutional supports for social enterprise development have been underdeveloped in Japan. National, regional, and local public sectors and private intermediary organizations do provide some support programs that facilitate social entrepreneurs' activities and assist in building their networks. Nevertheless, the actual impact of these support programs and intermediary organizations on the social enterprise movement has been quite limited. More importantly, these efforts have not been interrelated and have lacked a comprehensive and strategic perspective, which may result in the underdevelopment of social enterprise as a sector. Such an underdeveloped environment of institutional supports appears to be related to the lack of structure and networks and the sense that social enterprise is not yet a sector in Japan.

EXAMPLES OF SOCIAL ENTERPRISES IN JAPAN

In this section we present two examples that are representative of the two most common and successful forms of social enterprise in Japan. They are involved in social and work-integration activities for the disadvantaged and homeless. Both cases are widely viewed as successful cases by scholars and practitioners. Our research method involved semi-structured interviews with managers and staff. Our research focused on the nature of the business, the organizational structure of the various organizations involved, and their interrelationship, resources, and relations with various stakeholders.

Example 1: NPO Sanagitachi Project

In 1983, three homeless men were killed by juveniles in a park in the City of Yokohama, Kanagawa prefecture. This incident raised public interest in the homeless. In the same year, the NPO Sanagitachi Project was founded by voluntary supporters and homeless people in the Kotobuki area of Yokohama as a nonprofit organization meant to address issues affecting homeless people and to support their self-sufficiency.

The Kotobuki area used to be the day laborers' district of Yokohama and one of the most deprived urban areas in Japan. There are about 120 lodging buildings and 8,000 rooms for day laborers and people who are homeless. The population in the Kotobuki area was estimated at about 6,000 in 2006. Eighty percent of the population in Kotobuki receives public assistance from the national welfare system, and about 50 percent are over the age of sixty. Its population has been aging rapidly.

The NPO Sanagitachi Project itself was incorporated as an NPO hōjin in 2001, and it can be considered an "A-NPO" type of social enterprise according to our categorization. The NPO Sanagitachi Project operates Sanagi Gathering Place and Sanagi Restaurant to provide services such as meals, clothing, medical care, housing, information services, consulting, and job training to the homeless people of the Kotobuki area. These services are delivered in collaboration with a local medical clinic and one of the largest convenience chain stores in the area. Since 2006, the NPO Sanagitachi Project, in collaboration with the Yokohama municipal government and community, has also been engaged in a campaign of planting flowers around the Kotobuki area in order to tackle the problem of illegal waste disposal.

Additionally, the NPO Sanagitachi Project launched a commercial venture called Yokohama Hostel Village (YHV) in order to create employment opportunities for the homeless and regenerate the deprived neighborhood. Funnybee Co., Ltd., is a joint-stock company that was founded by a member of Sanagitachi in 2004. It runs YHV, which offers around thirty rehabilitated rooms of a single-room-occupancy hotel at an inexpensive rate for tourists, including foreign tourists. Funnybee can be regarded as a "B-Company" type of social enterprise.

Revenue for the NPO Sanagitachi Project comes from a City of Yokohama grant, business grants, donations, membership fees, and earned income (Sanagi Restaurant). In fiscal year 2006 the total income of the NPO Sanagitachi Project was about 40 million yen (260,000 Euros, £200,000, or US$400,000). In contrast, Funnybee's only source of income is earned income from the hostel fees tourist pay. Its total income is about 9 million yen (60,000 Euros, £45,000, or US$90,000). Four people are employed by the NPO Sanagitachi Project and work for the Sanagi Gathering Place and Sanagi Restaurant. About seventy volunteers participate in part-time support activities, and about twenty homeless people participate in activities and job training there. Two people are employed by Funnybee, and about twenty volunteers manage its operations. This shows that the human resource structure of social enterprises is mixed as well.

The NPO Sanagitachi Project and Funnybee are managed collaboratively, and they utilize various resources, including nonmarket and market resources, and different legal entities, such as an NPO hōjin and a joint-stock company. In addition, they have partnerships with other local stakeholders, including local medical clinics, municipal governments, and business enterprises. However, the market range is highly concentrated in their narrow initial mission, although Funnybee has been engaged in attracting foreign tourists and youth from outside the Kotobuki area. Thus, the potential for Funnybee's sustainable business growth seems to be unclear. In addition, the NPO Sanagitachi Project and Funnybee do not have strong relationships with other nonprofit organizations or social enterprises through which information on common experiences and general issues could be shared.

Example 2: Palette

The purpose of Palette is to support people with intellectual and developmental disabilities so they can live independently, work, and participate in social activities. Palette was founded in 1983 as a nonprofit organization designed to function as a gathering place where people with intellectual and developmental disabilities could meet on a daily basis. Palette manages two workshops: Palette Bakery, which was founded in 1985; and Sri Lanka Restaurant Palette (Restaurant Palette), which was founded as a subsidiary, joint-stock company in 1991. Palette also operates a residential home for people with intellectual and developmental disabilities that was founded in 1993. Palette's offices and workshops are all located in the Ebisu area of the Shibuya ward in Tokyo. Palette was incorporated as an NPO hōjin in 2002. According to our categorization, Palette as a whole is an "A-NPO" type of social enterprise, and Restaurant Palette is a "B-Company" type.

Palette Bakery and Restaurant Palette are new types of workshops for disadvantaged people. Although the former receives funding from the welfare system as a sheltered workshop, it is operated as a commercial bakery and therefore also exists in a market environment. The latter is managed as a business enterprise, specifically as a joint-stock company. Both are less dependent on public funding than other social welfare programs are. In addition, they focus more on the generation of commercial market resources in order to pursue work integration that enables employed disadvantaged people to earn incomes comparable to those of other workers.

Palette Bakery is engaged in the production and sale of cookies and cakes for individual and corporate customers. In 2005, its revenue came from approximately 20 million yen (130,000 Euros, £100,000, or US$200,000) in government grants and approximately 20 million yen in commercial income. Therefore, its total revenue was approximately 40 million yen (260,000 Euros, £200,000, or US$400,000). Restaurant Palette serves Sri Lankan curry dishes. Its income of approximately 20 million yen (130,000 Euros, £100,000, or US$200,000) in fiscal year 2005 was generated entirely from commercial sources. However, its income stream has fluctuated because the restaurant has to compete with many other restaurants in the area.

About 60 percent of the total income of Palette (an NPO hōjin) comes from government grants, and 26 percent comes from earned income (cookie sales). The rest of its income comes from business grants, donations, and membership fees. The total revenue is approximately 100 million yen (700,000 Euros, £500,000, or US$1 million). This total does not include the income generated by Restaurant Palette. In effect, Restaurant Palette is managed as a subsidiary of the Palette NPO, despite its legal status as an independent corporation.

As noted, Palette utilizes the social enterprise activities of its two workshops in order to provide employment opportunities for the disadvantaged. Restaurant Palette created four jobs, including two jobs for the intellectually disadvantaged, without receiving government grants. Palette Bakery created ten jobs by combining government grants and commercial resources and provides training for the intellectually disadvantaged with the help of three employed, nondisabled staff and some volunteers. The salaries paid to disadvantaged workers in both workshops are higher than in traditional sheltered workshops.

With the exception of Palette Restaurant, a major portion of Palette's resources comes from government funding. For this reason, Palette suffers from institutional pressures and current radical changes in public welfare policies for disadvantaged people. Changes that are producing these difficulties include the introduction of a quasi-market system by the national government, whereby clients of social services will be funded instead of the social service programs, and those clients will be expected to contribute to the cost of their services. The result is a reduction in assured program funding that instead favors competition for clients among various programs and the requirement that clients spend some of their limited discretionary resources on services.

On the other hand, Palette Restaurant and Bakery both suffer from commercial market pressures, namely market risk and fluctuation, and a persistent pressure that is related to commercial survival with a disadvantaged workforce. In this situation, Palette has been engaged in developing relationships with business enterprises in order to obtain business grants and find customers who are supportive of business enterprises and recognize their social missions.

KEY FINDINGS FROM THE EXAMPLES

We identified some key findings from the data on these two Japanese social enterprises. First, these social enterprises can contribute to the creation of employment opportunities and social cohesion for socially excluded and disadvantaged people by using the commercial market in innovative ways. Due to the effective use of the commercial market, social enterprises benefit from an unusual degree of organizational flexibility and independence from government: it enables them to develop new businesses more flexibly and to eliminate institutional pressures from public agencies and their regulations, which can be often described as "institutional isomorphism" (DiMaggio & Powell, 1991). Second, these social enterprises utilize the hybridization of organizational and resource structures strategically. That is, multiple resources, including market resources such as sales of goods and services, and nonmarket resources, such as volunteering, business grants, and donations, are mobilized. In addition, their organizational structures take on a hybrid character in the sense that they use different organizational forms such as nonprofit corporations and companies to combine social service and commercial divisions in an integrated way.

However, we can point out several main drawbacks even in these successful cases. First, each social enterprise operates only in a restrictively small local area. The limited capacity of their local markets can constrain their expansion and sustainable development, as a study on U.K. cases found (Amin, Cameron, & Hudson, 2003). Second, as the Palette case shows, social enterprises, particularly those that operate in the field of welfare services, tend to suffer from institutional and market pressures. The institutional pressures come from the contractual relationships with government, and the market pressures come from the "quasi-markets" in which different for-profit and nonprofit service providers compete with each other. This means that even successful social enterprises such as Palette tend to be embedded in a competitive market and institutional framework dominated by the government. In our view, this tendency has been amplified by the limited hybridization of organizational and resource structures of social enterprises and the lack of collaborative and support networks in Japan. In other words, these market and institutional pressures would decrease if Japan had more collaborative and supportive networks in an organized social enterprise sector. Social enterprises could also utilize more diverse resources, including both market and nonmarket incomes.

A third drawback is that social capital resources (Bode, Evers, & Schulz, 2004) such as donations, volunteering, solidarity and mutual support, and partnerships with other organizations seem to be relatively scarce in Japan compared with successful cases of social enterprises in Europe and the United States. This is related to the poor tax benefit system for nonprofits in Japan, underdeveloped infrastructure organizations, and the poor supportive environment for social enterprises. Such social capital resources are essential for retaining social mission–oriented businesses and diversity.

CONCLUSION

In conclusion, the social enterprise movement in Japan can be regarded as being in the germ stage of its development. In recent years the concept of social enterprise has increasingly attracted public interest, but there is no widely and commonly accepted definition of the concept. It has been vaguely conceptualized and can include different organizational and legal forms such as nonprofit corporations, cooperatives, and joint-stock companies. In addition, a sectoral identity has not been cultivated. Nevertheless, it is clear that the emerging social entrepreneurs and enterprises have provided an alternative model for traditional nonprofit organizations, business enterprises, and public-private partnerships in Japan even though the actual progress of the social enterprise movement seems to be slow. The social and economic impact of social enterprises on Japan has been highly limited, but specific, deprived local communities and socially excluded and disadvantaged people can benefit from social enterprises.

Our study also explored some drawbacks for social enterprises in Japan. These include the limited capacity of the local markets in which social enterprises operate, vulnerability to institutional and market pressures, and scarce social capital resources. If social enterprises hope to retain their hybrid character by reconciling their social mission and business methods and to maintain sustainable development, they need to address these drawbacks strategically and collaboratively. More specifically, social enterprises need to mobilize multiple resources from government, the market, and social capital or utilize different organizational forms in order to reduce institutional and market pressures. Another important challenge is the need for more collaborative networks as well as supportive institutional frameworks beyond individual organizations and localities. These supportive networks can help promote public awareness of social enterprises, share best practices among social entrepreneurs, and create a sense of identity as a sector with common values.

NOTES

1. In the Japanese context, earned income includes income from government and private contracts and commercial activities. In terms of the composition of earned income in the data, 70 percent of the total earned income comes from government contracts, 28.7 percent from commercial activities, and 5.4 percent from private contracts (Keizai Sangyo Kenkyujo, 2005).

REFERENCES

Amin, A., Cameron, A., & Hudson, R. (2003). The alterity of the social economy. In A. Leyshon, R. Lee, & C. C. Williams (Eds.), *Alternative economic spaces* (pp. 27–54). London: Sage.

Bode, I., Evers, A., & Schulz, A. (2004). A third way to employment and integration? Social enterprises in Europe between workfare and welfare. In A. Zimmer & C. Stecker (Eds.), *Strategic mix for nonprofit organizations: Vehicle for social and labour market integrations* (pp. 203–226). New York: Kluwer Academic/Plenum Publishers.

Borzaga, C., & Defourny, J. (Eds.). (2001). *The emergence of social enterprise.* London: Routledge.

Dees, J. G., Emerson, J., & Economy, P. (2001). *Enterprising nonprofits: A toolkit for social entrepreneurs.* New York: John Wiley & Sons.

DiMaggio, P. J., & Powell, W. W. (1991). The iron cage revisited: Institutional isomorphism and collective rationality in organizational fields. In W. W. Powell & P. J. DiMaggio (Eds.), *The new institutionalism in organizational analysis* (pp. 63–82). Chicago: University of Chicago Press.

Frumkin, P. (2002). *On being nonprofit*. Cambridge: Harvard University Press.

Hosouchi, N. (1999). *Komyuniti bijinesu (Community business)*. Tokyo: Chūō daigaku shuppannbu.

Keizai Sangyo Kenkyujo (2005). *NPO hojin ankeito chousa kekka 2004 (The research report on the national survey of the specified nonprofit corporations)*. Tokyo: Keizai Sangyo Kenkyujo (RIETI).

Kerlin, J. A. (2006a). Social enterprise in the United States and abroad: Learning from our differences. In R. Mosher-Willliams (Ed.), *Research on social entrepreneurship: Understanding and contributing to an emerging field* (pp. 105–125). Indianapolis: ARNOVA.

———. (2006b). Social enterprise in the United States and Europe: Understanding and learning from the differences. *Voluntas, 17*(3), 247–263.

Leadbeater, C. (1997). *The rise of the social entrepreneur*. London: DEMOS.

Machida, Y. (2000). *Shakai kigyōka (Social entrepreneurs)*. Tokyo: PHP.

Nyssens, M. (Ed.) (2006). *Social enterprise: At the crossroads of market, public policies and civil society*. London: Routledge.

Pekkanen, R., & Simon, K. (2003). The legal framework for voluntary and non-profit activity. In S. P. Osborne (Ed.), *The voluntary and non-profit sector in Japan* (pp. 76–101). London: Routledge.

Social Enterprise London (2001). *Introducing social enterprise*. London: SEL.

Sumitani, S., Oyama, H., & Hosouchi, N. (Eds.). (2004). *Sōsharuinkurūjon to shakaikigyō no yakuwari (Social inclusion and social entrepreneurs)*. Tokyo: Gyousei.

Tanimoto, K. (Ed.). (2006). *Sōsharu Entâpuraizu (Social Enterprise)*. Tokyo: Chuōkeizaisha.

Tsukamoto, I. (2004). NPO to shakaiteki kigyō (NPO and social enterprise). In I. Tsukamoto, S. Furukawa, & T. Amemiya (Eds.), *NPO to atarashii syakai dezain (Nonprofit organizations and new social design)* (pp. 237–255). Tokyo: Doubunkan.

———. (2006). Shakaiteki kigyō: Eiri to hieiri no haiburiddo (Social enterprise: Hybrid organization of for-profit and nonprofit). In K. Harada & I. Tsukamoto (Eds.), *Bōdaresukasuru CSR (CSR beyond the border)* (pp. 237–258). Tokyo: Doubunkan.

Tsukamoto, I., & Nishimura, M. (2006). The emergence of local non-profit-government partnerships and the role of intermediary organizations in Japan. *Public Management Review, 8*(4), 567–581.

———. (2007). *Commercializing nonprofit organizations and social enterprise activities*. Paper presented at the 11th annual conference of IRSPM (International

Research Society for Public Management), University of Potsdam, Potsdam, Germany, April 2–4.

Young, D. R. (1986). Entrepreneurship and the behavior of nonprofit organizations: Elements of a theory. In Susan Rose-Ackerman (Ed.), *The economics of nonprofit institutions: Studies in structure and policy* (pp. 161–184). New York: Oxford University Press.

——. (2003). Entrepreneurs, managers, and the nonprofit enterprise. In H. Anheier & A. Ben-Ner (Eds.), *The study of the nonprofit enterprise* (pp. 161–168). New York: Kluwer Academic / Plenum Publishers.

JANELLE A. KERLIN

A Comparison of Social Enterprise Models and Contexts

In countries around the world, the term "social enterprise" is becoming increasingly associated with the broad idea of commercial revenue generation in the service of charitable activities. However, as the preceding chapters show, the concept is also becoming connected to a certain set of organizations and activities, both old and new, that appear to be related to the regional context at hand. This suggests that as the concept grows in popularity, the resources and institutions that become involved in its promotion and development increasingly reflect the broader environment. This chapter proposes to test this thesis to find out whether differences in social enterprise in various regions of the world are, at least in part, reflections of the regional socioeconomic contexts in which the term has come to rest. To accomplish this, we match the regional and country information gathered in this volume with data from a number of international social and economic databases.

HISTORICAL CONTEXTS FOR THE DEVELOPMENT OF SOCIAL ENTERPRISE

Though there are few statistics on the prevalence of social enterprise in different regions of the world, Salamon et al. (2004) provide some evidence that it is a prominent phenomenon among nonprofit organizations. Their research also suggests that the context of social enterprise can influence its occurrence. In their study of thirty-four countries around the world, Salamon et al. (2004) found that on average 53 percent of nonprofit income comes "from fees and charges for the services that these organizations provide and the related commercial income they receive from investments, dues, and other commercial sources" (p. 30). Indeed, fees in twenty-four of the thirty-four countries represented the dominant source of revenue for these organizations. In particular, they note that the dominance of commercial revenue was most prevalent among transitional and developing countries where the civil society sectors are small. For these countries, fees represented, on average, 61 percent of civil society organization income, compared to 45 percent for developed countries (Salamon et al., 2004). What these findings hint at is how a region's history can affect the social and economic factors that ultimately mold social enterprise activity. This section provides a brief review of the historical contexts that shared in shaping the socioeconomic conditions that influenced the emergence and characteristics of social enterprise in the seven regions and countries under consideration.

The general theme underlying the emergence of social enterprise in all seven regions and countries is the absence of state social programs or funding, due to either the retreat or poor functioning of the state. The United States, Western and East-Central Europe, and South America all experienced, to differing degrees, a withdrawal of state support in the 1980s and/or 1990s. In the United States, scholars attribute the beginning of the contemporary social enterprise movement to government cuts in funds supporting nonprofits. A slowdown in the U.S. economy in the late 1970s resulted in government deficits in the 1980s that, in turn, brought on government cuts in funds for nonprofits by the Reagan administration. These cuts are estimated to have affected a wide array of nonprofits, not just those involved in human services. According to some scholars, nonprofits seized upon the idea of commercial revenue generation as a way to replace the loss of government funds (Crimmins & Keil, 1983; Eikenberry & Kluver, 2004; Salamon, 1993, 1997).

In Western Europe, too, a faltering economy was at the root of the emergence of contemporary social enterprise. However, the consequences played out in a slightly different form. As unemployment grew and government revenue fell, government employment programs in Western Europe were increasingly found to be ineffective. Moreover, given dwindling resources, many Western European governments resorted to retrenchment of their welfare states, which had become large and cumbersome over time. Reforms were characterized by decentralization, privatization, and a reduction in services. The social enterprise movement was in part a response to the unemployment problem, as one of its main initiatives was work integration of the unemployed, often through social cooperatives. Social enterprises also stepped in to provide human services the welfare state was no longer directly responsible for (Borzaga & Defourny, 2001).

In East-Central Europe, social enterprise was also spurred on by a withdrawal of the state, though in this case the cause was the fall of communism. Here the withdrawal of the state was much more dramatic and was compounded by an already weak civil society undercut by communist rule. In addition, the transition to a market economy brought large increases in unemployment. The international community responded to these crises with sizable amounts of foreign aid as well as policy recommendations. A small but growing number of East-Central European social reformers seized upon social enterprise (borrowing mostly from the West European model) as a viable solution and received support for its development from international sources. Though still largely framed as an unemployment and human service tool, the concept of social enterprise in East-Central Europe is already beginning to reflect the realities present there (Leś & Kolin, this volume).

On the other hand, Argentina experienced a withdrawal of the state due to "Washington Consensus" structural adjustment programs instituted as a part of market reform. Not only did reforms shrink universal social benefit programs; changes in the economy also resulted in rising unemployment. Roitter and Vivas in this volume conclude that social enterprises in Argentina "highlight problems related to poverty, income inequalities, and production conditions that were no longer being addressed by the economic sphere and the public sector." Indeed, social enterprise in Argentina has become associated with a broad range of cooperatives and mutual benefit societies to address unemployment and social exclusion.

By contrast, the histories of Zimbabwe and Zambia are marked by poor economies and a persistent lack of state support. This situation was compounded by structural adjustment programs similar to those in Argentina. Here, employment-oriented social enterprises emerged after structural adjustment programs resulted in unemployment rates reaching 60 to 80 percent. Large amounts of international aid increasingly went to nonstate actors as state institutions' capacity to manage the economy fell into doubt (Masendeke & Mugova, this volume). According to Chabal and Daloz (1999), this focus of international aid on nonstate actors was the single most important factor leading to the development of social enterprise through international NGOs. Rather than cooperatives, international aid focused on microcredit for small businesses, though lack of state reforms in certain areas continues to constrain their success.

Southeast Asia has also long been associated with high rates of poverty and unemployment inadequately addressed by government welfare programs. These problems were exacerbated by the Asian financial crisis in the late 1990s. Recently, however, some economies in the region have begun to show signs of growth, along with a burgeoning interest in social enterprise. Indeed, the term "social enterprise" is just now starting to be associated with revenue-generating activities for social as well as sustainable development. In Southeast Asia, social enterprises, whether for-profit or not-for-profit, are small social ventures that simultaneously address unemployment, provide needed services, and protect the environment (Santos et al., this volume).

In Japan, interest in social enterprise was spurred on by a series of events and changes in law that revealed the limitations of government. Volunteer efforts following the Hanshin-Awaji Earthquake of 1995, spurred on by a weak government response, awakened a new interest in grassroots non-profit organizations that led to the passage of a 1997 law making it easier to establish nonprofits. Entrepreneurs with social objectives have seized upon the new nonprofit law to develop social enterprises. Also, a 2003 revision in local government laws resulting in a decline in local communities turned local policy makers to social enterprises for help with revitalization and social integration. The business community's recent interest in corporate social responsibility has also resulted in their increasing involvement in social enterprise activities (Tsukamoto & Nishimura, this volume).

DIFFERING CHARACTERISTICS OF SOCIAL ENTERPRISE IN SEVEN WORLD REGIONS AND COUNTRIES

The chapters in this volume not only outline the circumstances that spurred on social enterprise; they also reveal important details about the characteristics of social enterprise in their locations. The analysis in this section makes use of this information to formulate models of social enterprise for each of the seven regions/countries. To create these models, the seven social enterprise descriptions are compared across six variables that help characterize differences in social enterprise: outcome emphasis, program area focus, common organizational type, legal framework, societal sector, and strategic development base. Because the present analysis is a comparison, regions/countries were characterized *relative to the other regions and countries in the study*. The following section provides explanations of the six variables and examples of how regional characteristics were determined relative to the variables. Table 9.1 provides an overview of these characteristics for all regions and countries.

TABLE 9.1. *Comparative Overview of Social Enterprise in Seven World Regions and Countries*

	United States	Western Europe	Japan	East-Central Europe	Argentina	Zimbabwe/Zambia	Southeast Asia
Outcome emphasis	Sustainability	Social benefit	Social/Economic benefit	Social benefit	Social/Economic benefit	Self-sustainability	Sustainable development
Program area focus	All nonprofit activities	Human services/Employment	Services/Employment	Human services/Employment	Human services/Employment	Employment	Employment/Services
Common organizational type	Nonprofit Company	Association/Cooperative	Nonprofit/Company	Association/Cooperative	Cooperative/Mutual benefit	MFI*/Small enterprise	Small enterprise/Association
Legal framework	Under discussion	Developing	Not yet considered	Developing	Not yet considered	Not yet considered	Not yet considered
Societal sector	Market economy	Social economy	Market economy	Social economy	Social economy	Market economy	Market economy
Strategic development	Foundations	Government/EU	Government	International donors/EU	Civil society	International donors	Mixed

The first variable, *outcome emphasis*, focuses on the overall immediate goal in implementing a social enterprise activity relative to other regions' emphases. Thus, for example, Zimbabwe and Zambia focus on self-sustainability as an immediate outcome, probably due to the lack of other forms of funding and an emphasis on economic development. In Western Europe, on the other hand, the immediate outcome focus is on social benefit, given the emphasis on employment and the reduction of social exclusion often supported by state funding. The variable of *program area focus* relates to the type of activity that is generally supported by social enterprise in a region. In the United States, basically all types of social activities can be supported by social enterprise to one degree or another. On the other hand, in East-Central Europe and many other regions, most of the programs associated with social enterprise are oriented toward employment or human service.

In many of the regions/countries, social enterprise is conducted via several different organizational types or legal arrangements. Thus the third variable, *organizational type*, refers to the most common legal form used to conduct social enterprise. For example, in Japan, the most common legal forms for social enterprise are the nonprofit and the company. In Argentina, however, the cooperative and mutual benefit society are most commonly used for social enterprise. Closely related to this discussion is whether or not a separate legal framework has been established for social enterprises, even if it is not the organizational form most often used for social enterprise in the region. Thus, *legal framework* is the fourth variable. Western Europe is the clear leader in this area, with legal designations for social enterprises established in several European countries, most recently the United Kingdom. Southeast Asia, on the other hand, has not begun to move in this direction; there is little or no discussion of the topic at present. The same is true for Japan, Argentina, and Zimbabwe and Zambia.

The fifth variable, *societal sector*, points to the sector that social enterprise is most commonly associated with. Here the focus is on the immediate environment in which the social enterprise activity operates or is perceived to operate. In Japan, where companies are equally involved in the concept of social enterprise and economic as well as social benefit is highlighted, the market economy is the most relevant sphere. In Argentina, where social enterprise has taken on a grassroots role of meeting citizen

TABLE 9.2. *The Emphasis of Social Enterprise in Four Areas: Market (M), Civil Society (CS), State (S), and International Aid (I)*

	United States	Western Europe	Japan	East-Central Europe	Argentina	Zimbabwe/ Zambia	Sout Asia
Outcome emphasis	M	CS	CS, M	CS	CS, (M)	M	M
Common org. type	CS, (M)	CS, (M)	CS, M	CS, (M)	CS, (M)	M	M, C
Societal sector	M	CS	M	CS	CS	M	M
Strategic development base	M	S	S	I, (S)	CS, (I)	I	I, M
Social enterprise model	Market/ Civil society	Civil society/ State	Civil society/ Market/ State	Civil society/ Int'l aid	Civil society	Market/ Int'l aid	Marl Civil soci Int'l

Note: Letters appearing in parentheses indicate the lower prominence of a given area.

needs, it falls into that part of civil society commonly referred to as the social economy (the same as in East-Central and Western Europe).

Finally, the sixth variable, *strategic development base*, focuses on the source of funding and development initiatives for social enterprise in a given region. In the United States this base is clearly the private foundation and business world, with limited government involvement. In Zimbabwe and Zambia, by contrast, this base mostly consists of international aid programs implemented by foreign organizations and governments.

The next step in creating the regional/country social enterprise models was to relate the regional characterizations in table 9.1 to the four factors most often associated with the functioning of social enterprise: market, civil society, international aid, and state (see chapter 1 this volume).[1] Thus, table 9.2 synthesizes the regional characterizations in table 9.1 with the emphasis they place on the four factors. For example, for the variable *outcome emphasis* we asked: what *immediate* benefit is social enterprise oriented toward in the region? Is it more of a market benefit in terms of revenue, or is it considered more of a civil society benefit in support of a collective group of citizens? For common *organizational type* we asked the question: are the most visible organizational types used for social enter-

ᴜʀᴇ 9.1. *Relative Placement of Social Enterprise for
·en World Regions and Countries with Regard to Market,
·te, Civil Society, and International Aid*

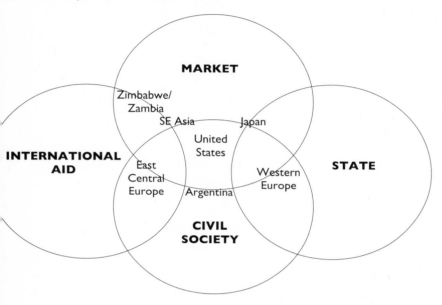

prise more civil society–based or market-based? The relevance of the last two factors, *societal sector* and *strategic development base*, to the four factors is readily apparent. Two variables, *program focus* and *legal framework*, were not considered because they were found to focus similarly on one of the four factors across all geographic locations. The last row in table 9.2 shows the composite model for social enterprise for each region/country. Figure 9.1 illustrates these findings by showing where social enterprise in each region falls with respect to other regions for market, civil society, international aid, and state.

THE SOCIOECONOMIC ENVIRONMENT
FOR SOCIAL ENTERPRISE

The socioeconomic environment for social enterprise in the seven world regions and countries was also found to vary significantly across the four areas of market, international aid, state, and civil society. Data for each of these areas was collected from a number of sources, including the

FIGURE 9.2. *Countries Included in the Three World Regions*

Western Europe	East-Central Europe	Southeast Asia
Austria	Albania	Bangladesh
Belgium	Bosnia & Herzegovina	Cambodia
Denmark	Bulgaria	Indonesia
Finland	Croatia	Laos
France	Czech Republic	Malaysia
Germany	Hungary	Philippines
Ireland	Macedonia, FYR	Singapore
Italy	Poland	Thailand
Netherlands	Romania	Vietnam
Norway	Serbia & Montenegro	
Portugal	Slovak Republic	
Spain	Slovenia	
Sweden		
Switzerland		
United Kingdom		

World Bank's World Development Indicators, Transparency International, Freedom House, and the Johns Hopkins Comparative Nonprofit Sector Project. For each of the four areas, one to two indicators were used to represent the general presence or functioning of that area, as shown in table 9.3 (footnotes for each indicator provide detailed information on data sources, definitions, and exceptions). The regional values and scores for each indicator shown in the table are composites of individual country information. The countries included in each of the three regions are found in figure 9.2.

These regional composite figures were each given a rating of one to four to reflect their position relative to one another, with one being the lowest and four the highest (these ratings are found in parentheses next to the composite figures). An overall rating was then given for each of the four areas, which in most cases involved taking the average of the ratings for the composite figures. These overall ratings are found in bold in table 9.3, along with the relevant description of that rating, ranging from weak to strong.

9.3. *Ratings of the Socioeconomic Environments in World Regions and Countries*

	United States	Western Europe	Japan	East-Central Europe	Argentina	Zimbabwe/ Zambia	Southeast Asia
P, PPP, per ternational	$36,465 (4)	28,072 (4)	26,884 (3)	11,039 (2)	7,483 (1)	1,383 (1)	6,501 (1)
ed capital n, per	$6,616 (3)	4,492 (3)	9,182 (4)	895 (1)	897 (1)	64 (1)	275 (1)
unctioning	3.5 Strong	3.5 Strong	3.5 Strong	1.5 Weak	1 Weak	1 Weak	1 Weak
onal aid, per	n/a	n/a	n/a	$72	2	54	15
onal aid	None	None	None	4 Strong	1 Weak	3 Mostly strong	1 Weak
of n/ health ending, %	6.5% (4)	6.4 (4)	5.0 (3)	5.0 (3)	4.0 (1)	3.3 (1)	3.9 (1)
on one[e] upt, 10 =	7.5 (4)	8.0 (4)	6.9 (3)	3.7 (1)	2.5 (1)	2.5 (1)	3.8 (2)
ability	4 Strong	4 Strong	3 Mostly strong	2 Mostly weak	1 Weak	1 Weak	1.5 Weak
rties[f] 7 = not free)	1 (4)	1 (4)	2 (3)	1.8 (4)	2 (3)	5 (1)	4.3 (1)
vil society[g] ore (1–100)	61 (4)	52 (4)	36 (2)	26 (1)	40 (2)	36 ? (2)	27 (1)
iety rating	4 Strong	4 Strong	2.5 Moderate	2.5 Moderate	2.5 Moderate	1.5 Weak	1 Weak

a–g appear at the end of this chapter.

Table 9.4 compares the different social enterprise models for each of the regions with their corresponding ratings for the four socioeconomic factors of market functioning, international aid, state capability, and civil society. The comparison finds, almost without exception, that the strongest socioeconomic factors for each region are reflected in that region's social enterprise model.

For the United States and Western Europe, both of which are strong in the three areas of market, state, and civil society, their social enterprise models reflect two of the three strengths. While both share the strength of civil society in social enterprise, the second strength for the United States is the market, while for Western Europe it is the state. This difference is likely explained by long traditions of market reliance in the United States and state intervention in Western Europe. Japan's mixed social enterprise model, showing characteristics of market, civil society, and state (likely influenced by Western Europe and United States models of social enterprise), plays on those same strengths in its environment.

Though closely following Western Europe in use and type, East-Central Europe varies in its source of support for social enterprise. The high levels of international aid that shore up this transitioning region are also found to be the main source of support for a small but growing social enterprise movement there. By contrast, in Argentina, civil society was the one socioeconomic factor that showed an elevated level and thus, not too surprisingly, civil society appears to completely define social enterprise in that region.

Southern Africa displays an interesting phenomenon: though social enterprise is accurately associated with high levels of international aid in the region, its association with the market does not match the weak market situation there. One explanation may be that international donors, interested in finding solutions for weak markets and poverty, are pushing the more market-oriented concept of social enterprise involving microcredit institutions and small enterprise, thereby making it a dominant model there. Finally, Southeast Asia, with its mixed social enterprise model, was found to be weak on all four socioeconomic factors. This widespread weakness may in fact explain why social enterprise in southern Africa shows no clear focus on any one area. Because all areas there are weak, social enterprise draws a little from where it can, resulting in a mixed social enterprise model.

CONCLUSION

Though a modern movement for social enterprise appears to be developing simultaneously in many places around the world, there are important regional differences in what the term means and how it is supported and developed. As the analysis in this chapter shows, differences in the regions appear to be explained at least in part by the variation in regional socioeconomic contexts. Importantly, social enterprise appears to draw on those dominant socioeconomic factors that offer the most strength in a given region or country. These findings suggest that the development of social enterprise follows along lines similar to those for the development of nonprofit sectors described by Salamon, Sokolowski, and Anheier's (2000) social origins approach.[2] Indeed, it appears that existing social structures and institutions shape and dictate the options available for the development of social enterprise, leading to different organizational models in different areas.

Several important practical implications arise from the global comparison of the social enterprise concept and its context. In addition to facilitating understanding among social enterprise actors from different regions, this comparison provides a basis for the exchange of innovative ideas. These might include both social enterprise activities and broader policies for their support. However, given the demonstrated importance of the context of social enterprise, the comparison also suggests that a transplanted idea should be matched with a context that closely resembles its original environment. For example, a social enterprise activity that draws heavily on civil society and the market in its originating region may be best suited for regions that have similar socioeconomic strengths. Where there is not a match, implementers should be alerted to the need to adjust the activity to make use of the dominant strengths of the region. Such matching or adjusting of transferred social enterprise initiatives to their new environment may lead to their improved sustainability.

Indeed, several of the studies in this volume illustrate that the concept of social enterprise as understood in one part of the world can be transferred to other regions and used to identify new and existing organizations that fit within the concept. These studies show, however, that the concept is often adjusted to fit with the immediate culture and environment, leading

TABLE 9.4. *Comparative Overview of Social Enterprise Models and Four Socioeconomic Factors for Seven World Regions and Countries*

	United States	Western Europe	Japan	East-Central Europe	Argentina	Zimbabwe/ Zambia	Southeast Asia
Social enterprise model	Civil society/ Market	Civil society/ State	Civil society/ Market/ State	Civil society/ Int'l aid	Civil society	Market/ Int'l aid	Market/ Civil society/ Int'l aid
Market performance	Strong	Strong	Strong	Weak	Weak	Weak	Weak
International aid	None	None	None	Strong	Weak	Mostly strong	Weak
State capability	Strong	Strong	Mostly strong	Mostly weak	Weak	Weak	Weak
Civil society	Strong	Strong	Moderate	Moderate	Moderate	Weak	Weak

to unique models. Specific social enterprise activities have also been transferred and developed in new contexts. The chapters on East-Central Europe, Japan, and Zimbabwe and Zambia best illustrate aspects of these processes. It is important to note that the discussions in these chapters indicate that viable transfers have been accomplished through the involvement, and many times the initiative, of the people and countries themselves.

Finally, though more detailed analysis is necessary, the research in this volume suggests that domestic and international actors interested in the development of social enterprise may also want to support the in-country replication of existing grassroots social enterprise initiatives and leverage specific regional or country strengths and structures in their support. Indeed, the in-country replication of local social enterprises and the shoring up of the strengths they draw on in their present environments may prove to be an important, effective approach to the rapid and sustainable expansion of social enterprise in diverse contexts.

NOTES

1. Nicholls (2006) uses market, civil society, and state to characterize and differentiate social entrepreneurship in different regions of the world. Nyssens (2006) also draws on these three elements in her discussion of social enterprise in Europe.

2. See the introduction to this volume for a discussion of the social origins approach.

NOTES TO TABLE 9.3

a. Source: World Development Indicators, World Bank, International Comparison Programme database, 2006. Data are from 2004. Notes: GDP per capita based on purchasing power parity (PPP), or GDP PPP, is gross domestic product converted to international dollars using purchasing power parity rates. An international dollar has the same purchasing power over GDP as the U.S. dollar has in the United States. GDP at purchaser's prices is the sum of gross value added by all resident producers in the economy plus any product taxes and minus any subsidies not included in the value of the products. It is calculated without making deductions for depreciation of fabricated assets or for depletion and degradation of natural resources. Data are in constant 2000 international dollars. Serbia and Montenegro was omitted due to lack of available data.

b. Source: World Development Indicators, World Bank national accounts data, and OECD National Accounts data files, 2006. Data are from 2004 except where indicated. Notes: Gross fixed capital formation consists of outlays on additions to the fixed assets of the economy plus net changes in the level of inventories. Fixed assets include land improvements (fences, ditches, drains, etc.); plant, machinery, and equipment purchases; and the construction of roads, railways, and the like, including schools, offices, hospitals, private residential dwellings, and commercial and industrial buildings. Inventories are stocks of goods held by firms to meet temporary or unexpected fluctuations in production or sales, and "work in progress." According to the 1993 SNA, net acquisitions of valuables are also considered capital formation. Data are in constant 2000 U.S. dollars. Gross fixed capital formation per capita is calculated by dividing total gross capital formation by the population estimate. The following countries were omitted due to lack of available data: France and Laos. Data for Switzerland and the United States are from 2003.

c. Source: World Development Indicators, Development Assistance Committee of the Organization for Economic Co-operation and Development, and World Bank population estimates, 2006. All data are from 2004. Notes: International aid per capita includes both official development assistance (ODA) and official aid and is calculated by dividing total aid by the midyear population estimate. The following countries were not included because they do not receive international aid: Austria, Belgium, Denmark, Finland, France, Germany, Indonesia, Ireland, Italy, Japan, the Netherlands, Norway, Portugal, Spain, Switzerland, Sweden, Thailand, United Kingdom, and the United States.

d. Source: World Development Indicators. Education spending data are from the United Nations Educational, Scientific, and Cultural Organization (UNESCO) Institute for Statistics. Health spending data are from the World Health Organization, World Health Report and updates, and from the OECD for its member countries, supplemented by World Bank poverty assessments and country and sector studies. Education spending data are from 2002 except for the following countries: Laos (2003), Thailand (2001), Zambia (2001), and Zimbabwe (2000). All health spending data are from 2003. Notes: Public expenditure on education consists of current and capital public expenditure on education plus subsidies to private education at the primary, secondary, and tertiary levels. Public health expenditure consists of recurrent and capital spending from government (central and local) budgets, external borrowings and grants (including donations from international agencies and nongovernmental organizations), and social (or compulsory) health insurance funds. The following countries were omitted from the public education spending total due to lack of available data: Bosnia and Herzegovina, and Serbia and Montenegro.

e. Source: Transparency International Annual Report's Corruption Perceptions Index (CPI), 2004. Notes: From Transparency International's 2004 Annual Report. "The Corruption Perceptions Index is a poll of polls, reflecting the perceptions of business people and country analysts, both resident and nonresident. The 2004 index draws on 18 surveys provided to Transparency International between 2002 and 2004, conducted by 12 independent institutions." The CPI score ranges from 0 (highly corrupt) to 10 (highly clean). Laos was omitted due to lack of available data.

f. Source: Freedom House (2005), *Freedom in the World*, survey for the period covering December 1, 2003, through November 30, 2004. Notes: The Civil Liberties Index score rates each country according to its residents' freedoms of assembly, association, education, religion, and expression. The score ranges from 1 (highest level of freedom) to 7 (lowest level of freedom).

g. Source: Johns Hopkins Comparative Nonprofit Sector Project via Salamon et al. (2004). Notes: The Global Civil Society Index Score is composed of three scores from three different dimensions of the civil society sector: capacity, sustainability, and impact. Capacity measures the ability of an individual country's civil society sector to mobilize. Sustainability measures the ability of the civil society sector to sustain such mobilization. Impact measures the contribution of the civil society sector to the broader society. Data for countries in this index were collected in 1995 for most of the countries and between 1997 and 2000 for the rest. No data was available for the following countries: Albania, Bosnia and Herzegovina, Bulgaria, Croatia, Denmark, Indonesia, Laos, Macedonia, Malaysia, Portugal, Serbia and Montenegro, Slovenia, Switzerland, Thailand, Vietnam, Zambia, and Zimbabwe. The following countries were substituted for Zambia and Zimbabwe: Kenya, Tanzania, and Uganda. Southeast Asia was represented in the data solely by the Philippines.

REFERENCES

Borzaga, C., & Defourny, J. (2001). Conclusions: Social enterprises in Europe: A diversity of initiatives and prospects. In C. Borzaga & J. Defourny (Eds.), *The emergence of social enterprise* (pp. 350–370). New York: Routledge.

Chabal, P., & Daloz, J. (1999). *Africa works: Disorder as political instrument*. Oxford: International African Institute in association with James Currey.

Crimmins, J. C., & Keil, M. (1983). *Enterprise in the nonprofit sector*. New York: The Rockefeller Brothers Fund.

Eikenberry, A., & Kluver, J. (2004). The marketization of the nonprofit sector: Civil society at risk? *Public Administration Review, 64*(2), pp. 132–140.

Nicholls, A. (Ed.) (2006). *Social entrepreneurship: New models of sustainable change.* Oxford: Oxford University Press.

Nyssens, M. (2006). *Social enterprise: At the crossroads of market, public policies and civil society.* New York: Routledge.

Salamon, L. (1993). The marketization of welfare: Changing nonprofit and for-profit roles in the American welfare state. *Social Service Review, 67*(1), pp. 16–39.

——. (1997). *Holding the center: America's nonprofit sector at a crossroads.* New York: Nathan Cummings Foundation.

Salamon, L. S., Sokolowski, W., & Anheier, H. K. (2000). *Social origins of civil society: An overview.* Working paper of the Johns Hopkins Comparative Nonprofit Sector Project, no. 38. Baltimore: Johns Hopkins Center for Civil Society Studies.

Salamon, L., et al. (2004). *Global civil society: Dimensions of the nonprofit sector, volume 2.* Bloomfield, CT: Kumarian Press.

Index

Page numbers in italics refer to figures or tables.

Abbas, Muchtar, 83
Abed, Fazle Hazan, 71
AbilityOne program, 99
Abramovich, A. L., 144
ACA (Argentine Association of Cooperatives), 146
academia: vs. nonprofit practitioner perspectives, 87–90; support for social enterprise, 23, 45–46, 100, 174–75
Act on Social Cooperatives, 42, 50
ACT UP (AIDS Coalition to Unleash Power), 106
ACTUS (Association for Vocational and Social Reintegration of the Handicapped), 58–59
advocacy role of NGOs: Argentina, 148–49; East-Central Europe, 49; in social democratic model of association, 24, 25; Southeast Asia, 69; United States, 101, 105; Zimbabwe, 123
Agenzia Socialle, 30
Agricola M. S. Pantaleone Cooperative, 30
agricultural assistance services: Argentina, 146–47, 148; East-Central Europe, 39, 40, 53; Southeast Asia, 65, 70, 73–74, 76–77; United States, 93–94; Western Europe, 29; Zimbabwe and Zambia, 127, 136–37
AIDS Coalition to Unleash Power (ACT UP), 106
AIDS services, 105–6
Alter, Kim, 115, 116, 117
Anheier, H. K., 3–5, 195
Arboleda, Justino, 65
Argentina: analysis, 140, 145–58, 158n2;

conceptual issues, 139, 141–42; cooperatives, 139, 140, 144–57, 159n7; historical perspective, 139–45, 186; informal economic sector, 144, 158–59n3; legal frameworks, 142–44, 145, 152–54, 157; overview, 8–9; recuperated companies, 151–57; socioeconomic environment, *193, 194, 196*; supporting institutions, 144–46, 186
Argentine Association of Cooperatives (ACA), 146
Asia. *See* Japan; Southeast Asia
Association for Vocational and Social Reintegration of the Handicapped (ACTUS), 58–59
associations: Argentina, 146; citizen, 51; East-Central Europe, 41, 47, 49–50, 51, 58–59; Japan (hôjin), 167, 168, 169–70, 173; in social democratic model, 24, 25; Southeast Asia, 73, 74; United States, 100; Western Europe, 18, 22–23, 24, 29–30; Zimbabwe and Zambia, 115, 123, 125–26, 131. *See also* cooperatives; foundations; mutual benefit societies; nongovernmental organizations (NGOs); nonprofit organizations
Atmark Learning Co., Ltd., 170
Autre Terre ASBL, 28

Bacani, Senen, 73–74
Bangladesh, 66–67, 70–71, 75, 77, 78
Bangladesh Rural Advancement Committee (BRAC), 71, 75, 78
Barka (Polish Foundation of Mutual Help), 37
Basaglia, Franco, 29
Belgium, 18–19, 27–28

Ben and Jerry's, 93
The Big Issue Japan, 170
Bina Swadaya Foundation, 71–72, 73, 77
Boccoli, Felipe, 149–50
Bombal, I. G., 146
Boonngamanong, Sombat, 69
Boschee, Jerr, 88
BRAC (Bangladesh Rural Advancement
    Committee), 71, 75, 78
Bradach, J., 95
Brukman Company (18th of December
    Work Cooperative), 155–57
Bulgaria, 38
businesses. *See* for-profit businesses

Cabbages and Condoms Restaurants, 74
CAC (Center for Active Community), 174
El Calafate telephone cooperative, 150
Cambodia, 67, 75, 77
Campetella, A., 146
CAMPFIRE (Communal Areas Manage-
    ment Program for Indigenous
    Resources), 131
capacity building: Argentina, 144–45, 154,
    157; East-Central Europe, 45–46, 58;
    Japan, 179, 180–81; as social enterprise
    factor, 5; Southeast Asia, 78–79, 81; Zim-
    babwe and Zambia, 122, 134, 186
Caritas (Serbian religious network), 52
Cassano, D., 142
cause-related marketing, 92, 104
CCIJ (Consumer Cooperative Institute of
    Japan), 165, 174
Center for Active Community (CAC), 174
CFC (Couples for Christ), 79
Chabal, P., 122
charity vs. social enterprise models, 75, 101
citizen associations, 51
civil society: class and size of, 4; cross-
    country comparison, 185–86, *188*, 189;
    East-Central Europe, 41; size and non-
    profit sector, 4; as social enterprise factor,
    5; socioeconomic environment, 191–92,
    193, 195, *196*; Southeast Asia, 68, 70, 72;

United States, 94–95, 103; Western
    Europe, 17; Zimbabwe and Zambia, 126
Coalition for Social Enterprise, 20
co-branding, 92
Cocotech, 65
Collective Self-Finance Scheme (CSFS), 135–
    36
La Collina Cooperative Sociale, 30
Communal Areas Management Program for
    Indigenous Resources (CAMPFIRE), 131
communism's repression of nonprofit sec-
    tor, 39–40
Community Action Network, 23
community business (Japan), 164, 169
community interest company (UK), 19
community rehabilitation programs, 99
Community Wind Power Co., Ltd., 170
conceptual issues for social enterprise:
    Argentina, 139, 141–42; diversity in, 1–2,
    xv–xvi; East-Central Europe, 35–39;
    Japan, 163–66; overview, xii–xvi; South-
    east Asia, 64–67; United States, 87–94;
    Western Europe, 12–16; Zimbabwe and
    Zambia, 114–19
Confederación Intercooperativa Agroper-
    cuaria (CONINAGRO), 146–47
Consorzio per I'Impresa Sociale, 27–28
Consumer Cooperative Institute of Japan
    (CCIJ), 165, 174
contracting out public services to social
    enterprises, 21–22, 44, 49, 55
cooperatives: Argentina, 139, 140, 144–57,
    159n7; East-Central Europe, 41, 42, 43–
    44, 45, 47–48, 50, 52–53, 58–60; Japan,
    165, 169–70, 171, 172, 174; Southeast
    Asia, 67, 72–73; Western Europe, 12, 15,
    17, 18–19, 20, 29–31; Zimbabwe and
    Zambia, 114, 126–27. *See also* social
    cooperatives
corporate philanthropy, 69, 88, 94, 170
corporate social responsibility (CSR), 13, 88,
    93, 116, 131, 170
corporations. *See* for-profit businesses
corporatist regimes, 4, 24

Co-terre safs, 28
Couples for Christ (CFC), 79
Crea Cooperative Sociale, 30
credit and loan unions (Argentina), 147
credit availability, group credit method, 66–
    67. *See also* microcredit lending
cross-regional comparison: and definitional
    issues for social enterprise, 1–2; of social
    enterprise, 184–87, *188*, 189–92, *193*,
    195, 196, 197; and social science
    research, 3. *See also individual regions or
    countries*
CSFS (Collective Self-Finance Scheme), 135–
    36
CSR (corporate social responsibility), 13, 88,
    93, 116, 131, 170
Czech Republic, 41, 44

Dacanay, Marie Lisa, 64, 78
Daloz, J., 122
DAPP (Development Aid from People to
    People), 116, 118–19
Datamation Consultants, 77
DDD (Digital Divide Data), 67
Dees, J. G., 163
Defourny, J., 12, 15, 140, 141
democratic governance of organizations, 15,
    36, 55, 60, 78, 120, 141, 158. *See also*
    cooperatives
Denmark, 20
Department for International Development
    (DFID), British, 130–31, 132
Development Aid from People to People
    (DAPP), 116, 118–19
DGCI (General Direction to Cooperation
    and Development), 28
Digestus Project, 19
Digital Divide Data (DDD), 67, 77
disabilities, services for persons with, 53–54,
    58–60, 99, 177–79
disadvantaged groups, helping: Argentina,
    141, 143, 144, 152, 158n2; East-Central
    Europe, 35, 39, 42, 50, 52–53, 54, 55;
    Japan, 166, 175–79; Southeast Asia, 66–

68, 70, 71, 76–77, 79–84; United States,
    103, 105–7; Western Europe, 18, 22, 26–
    28, 31; Zimbabwe and Zambia, 114, 116,
    117, 122, 123–24, 134–35
disaster relief projects, 71, 77–78
distribution of wealth, 35, 76, 123
dual-purpose (hybrid) businesses, 87–88,
    93–94

earned income for social enterprises: Argen-
    tina, 147–48; East-Central Europe, 48–
    49; Japan, 168, 176, 178, 181n1; sources
    overview, 184–85; Southeast Asia, 74;
    United States, 90–93, 103–5; Western
    Europe, 28, 30; Zimbabwe and Zambia,
    114, 116, 121
East-Central Europe: analysis, 45–59; con-
    ceptual issues, 35–39; historical perspec-
    tive, 39–41, 185–86; Lastavica NGO
    example, 57–58; legal framework, 36,
    41–45, 50, 54, 55; organizational forms,
    35–37; overview, 7; socioeconomic
    environment, *193, 194, 196*; supporting
    institutions, 39, 45–55, 185–86; WWW
    Promotion example, 58–59
economic dimension, social enterprise's role
    in: Argentina, 140, 143–44, 158–
    59nn1,3; cross-regional summary, *188*,
    189–90, 191–92, *193, 195, 196*; East-
    Central Europe, 35, 38–39, 43, 47–49,
    58; Southeast Asia, 65, 74–75; United
    States, 15–16; Western Europe, 15–16;
    Zimbabwe and Zambia, 116–17, 129–30
Economy, P., 163
Ecumenical Support Services (ESS), 123
education and training services: Argentina,
    145; East-Central Europe, 45–46, 48, 53–
    54, 55; Japan, 170; Southeast Asia, 67,
    68, 69, 71, 75, 77; United States, 98, 100;
    Western Europe, 18, 27–28; Zimbabwe
    and Zambia, 151
18th of December Work Cooperative (Bruk-
    man Company), 155–57
Emerson, J., 163

EMES criteria, 35, 36
EMES Research Network, 12–16, 23, 163–64, 165
employment services: Argentina, 141, 151–57; East-Central Europe, 37, 42, 44, 47–48, 50, 53–54, 58–60; Japan, 166, 170, 178; Southeast Asia, 67, 68, 77; United States, 99; Western Europe, 17–18, 19–20, 27–28, 29–31; Zimbabwe and Zambia, 117, 119
empowerment strategy: East-Central Europe, 59; Southeast Asia, 64–65, 66, 67, 72, 74, 82; Zimbabwe and Zambia, 115, 131
ENDA (Environmental Development Agency), 132
Entrepreneurial Development Trust, 117
entrepreneurial dynamic in social economy. *See* social enterprise; social entrepreneur/entrepreneurship
Entrepreneurs School of Asia (ESA), 77
entrepreneur support model (Africa), 117
Entre Ríos Confederation of Cooperatives, 146
environmental considerations, 65–66, 90, 155
Environmental Development Agency (ENDA), 132
EQUAL Development Partnership, 46, 48
ESA (Entrepreneurs School of Asia), 77
Esping-Anderson, G., 4
ESS (Ecumenical Support Services), 123
Europe. *See* East-Central Europe; Western Europe
European Research Institute on Cooperative and Social Enterprises (EURICSE), 45
European Union (EU), 19, 22, 40, 50, 54

Fajn, G., 152
farming assistance services. *See* agricultural assistance services
501(c)(3) charity legal framework, 101
501(c)(4) social welfare legal framework, 101

Florence nonprofit organization, 168–69
for-profit businesses: Argentina (recuperated companies), 145, 151-157; Japan, 170, 171–72, 173–74, 176–77, 179; partnerships with NGOs/nonprofits, 65, 91, 92–93, 94, 104; small and medium-sized enterprises, 36, 42, 54, 66, 134–35, 147; Southeast Asia, 65, 66; as subsidiaries for income production, 90–92, 170, 171, 176, 177–78; United States, 87–88, 90–94, 97–102; Zimbabwe and Zambia, 125, 130–31, 132, 133–34. *See also* microcredit lending
Foster, W., 95
foundations: Argentina, 142; East-Central Europe, 37, 47, 49–50; Japan, 167; Southeast Asia, 65, 69, 71–72, 73, 77; United States, 89, 98, 100
France, 18, 19, 26
Frumkin, P., 167–68
La Frutera Inc., 73, 76
Funnybee Co., Ltd, 176–77

Gawad Kalinga, 68, 73, 74, 77–78, 79–82
General Direction to Cooperation and Development (DGCI), 28
Georgia Justice Project (GJP), 106–7
global comparative perspective, 2–3. *See also* cross-regional comparison
Global Knowledge Partnership (GKP), 69
governmental institutions: Argentina, 142, 143–46, 148–49; cross-regional comparison, 185–87, *188*, 190, 191–92, *193*, 195, *196*; East-Central Europe, 37, 39–40; Japan, 169, 173, 176, 177, 178–79; Southeast Asia, 66, 68, 70, 72, 73, 74–76, 80, 83–84; support for social enterprise, 3, 4, 5; United States, 95, *96*, 97, 98–99, 102, 104; Western Europe, 16, 19–23, 24–27; Zimbabwe and Zambia, 115–16, 120–25, 122, 186. *See also* legal frameworks; supporting institutions
Grameen Bank, 66–67, 77
Greece, 18

group credit method, 66–67
Groupe Terre, 27–28

health care services: Southeast Asia, 70–71,
73, 74, 77, 80; United States, 105–6;
Western Europe, 18, 30
historical perspectives: Argentina, 139–45,
186; cross-regional comparison, 184–87;
East-Central Europe, 39–41, 185–86;
Japan, 166–70, 187; social entrepreneur/
entrepreneurship, xi–xii; Southeast Asia,
67–72, 186–87; United States, 94–97,
185; Western Europe, 16–19, 185; Zimbabwe and Zambia, 119–25, 186
Hivos (Humanist Institute for Cooperation
with Developing Countries), 130
Hockerts, K., 2
hôjin (Japanese nonprofits), 167, 168, 169–
70, 173
Hokkaido Green Fund, 169–70
Hosouchi, N., 164
housing projects, 68, 79–82, 92, 105–6
Housing Works, 92, 105–6
Housing Works Bookstore Café, 106
Housing Works Thrift Shops, 106
Humanist Institute for Cooperation with
Developing Countries (Hivos), 130
Hungary, 41
hybrid (dual-purpose) businesses, 87–88,
93–94

IDE (International Development Enterprises), 136–37
Il Posto Delle Fragole Cooperative, 30
Imwasan, Bambang, 72
INAES (National Institute of Activism and
Social Economy), 144–46
Indonesia, 75
informal economic sector, 129–30, 144, 158–
59n3
Institutio Movilizador de Fondos Cooperativos, 147
integration, socioeconomic: Argentina, 148–
49, 152; East-Central Europe, 36, 37, 42,

48, 58–59; Japan, 166, 169; Western
Europe, 17–18, 19–20, 26
intermediation strategy, 64, 65, 66, 67
internal commercial venture (U.S.), 90
international aid: Argentina, 143–44; cross-
country comparison, 188, 189; East-
Central Europe, 37, 51–52; as social
enterprise factor, 4, 5; socioeconomic
environment, 191–92, 193, 195, 196;
Southeast Asia, 75; Zimbabwe and Zambia, 121–22, 130–31, 135
international comparative perspective, 2–3.
See also cross-regional comparison
International Development Enterprises
(IDE), 136–37
INTI (National Institute of Industrial Technology), 145
Ireland, 22, 26
Italy, 12, 19, 27–28

Japan: analysis, 175–81, 181n1; conceptual
issues, 163–66; diversity of, 170–72; historical perspective, 166–70, 187; legal
frameworks, 164, 166, 167–68, 169,
172–73; overview, 9–10; Palette example,
177–80; Sanagitachi Project example,
175–77, 179–80; socioeconomic environment, 193, 194, 196; supporting institutions, 169, 173–75, 176, 177, 187
Java, 71–72
Javits-Wagner-O'Day (JWOD) Act, 99
Jensen, Jane Broen, 116
Juboken Enterprises, 65
JWOD (Javits-Wagner-O'Day) Act, 99

Kalinga Luzon, 74
Kanto Bureau of METI, 173
Kerlin, J., 97, 104
King, R, 127
Kobayashi, Kaori, 65

labor policies (Western Europe), 19–20, 26
LAG (Lobbying and Advocacy Group), 123
Landrieu, Mitch, 99–100

Laos, 67, 75
Lastavica NGO, 57–58
Latin America. *See* Argentina
Lavoratori Uniti Cooperative, 30
Law on the Agency for the Development of Small and Medium-Sized Enterprises (SMES), 54
Law to Promote Specified Nonprofit Activities (NPO Law), 167
Leadbeater, C., 164–65
legal frameworks: Argentina, 142–44, 145, 152–54, 157; democratic governance of organizations, 15, 36, 55, 60, 78, 120, 141, 158; East-Central Europe, 36, 41–45, 50, 54, 55; Japan, 164, 166, 167–68, 169, 172–73; by region, *188*, 191; Southeast Asia, 72–74; United States, 101–2; Western Europe, 18, 27, 30–31; Zimbabwe and Zambia, 123, 125–30. *See also* organizational arrangements
liberal regimes, 4, 24–25. *See also* United Kingdom; United States
Light, P. C., 89
Light Engineering Workshops, 134–35
limited liability company (LLC) (U.S.), 101–2
limited liability cooperatives (Africa), 126
limited profit distribution criterion, 14
Lithuania, 42
LLC (limited liability company) (U.S.), 101–2
Lobbying and Advocacy Group (LAG), 123
low-profit limited liability company (L³C) (U.S.), 102
Łuksja, 59–60

Machida, Y., 164–65
Mair, J., 2
Maireang Farmers' Group, 76–77
Makumbe, J., 116
Malaysia, 69, 74–75
Manchester-Bidwell Corporation, 92
manufacturing in Argentina, social enterprises in, 151–57
market-based approaches: Argentina, 140–

43, 155, 157–58, 158n2; East-Central Europe, 35, 38–39, 49, 55; Japan, 168, 177, 178, 179–80; United States, 87–88, 103–4; Western Europe, 13, 18, 21–22, 24–25, 29; Zimbabwe and Zambia, 117, 121, 133–35
market economy, *188*, 189–90, 191–92, *193*, 195, *196*. *See also* Japan; Southeast Asia; United States; Zimbabwe and Zambia
market functioning as social enterprise factor, 4, 5, 194, *196*
marketing partnerships, nonprofit/for-profit, 92–93, 104
market intermediation (Africa), 117, *120*
market linkage model (Africa), 116–19
MCYS (Ministry of Community Development, Youth, and Sports), 70
MDA (Mine Workers Development Agency), 132
membership organizations. *See* associations
MFIS (microfinance institutions) (Africa), 125, 130–31, 132, 133–34
microcredit lending: Southeast Asia, 66–67, 72, 83–84; Zimbabwe and Zambia, 125, 130–31, 132, 133–34
microfinance institutions (MFIS) (Africa), 125, 130–31, 132, 133–34
Mine Workers Development Agency (MDA), 132
Ministry of Community Development, Youth, and Sports (MCYS), 70
Mirror Foundation, 69, 77
mission and social enterprise: Argentina, 141–42; Japan, 165–66, 167, 170, 180–81; Southeast Asia, 66, 73; United States, 87–88, 93–94, 101, 103; Western Europe, 12, 14, 15–16, 19, 21–22, 26; Zimbabwe and Zambia, 114, 115–16
Mitra Usaha Mandiri (MUM), 77, 82–84, 90–91, 93–94
MNER (Movimiento Nacional de Empresas Recuperadas), 151–57
Moore, Barrington, 4
Morato, Eduardo, 64

Movimiento Nacional de Empresas Recuperadas (MNER), 151–57
Moyo, S., 116
multiple stakeholder ownership, 15, 19
MUM (Mitra Usaha Mandiri), 77, 82–84
mutual benefit societies: Argentina, 139–40, 144–45, 146; East-Central Europe, 36, 37, 51, 59; Zimbabwe and Zambia, 125–26
Mwengo, 123

National Association of Nongovernmental Organizations (NANGO), 123
National Constitutional Assembly (NCA), 123
National Institute of Activism and Social Economy (INAES), 144–46
National Institute of Industrial Technology (INTI), 145
Native Welfare Society, 125–26
NCA (National Constitutional Assembly), 123
NEC, 170
Net Impact, 101
New Community Corporation, 92
New Horizon Landscaping, 107
NGOs (nongovernmental organizations). See nongovernmental organizations (NGOs)
Nigeria, 127
nondistribution constraint on nonprofit organization, 13, 14, 43, 101
nongovernmental organizations (NGOs): advocacy role of, 24, 25, 49, 69, 101, 105, 123, 148–49; East-Central Europe, 38, 51, 57–58; vs. social enterprises, 115–16; Southeast Asia, 65, 68, 76; Zimbabwe and Zambia, 114, 122–25, 127–29. See also nonprofit organizations
nonprofit conglomerate, 91–92
nonprofit organizations: vs. academic perspective, 87–90; Argentina, 141–42; East-Central Europe, 38–41, 46–50; for-profit subsidiaries of, 90–92, 170, 171, 176, 177–78; Japan (hôjin), 164, 166,

167–70, 171, 172, 173, 174–77; non-distribution constraint, 13, 14, 43, 101; partnerships with for-profit businesses, 91, 92–93, 94, 104; quid pro quo organizations, 92–93; research on, 100; size of nonprofit sector, 3, 4; Southeast Asia, 68, 73, 75–76, 78; United States, 13–16, 87–93, 95, 96, 97, 102–5, 103; use of social enterprise, 184–85; Western Europe, 12, 13–16, 17, 25–26, 36; Zimbabwe and Zambia, 115, 116–17
Nordic countries, 24, 25
NPO Law (Law to Promote Specified Non-profit Activities), 167
Nyssens, M., 12

Office of Social Entrepreneurship, 99–100
Ogura, Masao, 170
O'Hara, P., 22
Open Research Center Project, 174
organizational arrangements: democratic governance, 15, 36, 55, 60, 78, 120, 141, 158; for-profit businesses, 90–94, 104, 170, 171, 176, 177–78; mutual benefit societies, 36, 37, 51, 59, 125–26, 139–40, 144–45, 146; by region, 188, 189, 190–91; religious-based, 51–52, 73, 79; self-help groups, 38, 51, 72. See also associations; cooperatives; foundations; non-governmental organizations (NGOs); nonprofit organizations
Osaka Social Entrepreneurs Support Program, 173
outcome emphasis by region, 188, 189

Paglas, Datu Ibrahim Toto II, 73–74
Paglas Corporation, 73–74, 76
Palette, 177–80
Palette Bakery, 177, 178
Pan-terre safs, 28
partnerships, nonprofit/for-profit, 91, 92–93, 94, 104
PBSP (Philippine Business for Social Progress), 68, 73

PDA (Population and Community Development Association), 74
peace-building, 73–74, 78
Peoplink, Inc., 92
Philanthropy (Serbian religious organization), 52
philanthropy, private, 69, 88, 94, 131, 170
Philippine Business for Social Progress (PBSP), 68, 73
Philippines, 64, 65, 67–68, 73–74, 77–78, 79–82
Pittsburgh Social Innovation Accelerator, 98
Poland: cooperatives, 20, 41, 42; leadership in social enterprise, 44–45; preschool centers, 38; social enterprise analysis, 46–50; social integration mission, 20, 36, 37, 42; Łuksja, 59–60; WWW Promotion, 58–59
Policy Research Institute for the Civil Sector, 165
Polish Foundation of Mutual Help (Barka), 37
political considerations: Argentina, 140, 148–49; East-Central Europe, 41–42, 43–44, 53; Japan, 167; Southeast Asia, 68, 69, 70, 78; United States, 105; Western Europe, 19–20, 26; Zimbabwe and Zambia, 119–20, 122–30
Pollak, T., 97, 104
Population and Community Development Association (PDA), 74
Portugal, 18, 26
poverty alleviation. See disadvantaged groups, helping
Practical Action, 117, 119, 132–33, 134–35
Prae Phan Womens' Weaving Group, 77
PRI (program related investment), 102
private sector: decentralization of social programs to, 143–44; philanthropy, 69, 88, 94, 131, 170. See also for-profit businesses; nongovernmental organizations (NGOs)
Private Voluntary Organisations (PVO) Act, 123, 127

producers groupings, xiv. See also cooperatives; worker collectives
profit-oriented businesses. See for-profit businesses
program area focus by region, 188, 189, 191. See also employment services; social services
program related investment (PRI), 102
El Progreso Agricola, 146
public authorities. See governmental institutions
Puravida Coffee, 93–94
purpose and social enterprise. See mission and social enterprise
PVO (Private Voluntary Organisations) Act, 123, 127

quid pro quo organizations, 92–93

Raftopoulos, B., 116
Raweewan, 70
Rebón, J., 153
Récol' Terre safs, 28
recuperated companies (Argentina), 145, 151–57
recycling business, 65–66
relief projects, 71, 77–78
religious-based organizations, 51–52, 73, 79
research considerations, 3, 23, 45–46, 100, 174
resource mobilization strategy, 64, 66, 67
revenue generation, 16, 103–4, 123, 168–69. See also earned income for social enterprises
River Ambulance Project, 70–71, 73
Robinson, J., 2
Romania, 38
rural development: Argentina, 146–47, 148; East-Central Europe, 37, 38; Southeast Asia, 65, 68, 71, 73–74, 75, 76, 77–78; Western Europe, 22; Zimbabwe and Zambia, 121–22. See also agricultural assistance services

Sabaté, Federico, 142
Salamon, L. S., 3–5, 13–14, 95, 184, 195
Sanagi Gathering Place, 176
Sanagi Restaurant, 176
Sanagitachi Project, 175–77, 179–80
Santos, Joel, 64
SAPS (Structural Adjustment Programmes), 117, 121–22
Sasakawa Peace Foundation, 65
Seikatsu Club Seikyô, 169
SEKN (Social Enterprise Knowledge Network), 158n2
self-help groups, 38, 51, 72
Serbia, 36, 38, 41, 43–44, 50–55, 57–58
Shelter and Site Development, 81
SIJ (Social Innovation Japan), 174
Singapore, 66, 70, 75
Sit, Norma, 70
Sitsophary, Nhev, 67
Slovakia, 41
Slovenia, 38
small and medium-sized enterprises (SMES), 36, 42, 54, 66, 134–35, 147
social capital, 26, 103, 109n16
social cooperatives: East-Central Europe, 42, 43, 44, 50, 58–59; Japan, 165; Western Europe, 18, 19, 29–31, 36
social cooperative with limited liability (Greece), 18
social democratic regimes, 4, 24, 25
social development programs (Denmark), 20
social economy, 188, 189–90. See also Argentina; East-Central Europe; Western Europe
social enterprise: vs. charity model, 75, 101; vs. corporate social responsibility, 116; cross-regional comparison, 184–87, 188, 189–92, 191, 193, 195, 196, 197; overview, 1–10, xii–xvi. See also conceptual issues for social enterprise; individual regions or countries
social enterprise accelerators, 98
Social Enterprise Alliance, 23, 88, 100

Social Enterprise Coalition, 23
Social Enterprise Committee, 66, 70, 75
Social Enterprise Initiative, 99
Social Enterprise Knowledge Network (SEKN), 158n2
social entrepreneur/entrepreneurship: definitional issues, 1, 2, 64, 89; historical development of concept, xi–xii; Japan, 164–65, 167–68, 174; Southeast Asia, 75–76, 77, 79; United States, 89; Western Europe, 13–15, 23; Zimbabwe and Zambia, 117
social initiative cooperative (Spain), 18
Social Innovation Japan (SIJ), 174
social innovation school (Japan), 164–65
social origins approach, 3–5. See also socioeconomic context
social protection initiatives (Zimbabwe), 125
social purpose company (Belgium), 18–19
social purpose organization (U.S.), 90, 91
social services: disabilities, people with, 53–54, 58–60, 99, 177–79; East-Central Europe, 39, 44, 52, 57–58; health care, 18, 30, 70–71, 73, 74, 77, 80, 105–6; housing projects, 68, 79–82, 92, 105–6; Japan, 168, 170, 175–79; Southeast Asia, 64, 68, 70–71, 73, 74, 77, 79–82; United States, 92, 105–6; Western Europe, 18, 30; women, development of, 51, 53, 57–58, 77, 120–21, 170; Zimbabwe and Zambia, 114, 116. See also disadvantaged groups, helping
social solidarity cooperative (Portugal), 18
social work school (Japan), 165–66
societal sector by region, 188, 189–90, 191. See also market economy; social economy
societé co-opérative d'interêt collectif (France), 18, 19
socioeconomic context: analytical overview, 3–5; Argentina, 140, 145–58, 158n2; cross-regional comparison, 191–92, 193, 195, 196; East-Central Europe, 45–59; Japan, 175–81, 181n1; Southeast Asia, 76–84; United States, 103–7; Western

Europe, 24–31; Zimbabwe and Zambia,
131–37
Sokolowski, W., 3–5, 195
South Africa, 132
Southeast Asia: analysis, 76–84; conceptual
issues, 64–67; Gawad Kalinga example,
79–82; historical perspective, 67–72,
186–87; legal frameworks, 72–74; Mitra
Usaha Mandiri example, 82–84; overview, 7–8; supporting institutions, 74–
76, 186–87
Spain, 18, 20
Sri Lanka Restaurant, 177
Srithong, Payong, 70
stakeholders, 15, 36, 80, 151–57
state capacity, 5, 186–87, 191–92, 193, 195,
196
state institutions. *See* governmental
institutions
statist regimes, 4. *See also* Argentina; Japan
strategic development base by region, *188*,
190, 191. *See also* civil society; foundations; governmental institutions; international aid
Structural Adjustment Programmes (SAPS),
117, 121–22
subsidiaries of nonprofits, for-profit operations as, 90–92, 170, 171, 176, 177–78
supporting institutions: academia, 23, 45–
46, 100, 174–75; Argentina, 144–46,
186; East-Central Europe, 39, 45–55,
185–86; European Union, 19, 22, 40, 50,
54; Japan, 169, 173–75, 176, 177, 180; private philanthropy, 69, 88, 94, 131, 170;
Southeast Asia, 74–76, 186–87; United
States, 97–101, 185; Western Europe,
19–27, 185; Zimbabwe and Zambia,
130–31. *See also* foundations; governmental institutions; international aid
Swan Bakery & Cafe, 170
Sweden, 20

Tanimoto, K., 165, 174
Teenpreneur Challenge, 77

telephone cooperatives (Argentina), 149–50
Ten Thousand Villages, 92
Thailand, 65–66, 69–70, 74, 76–77
third sector: East-Central Europe, 36-52,
54-57; Japan, 164, 166; overview, 3, 4;
Western Europe, 12-13, 16-17, 24-25. *See
also* associations; voluntary sector
third sector school (Japan), 166
trade intermediary (U.S.), 91, 92
trading activity, U.S. vs. Western European
social enterprise, 15–16
training services. *See* education and training
services
Trento Centre for Local Development, 45
Tri-Terre safs, 28

UBIT (Unrelated Business Income Tax), 102
umbrella organizations, 22–23, 120–21, 123
unions, 29, 126, 147, 156
United Kingdom, 12, 19, 20, 24, 25, 165
United States: analysis, 103–7; conceptual
issues, 87–94; Georgia Justice Project
example, 106–7; historical perspective,
94–97, 185; Housing Works example,
105–6; influence on Japanese social
enterprise, 165; legal frameworks, 101–2;
overview, 8; socioeconomic environment, *193*, *194*, *196*; supporting institutions, 97–101, 185; vs. Western Europe,
13–16
Unrelated Business Income Tax (UBIT), 102
USAID, 131

Vietnam, 75
Virtue Ventures, 88
Vision 2020, 69, 74–75
voluntary sector, 24–25, 36, 40, 42, 51, 94–
95. *See also* associations; third sector

Wallonia Project, 28
war reconstruction, 73–74, 78
waste management, 65–66
wealth-creation framework, 65
We Have Jobs project, 46, 48, 60–61n5

welfare state context, 4, 16, 24–27, 40, 49, 143

Western Europe: analysis, 24–31; conceptual issues, 12–16; Consorzio per l'Impresa Sociale example, 29–31; Groupe Terre example, 27–28; historical perspective, 16–19, 185; legal frameworks, 18, 27, 30–31; overview, 6–7; socioeconomic environment, *193*, *194*, *196*; supporting institutions, 19–27, 185

WISES (work integration social enterprises), 17–18, 19–20, 26, 37, 48

WNJ (Workers' Collective Network Japan), 170

Wolk, Andrew, 99

women, development of, 51, 53, 57–58, 77, 120–21, 170

Wongcharoen, Somthai, 65

Wongpanit Company, 65

worker collectives, 151–57, 159n7, 170

Workers' Collective Network Japan (WNJ), 170

work integration social enterprises (WISES), 17–18, 19–20, 26, 37, 48

The Works, 106

WWW Promotion, 58–59

Yayasan Mitra Usaha (YMU), 82

Yokohama Hostel Village (YHV), 176

Yoshikuni, T., 126

Young, Dennis, 13–14, 88

Youth Life Ownership, Ltd., 70

Yunus, Mohammad, 66

Zimbabwe and Zambia: analysis, 131–37; Collective Self-Finance Scheme example, 135–36; conceptual issues, 114–19; historical perspective, 119–25; International Development Enterprises example, 136–37; legal frameworks, 123, 125–30; overview, 8; Practical Action example, 134–35; socioeconomic environment, *193*, *194*–195, *196*; supporting institutions, 130–31

Zimbabwe Association of Micro Finance Institutions (ZAMFI), 131

Zimbabwe Opportunities Investment Centre, 117